The Living Text of the Gospels represents an important new departure in Gospel studies and textual criticism. David Parker offers a way of reading the Gospels which treats seriously the fact that they first existed as manuscripts. Through an analysis of the different forms of a number of key passages, he demonstrates that the Gospels cannot be properly understood as texts without taking into consideration their physical existence as manuscripts, printed books and electronic text. In conclusion, he argues that the search for an original text of the Gospels overlooks the way in which the early church passed down its traditions.

It is an approach that challenges many of the assumptions of New Testament scholarship. But, at the same time, it does not assume any prior knowledge of the discipline, and can therefore be used as a unique alternative to traditional primers of New Testament textual criticism.

THE LIVING TEXT OF THE GOSPELS

THE LIVING TEXT
OF THE GOSPELS

D. C. PARKER

University of Birmingham

CAMBRIDGE
UNIVERSITY PRESS

PUBLISHED BY THE PRESS SYNDICATE OF THE UNIVERSITY OF CAMBRIDGE
The Pitt Building, Trumpington Street, Cambridge CB2 1RP, United Kingdom

CAMBRIDGE UNIVERSITY PRESS
The Edinburgh Building, Cambridge CB2 2RU, United Kingdom
40 West 20th Street, New York, NY 10011–4211, USA
10 Stamford Road, Oakleigh, Melbourne, 3166, Australia

© David Parker 1997

First published 1997

Printed in the United Kingdom at the University Press, Cambridge

Typeset in Baskerville 11/12½ pt

A catalogue record for this book is available from the British Library

Library of Congress cataloguing in publication data
Parker, D. C. (David C.)
The living text of the Gospels / D. C. Parker.
p.   cm.
Includes bibliographical references and indexes.
ISBN 0 521 59062 0 (hardback) ISBN 0 521 59951 2 (paperback)
1. Bible. N.T. Gospels – criticism, textual.   I. Title.
BS2555.2.P274   1997
226'.0486–dc21   96–44610   CIP

ISBN 0 521 59062 0 hardback
ISBN 0 521 59951 2 paperback

And generally let this be a rule, that all partitions of knowledges be accepted rather for lines and veins than for sections and separations.

Francis Bacon, *Of the Advancement of Learning* 2.9.1

Contents

Preface

This book offers a different way of reading the Gospels. It is a way which treats seriously the fact that they are manuscripts. We use the verb 'to pen' as a description of authorship. The Gospels were 'penned' for a millennium and a half. The reader is invited to see what the consequences are of starting with that fact.

The way in which this undertaking has been set out is to bring together things which are too often kept separate. In the first place, the book has been written as an exploration of the textual criticism of the Gospels. The attempt has been made to assume as little, and to explain as much, as possible. The approach is a practical one, introducing the discipline by the study of examples. It follows that the information is generally provided in order to illuminate a specific point. As a result, some of the material included in the established handbooks of the discipline is absent here. The reader who wants to find out more is directed towards them.

The book has been written with the growing conviction that, once the present approach has been adopted, much else in our understanding of the Gospels requires revision. What I have written differs from many introductions (I mean introductions generally, not those in this discipline) in that it is not a summary of the current state of affairs. Instead, it attempts to find new departures. Recent developments in biblical criticism have brought new challenges for textual criticism. There are even those who view it as a peculiarly obsolete aspect of western imperialism in its guise of the historico-critical method, as a dead member of a moribund body. I hope to convince one or two such individuals that textual criticism is ahead of them and not behind them.

But current fashions in New Testament studies are not as

significant as certain other contemporary developments. The technological revolution is of more far-reaching significance. It has changed for ever our relationship to the manuscripts and printed books in which the Gospels have hitherto been reproduced and read. Because we are on the threshold of a new age, I have done no more than try to catch a glimpse of what lies ahead. But this new dawn has thrown its own light over the landscape which I survey.

I have, therefore, attempted to write a book which will both describe the subject and offer new ways of looking at it.

It will be found that the focus of the chapters varies. Sometimes my concern is with New Testament studies and in particular with textual problems; sometimes with the use of passages in the early church and later; sometimes with the light that textual criticism can shed on biblical interpretation in contemporary life, sometimes with theological problems. I draw attention to this fact not in order to justify myself, but to encourage the reader not to decide in advance what is likely to be found in a book on textual criticism.

One subject of considerable interest has been totally omitted. The question of the non-canonical Gospels is an important one today, and there are places where it might have been usefully discussed here. But I determined to fix only on the canonical texts, on the grounds that because of their use in the church, both in the past and today, their textual history has been quite different from that of other, non-canonical, Gospels, and their theological significance evidently much greater.

One of my goals has been clarity. I have therefore tried to restrict the footnotes to a minimum. Apart from the obvious one of citing sources, there are three kinds of occasion on which I have included them. The first is where I am using someone else's ideas, and might give the appearance of their being my own. The second is where it seems likely that the reader may wish for more information than I have space to provide, and so needs to be directed to a source. The third is where I have wished to include detail which was not essential to the argument; such material is banished to the obscurity of a learned footnote.

I conclude these preliminaries by expressing my gratitude to those who helped me. In particular: Mark Goodacre, who read and commented on Chapter 7; Peter Harvey, who read the whole book and helped me to work out what I meant to say; my father, T. H. L. Parker, who also read the whole book, pointed out the places where I had not written what I meant to say, and offered many other helpful suggestions.

Parts of Chapter 5 and a few paragraphs of Chapter 12 are reworked from two articles in *Theology*. I am grateful to the publishers for permission to use the material.

And finally, a word of grateful and affectionate homage to the two men who encouraged and directed my youthful steps in New Testament textual studies: Matthew Black († 1994) and Ernst Bammel († 1996).

Abbreviations and frequently cited works

Aland, *Liste*	K. Aland (ed.), *Kurzgefasste Liste der griechischen Handschriften des Neuen Testaments*, Arbeiten zu Neutestamentliche Textforschung 1 (2nd edn, Berlin and New York, 1994)
Alands, *Text*	K. and B. Aland, *The Text of the New Testament: An Introduction to the Critical Editions and to the Theory and Practice of Modern Textual Criticism* (2nd edn, Grand Rapids and Leiden, 1989)
CBQ	*Catholic Biblical Quarterly*
GCS	Die griechischen christlichen Schriftsteller der ersten drei Jahrhundert (Berlin)
HTR	*Harvard Theological Review*
JBL	*Journal of Biblical Literature*
Jerome, *Letters*	Jerome, *Letters and Select Works*, ed. W. H. Fremantle, Nicene and Post-Nicene Fathers 6 (Oxford and New York, 1893)
JSNTSS	Journal for the Study of the New Testament Supplement Series
JTS	*Journal of Theological Studies*
Metzger, *Text*	B. M. Metzger, *The Text of the New Testament: Its Transmisson, Corruption, and Restoration* (3rd edn, New York and Oxford, 1992)
NTS	*New Testament Studies*
NTTS	New Testament Tools and Studies
PBA	*Proceedings of the British Academy*

SNTSMS   Studiorum Novi Testamenti Societas
                    Monograph Series
Westcott and Hort   B. F. Westcott and F. J. A. Hort (eds.), *The
                    New Testament in the Original Greek*, Vol. I,
                    Text, Vol. II, *Introduction* (Cambridge and
                    London, 1881)

CHAPTER I

The theory

To be a well-favoured man is the gift of fortune, but to write
and read comes by nature.

William Shakespeare, *Much Ado About Nothing*

Textual criticism is in essence the act of understanding what
another person means by the words that are laid before me. When I
sit at the meal table with my family I can observe, throughout the
talk, that what is said contains broken sentences, one word spoken
where another is intended, gaps and false starts. Occasionally a
little enquiry is needed to sort out a particular statement, and
sometimes confusion will provoke hilarity or fierce argument. But
generally we meet what is intended in what is said and are unaware
of the process by which we receive the words. Whether the words
are spoken or written is of secondary importance. But we speak of
the process as textual criticism when the words are laid before us in
written form.

Everybody who reads the newspaper is expert in textual
criticism, in coping with those distctive errors of omssion and
displaced lines, and jumbling of letrset. This sophisticated process
of recognizing nonsense and picking up the sense is so natural to us
the classical scholars of ancient Alexandria or the Benedictines of
that we perform it without thinking, unaware of our kinship with
St Maur. Textual criticism is not an arcane science. It belongs to all
human communication.

The matter will become a little more complicated when we
apply our critical faculties to another language than our own, in a
form spoken two millennia since.

The undertaking changes again when – the nub of the matter – the text concerned is preserved in a number of handwritten copies which differ from one another. Instead of our single printed newspaper with its distinctive types of error, we are now reading half a dozen handwritten copies of the sports page, each with its own variations on events. We will decide which we believe by looking for more information in the context, by asking ourselves which of the papers is more likely to have jumbled the figures, and by speculating on the probability: what we know of the teams, who was playing for them, and so on. The process is the same as the one I described in the first paragraph, except that it is made more complicated by the language, by the distance in time, and by the number of differing copies.

These are the processes which are at work as we compare the five and a half thousand catalogued manuscripts of the Greek New Testament. There is plenty of accidental error to be found among so many. And there is a large additional factor, which will occupy most of our time: the incidence of conscious alteration to the text, whose causes have to be understood.

Textual criticism of the New Testament has been damaged by the notion that it is best left in the hands of experts. This view is no doubt a part of a general division of knowledge into compartments. Certainly, this particular branch of knowledge is frequently treated as so recherché as to be beyond the comprehension of all but a very few people, devotees who bring rare gifts to a secret god. It is clear that there is a certain amount of knowledge necessary to practise this discipline. But harm has been done by the assumption that the discipline itself is off limits for anyone who has not devoted their life to it. That it has been unfortunate for the discipline is not my concern here. The greater harm lies in the attitude to the text which it has engendered. This attitude manifests itself in two beliefs. The first is that the text chosen by the editors of the main current Greek New Testament is virtually certain, and that all variations from it, even those which the edition places at the foot of the page as significant variants, may be ignored. We shall shortly find that such optimism is not shared by the editors of that edition, who are best placed to know the doubts and uncertainties which attended their decisions. There are certainly other reasons for this assumption that the text is reliable and that no more needs to be said.

One reason is the success, or perhaps one should say the confidence, of textual critics themselves. The edition of the Greek New Testament published in 1881 by Westcott and Hort is titled *The New Testament in the Original Greek*. Nobody does believe or has believed that this is literally true, except in that the New Testament was originally written in Greek. But such a phrase will make its mark. The discovery since 1881 of copies much older than those available to Westcott and Hort may have led to the belief that scholarship has subsequently approached even closer to the original text. Other writers will emphasise the degree of reliability of the text in all but a few places.

We have, however, to distinguish at any rate between the desirable and the attainable. Caution rightly prevails in the Introduction to the most commonly used edition of the Greek New Testament, the small blue volume known as Nestle–Aland:

Novum Testamentum Graece seeks to provide the reader with a critical appreciation of the whole textual tradition... It should naturally be understood that this text is a working text (in the sense of the century-long Nestle tradition); it is not to be considered as definitive, but as a stimulus to further efforts towards redefining and verifying the text of the New Testament.[1]

This text was agreed by a committee. When they disagreed on the best reading to print, they voted. Evidently, they agreed either by a majority or unanimously that their text was the best available. But it does not follow that they believed their text to be 'original'. On the whole, textual critics have always been reluctant to claim so much. Other users of the Greek New Testament accord them too much honour in treating the text as definitive.

The second belief is one that is more deeply held. To challenge it is to offer a vital theological question. This belief is that the purpose of textual criticism is to recover the original text. That this was for long their goal was also expressed by textual critics themselves. It is

[1] *Novum Testamentum Graece*, ed. K. Aland and B. Aland, 27th edn (Stuttgart, 1993), p. 45*.

expressed in the very beginning of one classic manual of the discipline:

The object of all textual criticism is to recover so far as possible the actual words written by the author.[2]

But, precisely because it has been taken as axiomatic, the idea that there is an original text to be recovered is one that we must examine with the utmost care. The issue is not one which concerns only the New Testament, so we shall approach it more broadly.

We are used to the idea that to read a book is to read the text as the author wrote it. The reality is more complicated. Of course, there are occasions when there may have been more than one edition. But – and this is to be stressed – there are also texts which *cannot* exist in an 'original' form. Two examples will help.

Many of Shakespeare's plays exist in several early printings; a Quarto (in which they are printed separately) and the First Folio, the first collected works. A few of them survive in two quarto printings. The often significant differences between these used to be measured for purposes of recovering the original definitive text of the play, and generally the older printing was called 'bad' or 'corrupt' and the later one 'good'. But recently a quite different way of interpreting the evidence has been proposed, that the two printings represent stages in the growth of the play. Shakespeare produces the first draft of a play, a written text. This is later printed. He then takes his play down to the Globe, and it goes into rehearsal. Some things don't work, and he cuts them; suggestions are made by the cast, and he develops them. The form of the play that is finally put on may be markedly different from the original draft. This later comes out as another printing. What is the original text? The question obscures the truth, and we need instead to find a new way of thinking about the different printed texts and the process which they represent. There is no *original* text. There are just different texts from different stages of production. One modern editor has solved the particularly acute problems of the text of *King Lear* by printing it twice as two separate plays, *The Tragedy of King*

[2] Kirsopp Lake, *The Text of the New Testament* (London, 1913), p. 1.

Lear and *The History of King Lear*.[3] The character of the materials justifies the editor's procedure:

The hypothesis that we possess, in Q[uarto] and F[olio], Shakespeare's original version and Shakespeare's revision of *King Lear* necessitates a radical departure from traditional editorial practice; but traditional editorial practice itself represents a radical departure from the early texts.[4]

The second example is drawn from a very different kind of text, produced two centuries later. As Susanna and the Countess, Figaro and the Count sing their way through their day of madness to their final reconciliation, textual criticism is – or should be – far from our minds. But somebody has had to provide a text from which they could learn their parts, and recent research has revealed interesting information about the relationship between what Mozart wrote and what we hear. Manuscript sources include the autograph score, sketches, and what was probably the official copy of the court theatre in Vienna. The kind of traditional textual criticism that is applied also to the New Testament will seek to discover which manuscript is a copy of which. The expected conclusion will be that the autograph is the source of the others, and is to be followed unless there is good reason to mistrust it. Not so, for revisions made *in rehearsal* will have been written in the performance copies and the theatre's official copy, but not in the autograph. In rehearsal, Mozart had in some places to exchange the vocal lines of Susanna and the Countess, in order to accommodate the singers' voices. We might reverse this change in favour of the autograph in order to realise Mozart's original intentions. But there are also many smaller changes to the two soprano parts, also probably made by Mozart in rehearsal because he felt that they

[3] William Shakespeare, *The Complete Works*, general editors Stanley Wells and Gary Taylor (Oxford, 1986). For the editors' approach to the textual criticism, see especially pp. xxxiii–xxxv. 'It is not simply that the 1608 quarto lacks over 100 lines that are in the Folio, or that the Folio lacks close on 100 lines that are in the Quarto, or . . . It is rather that the sum total of these differences amounts, in this play, to a substantial shift in the presentation and interpretation of the underlying action . . . We believe, in short, that there are two distinct plays of *King Lear*, not merely two different texts of the same play.' It is significant that although the theory adopted by Wells was first broached in 1931, it has gained currency only in the last twenty years.
[4] S. Wells and G. Taylor, with J. Jowett and W. Montgomery, *William Shakespeare: A Textual Companion* (Oxford, 1987), p. 509.

improved the music. We would therefore end up with a hybrid text, one that existed neither in Mozart's intentions nor in the manuscript authorities. The quest for an original text is, again, unhelpful.[5]

In both these examples, the task of textual criticism and the role of the textual critic have changed. Instead of eliminating material in order to recover a single original text, the editor analyses all the developments of the material in order to demonstrate the processes to which they owe their origin. The textual critic's task has not become less important because there is no definitive text to be recovered. There is a sense in which an editor's continuing importance has increased. For when it is assumed that there *is* an original text, the textual critic's task is very simple: to recover the original text. The user then offers grateful thanks for the definitive product, and gets on with the interpretation, while the editor goes in search of another text to polish off. But if the task does not consist in the recovery of an original text, then the study of the entire range of materials available will not cease with the publication of an edition. That is, the reader of Shakespeare can now, and indeed should, read *both* forms of *King Lear*, rather than a single hybrid version.

Both these examples are, while not simple problems to resolve, based on comparatively limited materials. They consist essentially of the comparison of two forms of the text. Greater complexity arises where an author's process of revision lasted over many years, or resulted in a complicated process of development. Such is the case with Wordsworth's *The Prelude*, and Joyce's *Ulysses*. The problem here is to distinguish between the various stages of the text. And, frequently, we may prefer a line or a sentence which the author came to reject. *The Prelude* was first published in 1850 in its latest form. The earliest version of 1805 may be read with a different pleasure.[6]

Such quite different textual traditions and problems, and those contemporary interpretations of Shakespeare and Mozart, encour-

[5] For this example, see Alan Tyson, *Mozart: Studies of the Autograph Score* (Cambridge, Mass. and London, 1987).
[6] See also S. Gill, 'Wordsworth's Poems: The Question of the Text', *Review of English Studies* N.S. 34 (1983), 172–90.

age us to see that the quest for an original text need not be the only option available to the modern textual critic, or the only expectation of the modern reader. Returning to the Gospels armed with these possibilities, we ask this question: are the Gospels the kinds of texts that have originals? This book will attempt to provide ways of answering. For the moment we shall content ourselves with a more general point. Almost all writers on theological, ethical and historical issues have taken it for granted that the New Testament evidence on which they are drawing for support is the original text of the writers. The importance of scrutinising this assumption cannot be stressed too highly. It is a principal theme of this book. The discovery that the assumption is mistaken will have profound consequences for contemporary understandings of Scripture. We shall find that textual criticism of the Gospels not only is a preliminary to their study, but also provides a new way of interpreting them. It does not simply provide the service of recovering the text; it also provides ways of describing the text.

The need for that security which is provided by authority is an aspect of human life which we have to recognise if we are to understand the nature of the enquiry before us. I do not claim immunity from that need. But I hope to demonstrate that there are sound historical reasons why the original text of the Gospels does not satisfy it.

One final word to this chapter. The task of textual criticism consists of collecting evidence and evaluating it. Its contribution in gathering information about early Christian documents is beyond question. It is evidently important then to discern the appropriate question and to ask it of the data. But an answer can certainly not always be provided, nor where it can is it always of as much significance as the question. In the following pages, the fact that such questions arise will frequently prove as fruitful for reflection as whatever answers may be attempted.

But enough of theory. It must follow, not precede, the practice.

CHAPTER 2

The materials

Nothing beside remains.   P. B. Shelley,

The description of the materials in the handbooks of textual criticism follows a well-established pattern.[1] I shall first follow that, as concisely as possible in order to provide information that will be relevant to this book, and then attempt a different approach. Individual manuscripts will not be described here. They will be introduced as they appear in subsequent chapters.

I

The materials are generally divided into three categories: Greek manuscripts, translations into other tongues, and quotations by early Christian writers. And each may be further divided.

Greek manuscripts

All known manuscripts are itemised in a list that is accepted as standard by everyone. The Institute for New Testament Textual Research in Münster, Westphalia, assumed reponsibility for the List, and for forty years has earned our gratitude by improving and updating it. A revised edition was published in 1994.[2] It provides for each manuscript a number, its contents, date, the material on

---

[1] Besides the handbooks of Metzger and the Alands, attention should be drawn to the recent Festschrift honouring Professor Bruce Metzger: *The Text of the New Testament in Contemporary Research: Essays on the* Status Quaestionis. *A Volume in Honor of Bruce M. Metzger*, ed. B. D. Ehrman and M. W. Holmes, SD 46 (Grand Rapids, 1995). In addition to a section written by a specialist in the field on each of the areas outlined below, there are chapters on other important aspects of the discipline.

[2] Aland, *Liste*. The first edition had appeared in 1963.

which it is written, the number of leaves that survive, the number of columns on a page and the number of lines in a column, the dimensions, and the library where it is held with its classmark. The List separates manuscripts into four groups: papyri, majuscules, minuscules and lectionaries. Each manuscript's number tells us to which group it belongs. This system was formulated at the end of the last century by C. R. Gregory, and replaced a more cumbersome system which had separate lists for manuscripts according to contents. According to the older system, one might have one number given to four different manuscripts severally containing the Gospels, Pauline Epistles, Acts and the Catholic Epistles, and Revelation.

There are 2,388 listed manuscripts which include the Gospels.[3]

Papyri are indicated by a P, in either roman (P) or black-letter (𝔓) font, followed by a number written either normally or superscript. These are all manuscripts written on papyrus, a kind of reed. This, a common writing material of the ancient world, was manufactured by pressing cut strips of the papyrus plant into two layers at right angles to each other. There are ninety-five papyri in the List, forty-five of them containing Gospel material.[4] The latest are of the seventh century, the earliest of the second. Until their discovery in the course of excavations (mostly in Egypt) in the past century, no manuscript older than the second quarter of the fourth century was known. Now with the most extensive of the papyri we have large portions of copies of the Gospels dating from the late second century and the first part of the third. These are P[45] (which contains parts of all the Gospels), P[66] (most of John) and P[75] (large parts of Luke and John). Their study has led to some extensive reconsideration of the ways in which the text was copied in the first four centuries.

Majuscules (more often called uncials[5]) take their name from the style of writing in which they are produced, a form that is the

---

[3] The figure of 2,361 is given in Alands, *Text*, p. 83 as correct in May 1988. I have revised it by adding manuscripts added to the List since then: one papyrus, six majuscules and twenty minuscules.

[4] There are in fact ninety-nine items listed, but two manuscripts are divided between two numbers, and one between three.

[5] The word 'uncial', which is of uncertain origin, is more properly applied to various Latin scripts in use at the same period.

source of modern Greek capital letters. Most of the papyri are also written in majuscule hands, but the manuscripts classed as majuscules are all written on parchment (animal skin). Their numbers are prefixed with a zero; thus 01, 02, 0234. The oldest of them are also denominated in two other ways. Before many were known, it was possible to assign to each an upper-case letter of the alphabet. When the total reached thirty-five (J is not present in the Latin alphabet, but some letters were used twice, such as E which is used for one manuscript of the Gospels and one of Acts), the upper-case letters unique to the Greek alphabet were used – Γ Δ Θ Λ Ξ Π Σ Φ Ψ Ω. When these had been exhausted, Tischendorf (the first western scholar to find and to study many of these manuscripts) began to use Hebrew letters. The system was becoming unworkable, and in the generation after Tischendorf, C. R. Gregory introduced the numbering system. But traces of the alphabetical system remain. All the first forty-five majuscules in the List are also known by a letter. The first has the first letter of the Hebrew alphabet, so it is given as א 01. The next thirty-four all have Latin letters, and the remainder have Greek.

The other convention is of naming important manuscripts. Most of those forty-five which have letters are also named, either from their provenance (such as Codex Sinaiticus or Codex Zacynthius), or by their present location (such as Codex Vaticanus or Codex Mosquensis), or by some other distinguishing epithet. A manuscript that has been reused (a palimpsest) is often called after the author of the text for whose writing it was reused (such as Codex Ephraemi Rescriptus, or Codex Climaci Rescriptus, severally named after the Syrian writers Ephraem and John Climacus).

Turning the pages of the List one soon notes that while the first fifty or so majuscules are either complete or very extensive, the remainder down to the last entry, 0306, rarely consist of a dozen leaves and generally only of one or two. A few have, like the papyri, been found in excavation. More are the results of thorough searches through libraries. Others, the chance debris of ancient collections, have been recovered from bindings of later books or were used as palimpsests. The best of them provide us with valuable materials. A few of them are older than any of the extensive majuscules. There are 196 majuscule manuscripts containing the Gospels. The principal of these, as the oldest complete manuscripts, constitute the main materials for the study of the text, and will be the copies to be most frequently discussed in the following pages. They are among our chief witnesses to the earliest forms in which the Gospels were preserved. But a greater number, 116 of them, are fragmentary and consist of only a few leaves.[6]

A sudden increase in the demand for books in the Byzantine empire during the course of the tenth century caused majuscule to be abandoned in favour of a more compact and economical style of writing.[7] This style is known as *minuscule*, and like majuscule it has given its name to a class of New Testament manuscripts. The name *cursive* is sometimes used, somewhat less correctly.[8] The List contains 2,856 manuscripts in this category; 2,145 contain the Gospels. They are simply given an arabic number with no further distinguishing symbol, so that the first is called 1 and the last 2856. They were produced between the tenth century and the invention of printing (though there are a number that are more recent than the first printed Greek New Testament of 1516, dating as they do from the sixteenth and seventeenth centuries). Most minuscules were written on parchment, but paper was increasingly commonly used from its introduction in the thirteenth century. A very few of them, comprising some of the longest known and the most significant, have a name.

By the tenth century – as far from the evangelists as we are from the tenth century – the Greek New Testament text had assumed a standard form. Almost everyone knew and wrote the text in the so-called Byzantine or Koinē, a type of text that had been becoming increasingly common since the sixth century. But we would be mistaken to conclude that these medieval manuscripts represent a late text and to decide therefore to ignore them. For one thing, the value of a manuscript depends not on its age, but (assuming it to be a good copy) on the age and significance of its exemplar, the manuscript from which it was copied. A tenth-century manuscript

---

[6] For a more detailed discussion of the majuscules, see my contribution to Ehrman and Holmes, *The Text of the New Testament*.

[7] It has been calculated that a majuscule copy of the Gospels would require the hides of fifty to sixty sheep or goats (Alands, *Text*, p. 77).

[8] The word 'cursive' ('running') better describes less formal hands, used for non-literary texts or by less expert scribes.

copied from one of the third century will be of more interest than one of the sixth produced from an exemplar only a little older than itself. Likewise, a tenth-century manuscript copied from one only a little older, but itself derived from one of the third century, will be of more interest than one of the sixth century descended by many copyings from one of the third. Since it is the act of copying that introduces change, the frequency of copying as well as the degree of accuracy will affect the value of a manuscript. We shall come across some late witnesses with an early text. Also, we shall find a strong conservatism among the manuscripts. Where there is variation among medieval manuscripts, the variants are sometimes ones that came into existence in the first couple of centuries of copying.

Many families and sub-groups of minuscules have been found. One or two of these contain a strong influence from early sources. The two which we shall meet most often are Family 1 and Family 13, abbreviated as either f^1 or fam^1 and f^{13} or fam^{13}. They are called Family 1 and Family 13 after the first member of each group in numerical order.

The final category of manuscript is the *lectionary*. It is designated by an italic *l* before its number (for example, *l*2133). Instead of a continuous text, a lectionary provides the readings required for church services, in the order in which they are required, according to different categories such as daily services, Sunday services and special days. Separate volumes were employed for the Gospels and for other collections of New Testament books. There are in fact lectionaries among the papyri, and the lectionary list includes a few majuscule manuscripts, although the vast majority are minuscule. But what distinguishes the lectionary list is that they are all written on either parchment or paper (not papyrus) and none contains a continuous text (against the majuscules and minuscules). There are 2,403 lectionaries in the List. The majority contain Gospel readings. The earliest is of the eighth century. The lectionary text is not identical with the Byzantine text of the minuscules. The two had separate lives, for lectionaries were usually copied from lectionaries and continuous text manuscripts from continuous text manuscripts. The study of the lectionaries is less developed than that of other classes of manuscript.

Such are the Greek New Testament manuscripts. In the following pages we shall be most frequently concerned with the oldest and with those containing the oldest materials.

The versions

The second category is of versions. The translation of the New Testament into other languages appears to have begun in the second century. We can follow the processes with more certainty from the third century. The most important versions are the Syriac, the Latin and the Coptic.

The origins of the Syriac are obscure. The oldest representatives of it are two manuscripts known as the Sinaitic and the Curetonian. Copied the one in the fourth and the other in the fifth century, they preserve a text current in the early third century. They both have large parts missing, but between them they cover most of the Gospels. Later, in the fifth century, an 'official' text was produced, following the textual norms of its day. This, the 'Peshitta' version, is the text still used in the Syrian churches. Of particular interest also is the Harklean, of the early seventh century. Because it is a scholarly and slavish translation, with careful marginal notes, it tells us much about the Greek text from which it was made, a text which turns out to be of considerable interest in itself. In addition, there are several other Syriac versions which we shall encounter occasionally.

The Latin versions can certainly be charted from the third century, although the oldest surviving manuscripts were copied in the second half of the fourth. The first to circulate are those known as the Old Latin. They are divided into the African and the European types. Many sub-groups can be found among the latter. Just as an 'official' version of the Syriac was produced, so an attempt was made to introduce an official Latin text. The time was slightly earlier – the end of the fourth century – when Pope Damasus commissioned a new version of the Gospels from Jerome. The result was a text based on Old Latin manuscripts, corrected against good Greek manuscripts. It is called the Vulgate. The success of this new authorised version was not instant, and Old Latin versions continued to be copied and to circulate long after the fourth century. The result of this was that many Old Latin manuscripts contain readings of the Vulgate, and many of the older Vulgate manuscripts were influenced by pre-Jerome forms of the text.

The origins of the Coptic versions are less certain, for our knowledge of the origins of Egyptian Christianity itself is slight. Only with the fourth century do we begin to get a clear picture. The Coptic versions are subdivided into the various dialects in which different manuscripts are written: Sahidic, Bohairic, Fayyumic, Achmimic, Sub-Achmimic and Middle Egyptian. Of these the first is the most important, and the second the most common. It is the text still used in the Coptic church. The few manuscripts in Middle Egyptian are of particular interest for the unusual text they contain.

Other versions, probably less ancient than these three, are also of value: the Armenian, the Ethiopic, the Georgian, the Gothic, the Old Slavonic.[9]

The versions are of value for several reasons. First, when we can recover the original wording of a translation we are then able to recover a good deal of the wording of the Greek manuscript or manuscripts which the translator used. Thus, a third-century version will be a witness to a Greek text of the third century or older – and we have seen already that manuscripts of that age are rare. Second, when this has been done, they give us information about the area in which a text circulated – a Syriac text in Syria, a Coptic text in Egypt, and so on. The biblical citations of Cyprian of Carthage in the middle of the third century enable us to recognise several later Latin manuscripts to represent the third-century African Latin version. Third, there will be places where the translation and its subsequent developments will provide us with evidence about the way in which the text was understood at a particular time and place.

These are the possibilities. There are problems in realising them. The first is that the versions all had their own separate history once they came into being. They did not remain unchanged, any more than the Greek manuscripts preserved the text of the autographs

---

[9] For a full study providing the history, character and bibliography of all the versions, see B. M. Metzger, *The Early Versions of the New Testament. Their Origin, Transmission and Limitations* (Oxford, 1977). The handbooks also contain introductory information, as does Ehrman and Holmes, *The Text of the New Testament*.

unchanged. This may be seen from the history of the Latin versions, for which we have a comparatively large number of early manuscripts. Augustine of Hippo said that every manuscript was as good as a fresh translation. The student of the Latin versions has first to separate out the tangled traditions of the various Old Latin and the Vulgate texts. Only when that has been done can the underlying Greek texts be reconstructed.

The second problem is that it is necessary to set aside those apparent distinctive readings in the Greek underlying the version which are in fact due to the necessity or the choice of the translator. There are, for instance, many changes in word order in the Latin versions. But they are generally to be regarded as the consequence of syntactical differences between Greek and Latin. One has therefore to be cautious in weighing the significance of Latin evidence when Greek witnesses differ over word order.

There are various symbols used for indicating the versions. Those used in this book need brief explanation.

The Syriac is shown by the letters syr or sy, followed by a superscript letter as follows: c and s for the Curetonian and Sinaitic manuscripts; p for the Peshitta; h for the Harklean.

The Old Latin is shown by Lvt (standing for *Vetus Latina*), followed by superscript lower-case letters indicating the manuscript(s) cited. The individual manuscripts will be introduced as occasion arises. The Vulgate is shown by Lvg followed by superscript capital letters for the manuscripts. Lvt or Lvg without superscript letters shows that all the manuscripts, or at least all those consulted, agree.

The Coptic versions are shown by cop followed by a superscript abbreviation for the dialect: sa bo ach fa are all self-explanatory; mae indicates the Middle Egyptian. A form such as cop[sa mss] indicates that some manuscripts of the Sahidic version support the reading in question.

The abbreviations for the other versions are self-explanatory.

Patristic citations

Our third category is of early Christian writers. The quotation of Scripture is found from St Paul onwards, and some kind of references to the first-century Christian writings from the begin-

ning of the second century. The very allusive citations of the
earliest writers are of little use for our purposes, and it is only from
the middle of the second century that we have materials that enable
us to reconstruct the text of the manuscript that the writer was
using, or at least of manuscripts with which he was familiar. Where
we can be sure of the Greek text known to a writer, we can be sure
of both the date and the place where that text was known. As with
the versions, the text of the fathers of the third and fourth century
can in theory be as valuable as that of a manuscript of that period.
And writers of a later period may often have had access to earlier
materials.

The problems in recovering an early writer's text can be severe.
For, like Greek manuscripts and versions, his writings will have
their own copying history. If they became condemned as heretical
or simply lost their appeal, their very survival will have been at
stake. Thus the text of the second-century writer Marcion can only
be reconstructed in part, from the writings of his opponents. Many
of the extensive writings of some of the most important early
writers, such as Clement of Alexandria and Origen, are lost. Other
authors are lost to us almost totally, such as the second-century
writer Papias. Sometimes a work survives only in translation; thus
much of the text of the second-century writings of Irenaeus,
originally in Greek, are available to us only in Latin. It is sometimes
the case that a critical edition of a work has yet to be made, and that
the only edition available is based on whatever medieval manuscripts a sixteenth- or seventeenth-century editor happened to
come across.

There are further specific problems in recovering the biblical
text known to the writer. Later copyists often altered the biblical
text into agreement with the form known to them. Longer
quotations, including the blocks at the beginning of a passage in a
commentary, were particularly vulnerable. We shall therefore
have to treat such passages with suspicion, especially when they
seem to agree with later standard texts. Even after this, we shall
need to be sure that the text was actually written in a manuscript
known to the writer. A preacher may change a text slightly in order
to bring out the point he wishes to stress. And always there is the
possibility that the writer is quoting loosely or from memory.

Thus, the reconstruction of the text known to an early Christian writer requires caution. But the results can be spectacular when the evidence has been gathered and analysed.

And we must not be altogether despondent about the material that has been lost. We should remember that many long-lost writings have been recovered in modern times, and that many texts have been critically edited. Frustrating though our lack of information often is, we can at least comfort ourselves that we have more at our disposal than our predecessors of a century ago.

Finally, the writings of the fathers can obviously be of great value – much more than the versions – in finding how the text was interpreted in the early church.

The fathers may be subdivided according to the language in which they wrote. Again, the Greek, Latin and Syriac are the most significant, as well as the most numerous.

2

Thus far the established pattern of describing the materials that contain forms of the text. The second presentation takes a different form. It attempts to describe the kind of witnesses that would have been available to readers of the Gospels at different periods. We have in each era to imagine that we are a person with the freedom to choose books unhampered by the realities of cost, availability or theological controversy. For present purposes we must also set aside the likelihood that for much of the period under discussion Gospel books are more generally likely to have been owned by communities and used for communities than to have been private possessions acquired for personal use.

We have already seen how the manuscripts are classified according to materials, script and contents. In what follows, the physical characteristics of the copies will be frequently mentioned. This aspect of the study of the Gospels will be discussed carefully in the final chapters.

We begin in the early second century. All four canonical Gospels are in existence. Only one tiny scrap of manuscript survives from this period, but it is enough to encourage us to believe that it is worth asking two questions: what, physically, did a Gospel book look like? and what did it contain? The physical question concerns writing material and format. As to material, we have a choice between papyrus and parchment. We may safely settle for the former, since that is the material on which all our manuscripts older than about 225 are written (there are not certainly more than seven of them). The choice of format is between roll and codex, the format for a book which we accept as normal. There are some important distinctions here. The preferred format for Jewish Scriptures was the parchment or leather roll; that for Greek and Latin literary texts was the papyrus roll. By contrast, all but six of the surviving New Testament texts generally agreed to have been produced before the year 300 are papyrus codices. Of the six exceptions, two are papyrus rolls (one contains the Gospels) and four are parchment rolls. It thus appears that from as early as we can ascertain, Christians preferred a distinct, not to say strange, format for the writings which were to become known as the New Testament.

It has even been proposed that the codex form was invented by Christians.[10] Several explanations have been suggested: that Mark, writing in Rome in the sixties, used a notebook to jot down material and ideas which he worked into a Gospel, and that this notebook form remained with it and, by association, was extended to other Gospels and to other writings such as those of Paul; that early Christians preserved a record of sayings and acts of Jesus by imitating the Jewish practice of transcribing oral teachings onto wax tablets; that the codex appealed because it was cheaper than the roll to produce; that it was the formation of the Pauline *corpus*, too large for a single roll, that led to the Christian preference for the codex. Against the theory that Christians invented the codex, it has been argued that there was a general transition from roll to codex, which happened more swiftly in Christian circles. Be that as it may,

[10] For the following arguments see C. H. Roberts, 'The Codex', *Proceedings of the British Academy* 40 (1954), 169–204; C. H. Roberts and T. C. Skeat, *The Birth of the Codex* (London, Oxford 1983); T. C. Skeat, 'The Length of the Papyrus Roll and the Cost Advantage of the Codex', *Zeitschrift für Papyrusforschung und Epigraphik* 45 (1982), 169–75; Harry Y. Gamble, *Books and Readers in the Early Church: A History of Early Christian Texts* (New Haven and London, 1995), pp. 49–66. The hypothesis against Christian invention of the format is advanced by J. van Haelst, 'Les Origines du Codex', in A. Blanchard (ed.), *Les Débuts du codex*, Bibliologia 9 (Turnhout, 1989), pp. 13–35.

the fact is quite clear that the use of the papyrus codex is a unique feature in the early production of the Gospels.

But by contrast to what has been proposed for Mark, Luke appears to have divided his account of Jesus and the early church into two volumes, his Gospels and Acts, so that they would fit conveniently on two rolls.

With regard to contents, it seems unlikely that the early second-century reader will have possessed more than one Gospel in any one book. In one other respect that reader will have read the texts quite differently from us: in the knowledge of a perhaps quite extensive body of oral traditions still circulating. In later chapters, we shall find examples of passages which were probably part of the oral tradition until the second century before they were added to the written tradition. It is important to be aware that the relationship between the written and the spoken word in the early church was quite different from that which we assume today. The Gospels were written rather to support than to replace the oral tradition.

In this first period, then, our reader either has only one Gospel, or has a pile of books, each containing one; possibly quite an awkward pile, if at least one of them was produced as a roll and at least one as a codex.

Let us move on to the year 200. By now, it is possible to possess a book containing more than one Gospel. There is even a papyrus of this period which may have originally contained all four Gospels.[11] Another surviving book (P75) contains Luke and John.

The Gospel books of this early period did not contain many aids for the reader. Written for the most part without any space between words and with very little punctuation, they lack any means of finding your place in the text. The most that you could hope for was page numbers, and (in a book containing more than one) a note telling you which Gospel was ending and which beginning. Anyone who has worked with such manuscripts will be familiar with the problems of orientation. Given the similarity of

---

[11] T. C. Skeat argues that a manuscript of about 200, whose remains are now divided between libraries in Oxford, Paris and Barcelona, is the oldest surviving copy of four Gospels in one codex. Although it is a single manuscript, it is listed as three separate ones in the List: P⁴, P⁶⁴ and P⁶⁷.

much of the material in the Synoptic Gospels, it may take some
time to find out which Gospel one is studying. It is clear that not all
the possibilities of the codex format were immediately recognised.

A significant mark of this period is that the reader has a wider
choice by now. In the middle of the second century, a book called
the Diatessaron had been produced by the Syrian writer Tatian. It
was a weaving together of the four separate Gospels into a single
narrative. Tatian was not the first to produce such a harmony, but
it was his that became the most popular in the ancient world. It was
translated many times, and formed the foundation of a tradition of
harmonies that was to last until the end of the Middle Ages. In
Syria, the Diatessaron became more popular than the separated
Gospels. But Tatian himself came quite soon to be regarded as a
heretic, and his great work increasingly to be either disregarded or
intentionally suppressed (in Syria over two hundred copies were
destroyed by a fifth-century reforming bishop). The result is that no
certain fragment of the Diatessaron survives. There is even dispute
about the language in which he first produced it. Was it Greek, or
Syriac, or even Latin? In order to recover Tatian's text we need to
study the representatives of the harmonies descended from him.
They divide into two branches. The eastern is represented by
harmonies in Arabic and in Persian. The western's main representatives are Latin and a large collection of medieval versions, in
various dialects of German, Italian (Venetian and Tuscan), Dutch
and Middle English (represented by a single manuscript once in the
possession of Samuel Pepys). In addition, there are other witnesses
which occasionally provide Diatessaronic readings. These include
such disparate documents as the Old Syriac Gospels and an Old
Saxon poem about Jesus called *The Heliand* ('The Saviour').[12]

One third-century fragment of a Greek harmony has been
believed to belong to the Diatessaron.[13] But the identification is by
no means certain, and I am now convinced that this fragment is not

---

[12] A recent full survey is provided by W. L. Petersen, *Tatian's Diatessaron: Its Creation,
Dissemination, Significance, and History in Scholarship*, Supplements to Vigiliae Christianae 25
(Leiden, 1994).

[13] The fragment was found at Dura Europos, a city on the Roman empire's Euphrates
frontier which was captured in 257. Archaeology provides firm evidence that the volume
was produced before 256–7; palaeography that it was made in the third century. A date of
around 220–30 is generally agreed.

a copy of Tatian's work. However, it remains the oldest extant fragment of a harmony, and I provide a translation, to illustrate the kind of form in which the Gospel story was perhaps best known to many down to the time of the Reformation. The presentation attempts to show how the four accounts are woven together. Since the text is fragmentary, the attempt to provide an English translation is all the harder, and I have not aimed at grammatical English.

The square brackets try to show the equivalent parts to the missing Greek letters; an x in bold type indicates a precise parallel; one in ordinary type means that something similar is found in that Gospel; angle brackets around an x indicate that the wording is found in only one or more manuscripts of that Gospel.

	Matthew 27.55–7	Mark 15.40–2	Luke 23.49–55	John 19.25, 31, 38, 42
[of Zebed]ee	**x**			
and Salome		**x**		
a[nd]	⟨**x**⟩	**x**	**x**	
the		⟨**x**⟩		
wives	**x**	**x**	**x**	
of those who followed [wit]h	x	x	x	
h[i]m		**x**	**x**	
from [Galil]ee	**x**		**x**	
to see			**x**	
the crucified one.				
Now it was			⟨**x**⟩	
[... da]y Preparation				x
the sabbath was dawn[ing.				**x**
Wh]en it was late	**x**	x		
on the D[ay of Pr]ep[ar]a[tion]		x		x
which is before the sabbath,		**x**	⟨x⟩	
there ca[me]	⟨**x**⟩			
a man	**x**			
w[ho w]as			**x**	
a member of the council,		**x**	**x**	
[fr]om Erinmathai[a]	x	x	x	x
a c[i]ty of [Judae]a,			⟨**x**⟩	
called	⟨**x**⟩		x	
Jo[seph],	**x**	**x**	**x**	**x**
g[o]od ri[ghteous],			⟨**x**⟩	
being a disciple [o]f Jesus				**x**

	Matthew	Mark	Luke	John
but se[cret]ly				x
for fear of the [Jew]s				x
and he		x	⟨x⟩	
awaited [the] k[ingdom] of God.		x	x	
He was not [cons]enting			x	
to the p[urpose]			x	

The reader may wish to browse in a synopsis or a Bible to work out how this composition was stitched together. Of particular interest are several unique wordings (note 'the wives of those who followed', 'the crucified one', and 'Erinmathaia') and the building up of phrases about the day of the week, with no attempt to make a grammatical sentence out of them.

Besides Tatian, another writer had produced a severely edited version of Luke's Gospel. The writer was Marcion, and his version of Luke was to continue in use in Marcionite churches for some centuries. We know also from writers such as Clement of Alexandria (writing in the period 180–215) that there were other Gospels in circulation as well as the canonical four. The books that readers used will have depended partly on the group to which they belonged. The Marcionite congregations used only Marcion's version of Luke. Various Gnostic groups used extra-canonical Gospels. Some churches used the Diatessaron. It is important to remember that the later concept of orthodoxy is in some respects an anachronism, for no one group in the church was in that position of power necessary if other groups are to be outlawed or prohibited. Instead, Christianity of this age consisted of a number of competing groups, approving and condemning one another as they saw fit.[14]

We move on from 200 to 300. By now it is commonplace to have the four Gospels in one book. It will still almost certainly be written on papyrus, though it might just be possible to find one on parchment. The style of handwriting may be of almost any kind used for copying books – there are no conventions as yet. There are no more aids for the reader than previously. The changes that

---

[14] The work to which this view of early Christianity is principally indebted is Walter Bauer, *Orthodoxy and Heresy in Earliest Christianity* (Philadelphia, 1971).

occurred at this time are of two kinds. The first is that in the course of this century the texts associated with particular centres have acquired more distinctive characteristics, and we see the first developments in the direction of standard, agreed texts. The process might be explained with a biological analogy: selective breeding enhances particular characteristics. Thus, the copy that you have will be likely to be more uniform with others in your ambience, and more distinctive from those used in other places. The second change is the Diocletianic persecution, which began in 303. Holy books had to be surrendered to be burned. Two consequences followed: a tightening up in the definition of holy books, encouraging the formation of the canon; and the loss of many Gospel books, leading to their scarcity. The consequences of this scarcity will be described shortly.

We move on to the middle of the fourth century. By now the Peace of Constantine (313) has caused dramatic changes to the church, and with that to the production of Christian books. The need to replace books lost during the persecution, the demand for more copies as the church grew, and increased wealth and hence freedom for scholarly and scribal pursuits all contributed to the change. There is now a much wider spread of demand, including that for de luxe books at the top end of the market. The change is perhaps best exemplified by a well-known passage in Eusebius of Caesarea's Life of Constantine (written in the late 330s). Eusebius received a letter from the emperor. He transcribed it in its entirety into his Life:

It happens, through the favouring providence of God our saviour, that great numbers have united themselves to the most holy church in the city which is called by my name. It seems, therefore, highly requisite . . . that the number of churches should also be increased. Do you, therefore, receive with all readiness my determination on this behalf. I have thought it expedient to instruct your Prudence to order fifty copies of the sacred scriptures (the provision and use of which you know to be most needful for the instruction of the Church) to be written on fine parchment in a legible manner, and in a commodious and portable form, by scribes thoroughly skilled in their art. The procurator of the diocese has also received instructions by letter from our Clemency to be careful to furnish all things necessary for the preparation of such copies; and it will be for you to take special care that they be completed with as little delay as possible. You have authority also, in virtue of this letter, to use two of the public carriages for their conveyance, by which arrangement the copies when fairly written will most easily be forwarded for my personal inspection; and one of the deacons of your church may be intrusted with this service, who, on his arrival here, shall experience my liberality. God preserve you, beloved brother![15]

It is impressive to see the imperial mind and machinery going into action with such meticulous attention to detail. Slightly less encouraging is the emperor's confidence in his abilities to assess the end product. A number of more specific points attract our attention: first, mass production of entire Bibles. Only a hundred years before, a book containing more than one Gospel was an innovation. Now we have fifty copies of the entire Scriptures. The order was also for copies on parchment. Virtually every extant copy of the Gospels older than the Peace of Constantine is on papyrus. Although papyrus did not go out of use for some centuries yet, from now on parchment is the preferred material, if you could afford it. Certainly, it was preferred for church use. The order is specifically for fine parchment – the best is expected. Finally, good professional scribes were to be employed. Accurate and beautiful copies were required. During the fourth century there developed the style of writing that is called biblical majuscule, or biblical uncial, a beautiful and economical hand that was to be used for most Greek biblical manuscripts during the ensuing centuries. Its character meets the requirements laid down by Constantine.

The custom of producing luxury books included purple manuscripts. The parchment was dyed a rich plum colour, and silver and even gold ink was used. Not everyone approved of such lavish adornment: Jerome condemned those who spent money on such books while Christ died in poverty at their gate. He emphasises that high-quality production is no guarantee of accuracy.[16]

---

[15] *The Life of the Blessed Emperor Constantine* (London, 1845), 4.36 (pp. 204f.) (translation slightly revised).

[16] Advising an enquirer: 'think less of gilding, and Babylonian parchment, and arabesque patterns, than of correctness and accurate punctuation' Jerome, Letter 107.12); 'Let those who will keep the old books with their gold and silver letters on purple skins ... loads of writing rather than manuscripts, if only they will leave for me and mine our poor pages and copies which are less remarkable for beauty than for accuracy' (Preface to his translation of Job from Hebrew into Latin).

Along with the changes in material and in script which have already been described, our fourth-century reader is fortunate in another way. A number of extremely useful aids for readers were devised. A scholar called Ammonius (his dates are unknown) had divided each Gospel into numbered paragraphs. Eusebius of Caesarea provided prefatory tables which allowed the reader to use these numbers quickly to find the parallel passage in the other Gospels. Other systems of paragraph division were introduced. Some manuscripts were copied in sense-lines, so that the sense was more easily found. Running titles became more common, so that it was easier to find one's way around the book. Colophons and titles at the beginning and end of books were developed.

Yet another element of choice to appear was the translation of the Gospels. The first stages of such translation may have been instantaneous translation after the reading of the Gospel in Greek. Such a practice in Jerusalem is attested by a pilgrim as late as the fourth century.[17] By the time of which I am now speaking, vernacular copies will have been the norm in many areas. Most of western Christianity had ceased to be Greek speaking and had adopted Latin by the beginning of the third century. The oldest Old Latin manuscripts that we possess date from shortly after the middle of the fourth century. In addition to Greek and versional manuscripts, a number of bilinguals have survived. The ones that concern us have Greek as one language, and as the other some have Latin and some Coptic. Sometimes they are the product of a bilingual community or district; sometimes they are testimony to the regard in which the original Greek was held. They may also be proof of scholarly interest in producing translations that are faithful to the Greek.

We may see that the user of reasonable affluence has a choice. At the top end is a high-quality copy professionally written on parchment; at the bottom end is the papyrus book; in between there are compromises. The parchment book was likely to contain more than the one made of papyrus, partly because the material was more robust and the page size could be larger, and partly because if you could afford parchment you could probably also

---

[17] *Egeria; Diary of a Pilgrimage*, tr. G. E. Gingras, Ancient Christian Writers 38 (New York, 1970), 47.3–4. The pilgrim's name will also be found spelt as Aetheria and Etheria.

afford more pages. It is interesting to see Jerome complaining about this as well, in a letter to a friend who had asked for copies of some Old Testament books which he did not possess. Jerome sternly tells him to be content with what he has and not to want too much. Our imaginary user, once he has made his choice, now has a book that is much easier to use. He is also likely to have had less difficulty getting hold of one in the first place.

The destruction of manuscripts in the Diocletianic persecution was followed by an increased demand. The few surviving manuscripts were the source from which the many new copies were derived. The range of texts represented by the majority of fourth-century copies is thus markedly narrower than the range of the previous centuries, although neither local nor all early forms were completely lost.

We move on more quickly now, to the sixth century. Biblical majuscule has become well established, and is even showing signs of decline. The conventions of manuscripts are firmly fixed. Textually, a trend that was already beginning in the fourth century has accelerated. The growth of influence of a number of key sees, particularly Antioch, Alexandria and Constantinople, led to a standardising of the text. Bishops' power was increasing, and one way of asserting power was to control the biblical text. In addition, such centres had the resources to produce copies. Our sixth-century reader is likely to have a copy of the Gospels whose text is well on the way to becoming the standard Byzantine text. We are far removed from the church of the second century; now, and for some time, there has been a structure and an authority in the catholic church which gives it confidence to banish heresy in the name of its catholicity. This is neatly encapsulated in the story of Tatian's Diatessaron. Theodoret became bishop of a town in upper Syria in 423, and found the Diatessaron in common use. Tatian was by now deemed heretical, and his work therefore came under suspicion. Theodoret had every copy destroyed, and replaced the Diatessaron with the separated Gospels. Theodoret had both the will and the power to eliminate texts which he condemned.

By now, the ornamentation of manuscripts has increased. It also becomes possible to own an illustrated Gospels. From this era dates the oldest such book, although there are other biblical manuscripts with miniatures from somewhat earlier. The provision of pictures places the text in a different light for the reader. This may best be illustrated by the example of a manuscript of the Pentateuch. It has a series of miniatures accompanying the story of Joseph. But the miniatures contain material and scenes which are found in Jewish apocryphal writings, and not in the written text of Genesis. Thus the entire manuscript, text and pictures, is telling a different story from that found in the text alone.[18]

From this time onwards, we could choose another innovation, a *catena* manuscript. This contains, around the text, a chain (in Latin, *catena*) of selections from patristic commentaries on the text. A page of such a manuscript contains more catena than biblical text.[19] This is the place at which we may also note other kinds of copies. Amulets, containing short phrases as a prayer or charm, were common. Less frequent, but still not uncommon, are copies of the Gospels which were used for fortune telling. Six of the surviving papyrus copies of John are in this category. A verse or short passage would be followed by a lot – a sentence detailing something to be done or avoided. Gospel manuscripts proper were sometimes converted to this use by the addition of such sentences in the margins.

Our next stopping place is in the tenth century. We are looking at an early minuscule manuscript. One thing is obvious – the page looks so different. A new script changes the text in the eye and mind of the reader. As we turn the pages, we find that there is more ancillary material. There is likely to be a series of prologues, containing information about the book and its author. The Eusebian canons and canon tables are present. The chapters now have titles, and there is a list of them at the beginning of each Gospel. The text itself has fuller punctuation. A colophon may give us the name of the scribe and the date on which he finished,

---

[18] K. Weitzmann, *Late Antique and Early Christian Book Illumination* (New York, 1977), Plates 25–8. The manuscript is the Vienna Genesis.
[19] The oldest surviving example is the majuscule Ξ 040, Codex Zacynthius. It has been variously dated to the eighth and the sixth centuries. Examination of the two scripts of the manuscript leads me to prefer the seventh century.

and ask us to pray for him. If we wish to, we may decide not to select a continuous-text manuscript, but to choose a lectionary instead.

Our remaining visits are all in north-west Europe. First, we become students in thirteenth-century Paris. At this stage in the culture of Latin Christendom knowledge of Greek and the Greek Bible is extremely rare. The Gospels are preserved solely in Latin dress, a version now with its own thousand-year-old history. The copy that we are looking at is one of many complete Bibles sharing a standard format and a standard text, for standardisation was the hallmark of the Paris Bible. Handy and comparatively cheap, it is the closest yet to mass production. The aids for the reader are very similar to those in the tenth-century Greek manuscript – prologues, lists of chapters (now the same chapters as we know today), fairly full punctuation.

We cross the English Channel and another century, into a parish church. Latin is the liturgical language. So, if we know no Latin are we unable to read or listen to the Gospels? In church, the story will be conveyed in the paintings and the windows and the homily. In private, vernacular versions may be used. In a country whose bishops had been made anxious by the views and activities of Wycliffe and his followers, a licence was necessary for the possession of an English Bible to be legal. Such licences were not easy to obtain.

As elsewhere, we have the choice between separate Gospels and a Harmony. Here, as a sample of the latter, are a few lines of the Pepysian Harmony. It covers the same passage as the third-century fragment which has been quoted above. I have modernised the spelling:

And sithen it was evensong time, come a noble rich baron, good and rightful, that had ten knights to his banner, that ne had nought assented to the counsel and the deeds of the Jews; for he was one of Jesus' disciples, privily, for dread of the Jews.[20]

---

[20] Altered from Marjery Coates, *The Pepysian Gospel Harmony* (London: Early English Text Society, 1922), p. 100. The ten knights are from the Latin word *decurio*, translating the Greek word which our modern versions render as 'a member of the council'.

We move on to the year 1516. In our hands, straight from Basle, is a copy of Erasmus' printed Greek New Testament, the first to be published. It has two columns to the page. One is the Greek text, constructed by Erasmus from the Greek manuscripts which he consulted in Basle University Library; and the second is his own Latin translation. The Greek and the new Latin offer a challenge to the supremacy of the official Vulgate. The excitement – and dismay – at this publication spreads across Europe. It is the supreme example of that Renaissance goal, the recovery of the Greek fountainhead of knowledge. It is also a part of a technological revolution: as many identical copies as can be sold may be produced. And this change in the nature of the copies led to a change in the perception of the texts contained in them. It gave the printed book an authority that had been beyond the reach of any manuscript. This development, to which we shall return in the final chapters, was of great significance.

In 1611, there has come to an end an important era in the production of the English Bible. Three principal survivors remain:[21] the Geneva Bible, extremely popular ever since its fashioning by exiles during the reign of Mary; the Authorised Version of 1611, and the Douai Bible, whose New Testament was published in 1582. The Gospels are now available on a scale hitherto inconceivable. These Bibles have chapter and verse divisions; they have prologues; they contain marginalia of various kinds; the first two of them are translated from modern Hebrew and Greek editions.

Finally, today. It is nineteen hundred years since the earliest Christians preferred codices to scrolls, a thousand since the minuscule script assumed supremacy, five hundred since copying gave way to printing. And now we lay aside our printed Greek New Testament, push a CD-ROM or diskette into the drive or log into the World-Wide Web, and summon up the electronic text, so that we may manipulate it on the screen. A revolution at least as profound as those of the second and the sixteenth century is under way. Its implications will be discussed at the end of this book. At

---

[21] One should mention also the version of Coverdale, still continuing in use today as the texts of the Epistles and Gospels in the Book of Common Prayer.

present the fact is emphasised, because it is becoming an essential part of the way in which we are now coming to understand the two-thousand-year-old tradition that has brought the Gospels to us.

CHAPTER 3

The practice

The golden rule is that there are no golden rules.
George Bernard Shaw, *Maxims for Revolutionists*

Such are the materials. What is the task of textual criticism? What kind of problems demand our attention? The reader who is used to the occasional note at the bottom of the page that runs 'Other ancient authorities read...', where a particularly significant or troublesome problem arises, may wonder what manuscript variation there is to demand so much attention. The kinds of problem and the scope of the variation are best shown by examining a specimen passage.

Translations of three manuscripts of Luke 6.1–10 will be studied and compared. The example is admittedly a particularly dramatic one, but I select it because it contains so much that can be considered. The examination will consist of two parts. The first will look in detail at the kinds of differences between the manuscripts, and describe ways of analysing them. The second will look at the cumulative effect of these differences, and at the distinctive character of each of the manuscripts. The investigation will therefore also show how text-critical studies are developed, by the accumulation of large amounts of small details in order to reach an assessment of a witness's character.

I set alongside each other three manuscripts of Luke 6 and graphically illustrate the variation between them. On the left is Codex Vaticanus. It is a manuscript of the entire Bible in Greek (one of only four surviving from antiquity). It has been in the Vatican Library since before 1475. It was copied towards the

31

middle of the fourth century, the Old Testament by two scribes and the New by one, in the hand known as biblical majuscule. The last pages were at some time lost, and replaced in the fifteenth century. It has long been agreed that for most of the New Testament it is the most reliable witness to the text preserved in Alexandria. This form of text shows clear evidence of having been produced with the scholarly care that had been developed at Alexandria by editors of classical texts, above all that of Homer. Its text was the foundation of the edition called *The New Testament in the Original Greek*, produced in 1881 by Westcott and Hort, itself the foundation of all subsequent critical editions. It is carefully copied, consistent in spelling and in presentation. It bears the hallmarks of a controlled text, in that the language and grammar of the writers seem sometimes to have been improved, and care has been taken to include no material that could have been added by copyists. The character of its text aside, its great age ensured that it received the attention it deserved. The manuscript is known by the letter B and the number 02.

The manuscript in the middle column is D 05, Codex Bezae. This witness was produced in about the year 400. It is a bilingual, its languages Greek and Latin. It was probably copied by a professional Latin scribe, for it has the reader's aids that would have been typical of a Latin book of the time. I have argued that it was produced in Berytus (Beirut), which at that time was an important centre for Latin studies (particularly of Roman law) in the eastern empire. It contained certainly the Gospels, Johannine epistles and Acts of the Apostles (portions of all of these survive), and possibly Revelation as well. As will become clear, its text is quite different in character from those flanking it. That character is best discovered by examining it. Our concern is at present only with the Greek text, but we shall find in time that its Latin version (one of the Old Latin, pre-Jerome versions) is also both important and interesting.

The third manuscript is known by the Greek letter Ω (*omega*) (Mount Athos, Codex Dionysiou 10, with the Gregory–Aland number 045). Copied in the sixth century, it is an early representative of the standard Byzantine text. This text, as we have seen, is the one that increasingly dominated, until it exercised a virtual monopoly in the Byzantine period.

The texts are printed with different typefaces and symbols to indicate the similarities and differences. The indicators are of two kinds.

The first is of wording. **Bold type** indicates wording that is unique to that manuscript. This may consist either of added wording, or the same lexical item as the others but with an alteration. Because of the nature of the Greek language, there are more of this second type than there would be in an English text. Of course, the difference cannot always be expressed in translation. *Italic type* indicates wording in which two manuscripts agree against the third. Roman type is used where all three have the same wording. † indicates that wording found in one or both of the other witnesses is not present in this one; ‡ that two of the witnesses lack wording found in the third.

The other indicators are of word order. <u>Double underlining</u> indicates that the word order is unique to that manuscript. <u>Single underlining</u> indicates that the word order is shared with one of the other two witnesses. Again, such differences cannot always be properly expressed in English.[1]

---

[1] The word which I have translated literally as 'second-first' has never been satisfactorily explained. The Authorised Version's 'the second sabbath after the first' has little apparent sense, though the suggestion I am about to make provides some. The only analogy in Greek literature is its use at a later date to describe Low Sunday. Here, it might simply be an error: Burkitt ingeniously suggested that a scribe wrote *sabbatobato*, repeating the last four letters of 'sabbath' by mistake; since *beta* in Greek numerals represents 2 and *alpha* 1, this was wrongly understood by a copyist as 'sabbath second-first', with the ending *to* as the last two letters of *proto*, 'first' (F. C. Burkitt, *The Gospel History and its Transmission*, 3rd edn (Edinburgh, 1911), p. 81n). Nobody has come up with anything better. Jerome's comment shows that the word has always baffled: 'My teacher, Gregory of Nazianzus, when I once asked him to explain Luke's phrase *sabbaton deuteroproton*, that is "the second-first sabbath"', playfully evaded my request saying: "I will tell you about it in church, and there, when all the people applaud me, you will be forced against your will to know what you do not know at all. For, if you alone remain silent, every one will put you down for a fool"' (Jerome, Letter 52, to Nepotian, section 8; from Jerome, *Letters*, p. 93).

It seems to me that the phrase must refer back to the previous sabbath incidents in Chapter 4; 4.31 could imply that Jesus went straight from Nazareth to Capernaum and taught there on the same day. The second sabbath after the first would then (on the analogy of Low Sunday) mean that the events of 6.1–11 occurred a week later.

B (CODEX VATICANUS)

¹*Now* it came to pass on **a** sabbath,
that <u>he</u> was going through
† cornfields,
and his disciples were
plucking and <u>eating</u> the
heads of grain, rubbing
them in their hands.
²But some of the Pharisees
said ‡,
'Why
are you doing
<u>what is not lawful</u>
<u>on the sabbath?'</u>
³*And* <u>answering them</u>
<u>Jesus said</u>
'Have you *not* read
what David did,
when he was hungry,
he and those
⁺⁄₋ *with* him?

⁴ *He entered* into
the house of God,
and **taking** ate the
shewbread, and gave
† to those with him,
which it *is* not lawful
to eat except only
the priests.'

⁵And he said to them †
<u>'The Son of man is</u>
<u>lord of the sabbath †.'</u>
⁺⁄₋

D (CODEX BEZAE)

¹**And** it came to pass on
a second-first sabbath
that <u>he</u> was going through
the cornfields.
Now <u>his disciples</u> **began**
<u>to pluck</u> the heads of grain
and rubbing
them in their hands <u>ate</u>.
²But some of the Pharisees
said *to* **him**
'**Look** what **your disciples**
are doing
<u>on the sabbath</u>
<u>which is not lawful.</u>
³**But** answering
<u>Jesus</u> **said** <u>to them</u>
'Have you **never** read
this that David did, *when* he
was hungry, he and those ⁺⁄₋
with him?
⁴⁺⁄₋ **Entering** into the house
of God,
and † he ate the shewbread,
and gave *also* to those with
him,
which it **was** not lawful to
eat except only
for the priests.

The same day, seeing
someone working on the
sabbath, he said to him,
'Man, if indeed you
know what you are
doing then you are
blessed.
But if you do not know,
then you are accursed
and a
transgressor of the law.'

Ω (CODEX ATHOUS DION.)

¹*Now* it came to pass on
the second-first sabbath
that <u>he</u> was going through
the cornfields,
and his disciples were
plucking the heads of grain
<u>and eating</u>, rubbing
them in their hands.
²But some of the Pharisees
said to **them**
'Why
are you doing
<u>what it is not lawful</u>
to do upon the sabbath?'
³*And* answering <u>them</u>
Jesus said
'Have you *not* read
what David did,
when he was hungry,
he and those
who were *with* him?
⁴**How** *he entered* into
the house of God,
and **took and** ate the
shewbread, and gave
also to those with him,
which it *is* not lawful
to eat except only
the priests.'
⁵And he said to them that
<u>'The Son of man is</u>
<u>lord of the sabbath also.'</u>
⁺⁄₋

(CODEX VATICANUS)	(CODEX BEZAE)	(CODEX ATHOUS DION.)
[6]*Now it came to pass on another* sabbath, *that he entered* the synagogue *and taught;* *and* there was <u>a man *there*,</u> *and his right hand was withered.* [7]*Now* the scribes and the Pharisees *watched him* ... [10]And looking around at <u>all of them</u> ‡, *he said to him* 'Stretch out your hand.' *And he did,* and his hand **was restored**. †	[6]**And when he entered again** <u>into the synagogue on a sabbath,</u> † **in which** there was a man **who had a withered hand,** [7]† the scribes and the Pharisees *watched him* ... [10]And looking around at <u>them all</u> **in anger,** **he says to the man** 'Stretch out your hand.' **And he stretched it out** and his hand *was* *restored* *like* also the other one. [5]<u>And he said to them that 'The Son of man is lord even of the sabbath.'</u>	[6]*Now it came to pass on another* sabbath *that he* *entered* the synagogue *and taught;* *and* there was <u>*there* a man,</u> *and his right hand was withered.* [7]*Now* the scribes and the Pharisees **watched** † ... [10]And looking around at <u>all of them[‡]</u>, *he said to him* 'Stretch out your hand.' *And he did,* and his hand *was* *restored* **whole** *like the other one.*
[11]But they were filled with fury ...	[11]But they were filled with fury ...	[11]But they were filled with fury ...

Variation of word order within verse 5 is here recorded separately, for the sake of clarity:

B (CODEX VATICANUS)	D (CODEX BEZAE)	Ω (CODEX ATHOUS DION.)
[5]And he said to them † 'The Son of man is <u>lord of the sabbath</u> †.'	And he said to them *that* 'The Son of man is <u>lord even</u> of the sabbath.'	And he said to them *that* 'The Son of man is <u>lord of the sabbath *also*.</u>'

THE TYPES OF VARIATION

1.   The most obvious difference is in the addition and omission of material. We can find an example in every verse.

verse 1   the odd word 'second-first' found in D and Ω
            'began to' in D
verse 2   'to him' in D and 'to them' in Ω are neither in B
            the introduction of the disciples in D
            the verb 'to do' and a separate preposition in Ω

verse 3 the added verb in Ω
verse 4 the taking of the shewbread in B and Ω
     'also' in B and Ω
     the long addition in D
verse 5 'that' and 'also' in D and Ω
verse 6 'and taught' in B and Ω
     the statement that it was his *right* hand in B and Ω
verse 7 'Now' in B and Ω
     'him' in B and Ω
verse 10 'in anger' in D
     the comparison of his hands in D and Ω

2. Changes in word order. Again, there is an example in every verse. Most striking is the fact that verse 5 is found in a quite different place in D. In addition, D and Ω agree in the word order within the verse against B. Sometimes the changes seem quite insignificant. But where they are extensive, or occur in conjunction with other types of variation (as in verses 2 and 6), they are important.

3. The substitution of one wording for another may also be observed. It includes differences in the tense of the verb (for example 'said' in verse 2, and in the case of nouns (as in the very end of verse 4). In verse 3 Ω uses a different preposition meaning 'with' against the other two. The words that I translate 'now' and 'and' are used at the beginnings of verse 1 and verse 6.

Besides these smaller points, often matters of grammatical niceties, are some blocks where the wording varies:

verse 2 'Look what your disciples are doing' in D against the other
     two
verse 6 the whole introduction to the story is different in D from
     the other two
     the description of the man's condition is different in D
     from the other two
verse 10 'And he stretched it out' in D against the other two.

One should include here casual errors by the copyists. Ω omits a syllable of the word translated as **second-first**. It is not always possible to distinguish between copying errors and intentional changes. I digress to discuss this point.

The difficulty of distinguishing between intentional and unintentional errors is that it arises from a deficient understanding of human behaviour. In the 'Freudian slip', we have learned to recognise how the unconscious can control our spoken words. There are many places in manuscripts of the Greek New Testament where the scribe may have changed the sense unconsciously. In addition, there are problems of the way in which the written language fails adequately to represent the changing spoken language. For example, the two Greek words 'to us' (*hēmin*) and 'to you' (*humin*) were pronounced identically (*eemin*) in the period from which our manuscripts come. The result is frequent confusion, as may be found in any edition of the letters of Paul. The distinction between intentional and unintentional error is therefore best avoided. Only the production of complete nonsense can safely be called accidental. Intentional nonsense falls into a category of its own. Instead, one may speak of conscious or unconscious alteration.

Conscious alteration comprises the correction of the text being copied for various reasons: because the copyist knows another version of the text and believes that to be superior; because of the belief that the text being copied is in error and needs to be improved (this could include stylistic improvement, harmonisation to the text of another Gospel, theological correction and removal of nonsense reading). Unconscious alteration may be due to any of the reasons for conscious alteration and to other factors also. Some of these are apparently random. In typing out the text of verse 10 in the middle column, I first produced 'He said to the paralytic'. Others are due to the scribe's writing the word phonetically, as it was heard, rather than as it should be written. This phenomenon, known as itacism, includes the example of *hēmin* and *humin* that we have already noted.

Here the observations of the French scholar Alphonse Dain are worth following.[2] He divided the act of copying a text into four stages: reading the manuscript being copied, remembering it, repeating it, and writing it. It should be noted that since all reading in the ancient world was aloud, the third stage will have consisted in speaking the words audibly. Dain goes on to demonstrate how

---

[2] A. Dain, *Les Manuscrits*, Collections des Etudes Anciennes, 3rd edn (Paris, 1975), pp. 41–6.

each stage gives occasion to its own typical errors. The first includes misreading the text and the eye going back to the wrong place, leading either to repetition or to omission. The second, I suggest, is particularly prone to the unconscious alteration; the third leads to errors such as itacism; and in the fourth the pen can fail to follow the mind in quite bewildering ways.

Thus, with Dain's help we may chart the processes of copying, but we cannot always account for the consequences of them. On occasion there may be a number of possible reasons for a variant. But to return to Luke 6.

We have identified these kinds of differences – addition or omission of words, changes in order, and substitution of one word for another. The majority of these variants are small. After some time spent studying them, the whole shape of the text may be forgotten. It will be like studying a leaf under a microscope: its scale will change for us, and what is insignificant lying in the garden will become a whole world. This careful analysis of the text is an essential part of textual criticism. But no less essential is what follows, the analysis of the results to assess the whole character of the text. The cumulative result of a number of tiny changes may be more significant than that of one or two larger ones. We shall shortly discover this. Let us see what we have learned about each of our three witnesses.

Codex Vaticanus presents the shortest text – 134 words in Greek.[3] It also has the neatest and most elegant Greek of the three. Here is an economical text which has been organised and tidied. It is virtually identical with the text of the Revised Standard Version, so it will be familiar to most English-speaking readers.

Codex Bezae is markedly different. It has 171 words, or 143 not counting the story added after verse 4. It also moves verse 5 to the end of the story of the man with the withered hand. With these two differences a pair of stories loosely related to the theme of the sabbath has become a trio leading to the conclusion that 'The Son of man is lord of the sabbath also.' The added story about the man working on the sabbath is found only here and in no other manuscript or text. It will receive separate discussion below.

---

[3] I have not counted the words from verses 7 and 11.

In several other places Codex Bezae is markedly different. A substantial proportion of the readings in which it differs from B and Ω are wordings which it shares with the synoptic parallels in Matthew 12.1–13 and Mark 2.23–3.5. Fifteen were listed in our seven verses. It is important to appreciate the effect that these differences have on the story. The wording of its description of the activity of the disciples in verse 1, its introduction to the second story, and the words 'And he stretched it out' are all sharply divergent from the other two manuscripts. Finally, the simple addition of 'in anger' at verse 10 gives a quite different flavour to the scene.[4]

Compared with Codex Vaticanus, the Greek of D is less neat and stylish. The beginning of verse 4 translates literally as 'Entering into the house of God and he ate', which is no more good Greek than it is correct English. The text of D is about as far removed from that of B as one can get. Unlike a scholarly edition, it shows all the signs of being copied freely, of presenting a text that had gone on developing long after the Alexandrian text had become fixed.

Codex Ω has some characteristics of both the other manuscripts. It agrees with Vaticanus in the structure of the section (no man working on the sabbath, verse 5 after verse 4). But it also has a number of the words found in D but not in B. Thus its length is 150 words. That is, it is a fuller text than Codex Bezae if we except the added story.

Words found in B and Ω but not in D:

verse 4 reference to 'taking' (not identical wording)
verse 6 and taught
         right

Words included in D and Ω but not in B:

verse 1 second-first
         the
verse 3 article before Jesus

---

[4] The reading of the same manuscript in the story of the healing of a leper at Mark 1.41, where with a few Old Latin manuscripts it has 'moved with anger' rather than 'moved with pity', has been the subject of much attention, and it has been argued that it is original. This variant in Luke, which contains information found also in the parallel story at Mark 3.5, has been the subject of little attention, even in discussions of Mark 1.41.

verse 5 that
              also
verse 10 like the other.

It also adds a few words of its own:

verse   2 added verb and preposition
verse   3 who were
verse   4 how
verse 10 whole.

There are no words found in both B and D and not in Ω.

This text has the principal characteristic of one that is a gathering together of older materials: it is reluctant to lose anything of value. The absence of the story of the man working on the sabbath must indicate either that it was unknown to the compiler(s) of this text, or that they considered it to be an interpolation.

A brief characterisation of these three manuscripts would not be hard. The first is economical and scholarly; the second is extremely distinctive in what it contains and in its wording; the third is at pains to avoid missing out anything which might be of value, and is derivative of the first two.

No language has been used so far in this description that might suggest whether one of the three presented the original wording. The aim has simply been to describe and analyse the differences. But the time now comes to begin to look at the readings in the light of the matters which were discussed in the first chapter. We shall do so by enquiring into the causes of the readings which we have given.

First comes harmonisation, the alteration of the text of one Gospel so that it conforms to that of another. We shall find time and again that manuscripts alter the text of one Gospel to bring it into conformity with another. To take an extreme example, the manuscripts Sinaiticus, Vaticanus and Ephraemi Rescriptus – three of our 'best' – include at Matthew 27.49 the words 'But another, taking a spear, pierced his side, and there came out water and blood.' This is rejected by modern editors, on the grounds that it is a harmonisation to John 19.34. This seems to hold good, even though the wording is not identical, and even though in Matthew the event precedes Jesus' death. Such harmonisation must be intentional. But the reason will vary. Sometimes it is to remove an inconsistency, sometimes to add a detail; sometimes it is the unconscious recollection of a perhaps better-known parallel.

We at once find that a substantial number of the readings in D are due to harmonisation. The reader may prefer to test this first, before going through the following list of readings that are readily identifiable in the parallel passages Matthew 12.1–13 and Mark 2.23–3.5:

verse 1	And ... he	Mark
	the [cornfields]	Matthew/Mark
	Now	Matthew
	began to pluck	Matthew
verse 2	said to him	Mark
	Look ... lawful	Mark (some manuscripts)
verse 3	said	Mark (some manuscripts)
	never	Mark
verse 4	for the priests	Matthew (not identical)
verse 6	And ... again	Mark (in one manuscript)
	had a withered hand	Matthew (not identical)
verse 10	in anger	Mark (not identical)
	he says to the man	Matthew/Mark
	And he stretched it out	Matthew/Mark
	like the other one	Matthew (not identical).

The evident harmonisations in Ω are

verse 1	and eating	Matthew (in word order)
verse 2	to do up[on]	Matthew
verse 6	there a man	Mark (word order)
verse 7	watched	Mark
verse 10	whole like the other one	Matthew.

It is harder to find harmonisations in B. The omission of 'second-first' in verse 1 seems to be the only candidate. But harmonisation is almost invariably effected by alteration or addition, and not by omission.

More complicated are the readings where two of our three witnesses harmonise:

B and D:

| verse 3 | when | Matthew/Mark |
| | omit 'who were' | Matthew/Mark |

B and Ω:

| verse 3 | with | Matthew/Mark |
| verse 4 | he entered | Matthew/Mark |

D and Ω:

| verse 5 | Lord … sabbath | Mark. |

Should we take all these also as harmonisations? The problem is the application of rules of thumb. It is generally agreed that readings which harmonise are less likely to be original than those which preserve divergent texts. But it does not follow that every reading which makes the text of a Gospel less like the others is original. The possibility has also to be considered that a copyist has for some reason changed one of the Gospels in a way that makes it less like its parallels. The problems caused by these difficulties will be discussed more fully in Chapter 6.

The matter is more complicated, because the process is, to varying degrees, going on in all four canonical Gospels. Thus, there will often be several forms of each Gospel. We could draw up parallel columns for the different manuscripts of each Gospel's version of a story. I have suggested that 'never' in D in verse 3 is a harmonisation to Mark. But one Greek manuscript and several Old Latin ones of Mark there read 'Not'. Could it be that it is B and Ω which are harmonising Luke in order to adopt 'Not' from Mark, and that 'Never' is original to Luke, which has then been adopted by most manuscripts of Mark? Such an explanation is very improbable here. But there are also places where the situation is more complicated, and harmonisation might have occurred in either direction.

Harmonisation thus seems to account for a high proportion of the distinctive readings of Codex Bezae. The claim that one reading is a harmonisation leads, of course, to the assumption that its rival holds the field as original. The examination of the character of individual manuscripts is vital here. Once we have seen how often Codex Bezae borrows from Matthew and Mark, we shall be less inclined to trust it. But Codex Vaticanus hardly ever does, on the present evidence, and we must scrutinise much more carefully the apparent harmonisations, and ask whether it is not the other witnesses that are at fault in reading a text different from that of the other Gospels.

Another class of reading, often closely related to harmonisation, is stylistic improvement and the quest for clarity. Just as Matthew and Luke improved the style of Mark, so copyists improve the style of all three. And, where the text is obscure, a phrase borrowed from a parallel may help to make it plain. So in verse 2 we want to know whom the Pharisees are addressing. D supplies 'to him' from Matthew or Mark. Ω cannot do that without changing the wording of the question to the third person. So it supplies 'to them' from the context ('Why do *you* do...?'). It is possible to identify the characteristic features of the evangelists' styles, and from that evidence to argue that a reading which contains one or more of those features is more likely to be authentic. But one should also allow for coincidence, and for imitation. In addition, one has also to consider the changing tastes in Greek style of the ancient world. The neat Greek of Codex Vaticanus seems to owe something to Atticism, the trend from the third century onwards of trying to imitate the best classical Greek in defiance of the contemporary developments in the direction of Hellenistic Greek. It might therefore seem easy to suppose that a reading which is cruder is more likely to be original. But a contrary trend towards a more contemporary style appears to be present in Codex Bezae. Even some features which, it has been suggested, are Semitic and therefore more likely to be original to the Gospels may rather be an attempt to assume a less literary style. An example may be found in verse 4, with the construction 'Entering... and he...'. It has been proposed that this construction is a Semitism. But it is also found in vernacular Greek. Since the latter is a possibility, the former cannot be regarded as proven, and the general tendency towards revision encourages us to suppose that it is a part of the popular Greek which a reviser was introducing.

The general rule towards which we are inclining is that the reading is to be preferred which suits the author's style.

So far we have been quite easily eliminating readings which are unlikely to be Lukan. But we come now to a bigger difficulty: the evaluation of larger additions to the text. The addition is the story of the man working on the sabbath.

We need here to avoid confusing two quite separate questions. The first is whether the passage is authentic to Luke's Gospel. The second is whether it is an event that happened in the life of Jesus. Properly speaking, textual criticism is concerned only with the former. There may be many passages which undoubtedly belong within the Gospels but which are not records of events that happened to Jesus. And there may be stories which are not part of the canonical Gospels which are historically accurate. The two questions touch one another only if it can be demonstrated that a story was created at a later date than the compilation of the Gospels, for then it can be neither an original part of the Gospels nor a historical event.

The question whether the story is authentic to Luke has been answered in many ways.[5] In the sixteenth century it was actually introduced into the printed text, first by Robert Stephanus, who collected variants for the edition which he printed at Paris in 1550 (the first edition to cite variant readings) and then by Beza, the Genevan reformer in his edition of 1563. Beza subsequently changed his mind and omitted it in his later editions (1565 onwards), with a note on the matter.

The fact that the entire passage of Luke has been reordered in D leads one to suspect its inclusion here. On the other hand, one might point to groups of three stories on a theme within Luke (for example, the Lost Sheep, Lost Coin and Prodigal Son in Chapter 15). In deciding whether the story might be Lukan, the fact that it comes in only a single manuscript should not weigh too heavily, if reasons could be found for arguing that the tradition preferred to lose this story. For example, if it could be demonstrated to have been used to argue an antinomian case, then it might have been rejected by the opponents of such a view.

The possibility that it is an authentic episode in the ministry of Jesus has been carefully explored. One of the best-known cham-

---

[5] For the many and contradictory views expressed, see E. Bammel, 'The Cambridge Pericope: The Addition to Luke 6.4 in Codex Bezae', *NTS* 32 (1986), 404–26, pp. 405f.

pions of its authenticity is Joachim Jeremias.[6] The most detailed recent study is that of Bammel. He avoids stating directly that it is authentic, but draws attention to features which suggest that the story's origins lie more probably in the ministry of Jesus than in the early church. These include the fact that debate about the sabbath was significant in Jesus' controversies, but not in those of the early church. He also indicates that it is difficult to find a context for the passage in early Jewish Christianity. In addition, Bammel considers it unlikely that the story could have been formulated by Luke, who shows less interest in such questions than his predecessors, but he does not resolve the issue of Lukan authorship.

In attempting to decide in favour of a particular reading where there is variation, we have been applying a number of rules in a sophisticated way. There is no absolute rule which allows one to prefer a reading mechanically without careful reflection. Quite often, the critics will operate by principles which are in conflict with each other. This will be repeatedly true in the problems we shall be studying in subsequent chapters. The method which we have followed is to collect information about the readings distinctive to each witness, and to use that information to assess that witness's distinctive character. We shall then be reluctant to accept a reading of a manuscript which appears to follow its distinctive bent.

While the task of recovering the original text is traditionally the most important part of the discipline, as well as one which other scholars *expect* textual critics to perform on their behalf, it is not the only matter which is to be pursued. We saw in Chapter 1 that there are other possible approaches. That apart, textual critics have never been *solely* or even principally interested in the recovery of an original text. This is because the task of recovering an original text has always required the reconstruction of the way in which that text changed as it was copied. The study of the history of the text in fact occupies far more time than that taken in establishing an original reading. In setting out a new approach to the textual criticism of the Gospels, we shall be building on this traditional aspect of textual criticism. In what follows, we shall study the way in which sayings and stories continued to be developed by copyists and

[6] *Unknown Sayings of Jesus* (London, 1957), pp. 49–54.

readers. This will establish a new approach to the textual criticism of the Gospels, and with that a new understanding of the nature and use of the Gospels themselves. The addition to Luke 6.4 might be taken as a parable to illustrate the issues.

There is one more matter to be discussed before we conclude this chapter. There is a marked degree of variation between the three manuscripts of Luke 6 which we have examined. In this variation, D stands out against the other two. We must ask how much variation is necessary for the text to become a different text. Does D really present us with the text of Luke 6.1ff., or does it give us another text? It is very important to take note of the fact that there are as many differences between D and B in Luke 6.1ff. as there are between the two texts in D of Mark 2.23ff. and Luke 6.1ff. This must be emphasised, for it is a matter that will be fundamental to some later chapters.

It is hard to recognise and then to express all the similarities and differences. But here is an attempt to do so. Bold type indicates that Luke D agrees with Luke B against Mark D in wording or word order; italics mean that it agrees with Mark D against Luke B in wording; square brackets indicate that it agrees with neither in wording; underlining that it agrees with Mark D in word order. † indicates that it agrees with Mark D in not containing a word that is in Luke B; ‡ that it agrees with Luke B in not containing a word found in Mark D. Normal type is used where all three agree.

There are 101 words in the Greek text of Luke in D. Twenty-nine agree with its text of Mark against B (twelve as different wording, fourteen in word order, two in both and one in omitting a word found in B), seventeen agree with B against its Markan text (ten in wording and seven in omitting words found in Mark, no agreements against Mark in order), and a further twelve are different from both. I have excluded three phrases with double problems ('and rubbing them in their hands ate', where it follows B in wording but not in order; 'Jesus said to them', which is partly B but also partly unique and different also in word order; and 'only', which follows B in including the word but not in construction). The remaining forty words are common to the three texts. It is no idle question to wonder what we have in these columns. Are there two

LUKE 6.1–5 B	LUKE 6.1–5 D	MARK 2.23–8 D
[1]Now it came to pass	[1]*And* it came to pass⁺⁺	[23]And it came to pass
on a	on **a** [second-first]	again on the
sabbath,	**sabbath**	sabbath
that he was going	that he was going	that he was going
through cornfields,	through *the* cornfields.	through the cornfields,
and his disciples were	[Now] **his** disciples *began to*	and the disciples began to
plucking and eating	*pluck* the heads of grain	pluck the heads of grain.
the heads of grain,	**and rubbing them**	
rubbing them in their hands.	**in their hands ate**.	
[2]But some of the	[2]But **some of the**	[24]But the
Pharisees said,	**Pharisees** *said* [to him]	Pharisees said
'Why are you	'*Look* what *your disciples*	'Look what your disciples
doing what is not lawful	*are doing* on the sabbath	are doing on the sabbath,
on the sabbath?'	which is not lawful⁺⁺.'	which is not lawful for them.'
[3]And answering	[3][But] answering	[25]And answering
them Jesus said	**Jesus** said **to them**	he said to them
'Have you not read	'Have you *never* read	'Have you never read
this that David did,	**this that** David did,	what David did,
when	when ⁺ ⁺ ⁺	when he had need,
he was hungry,	he was hungry,	and was hungry,
he and those	he and those ⁺	he and those who were
with him?	[with] him?	with him?
[4]He entered into	[4][Entering] into	[26]He entered into
the house of God,	the house of God,	the house of God,
and taking ate	† and he ate	and ate
the shewbread,	the shewbread,	the shewbread
and gave to those	and gave [also] to those	and gave to those
with him,	⁺ with him,	who were with him
which it is not lawful	[which] it [was]not lawful]	which it is not lawful
to eat except only	to eat except **only**	to eat except
the priests.'	*for the priests.*	for the priests?
	...	
[5]And he said to them	[5]**And he said to them**	I say to you
	[that]	
'The Son of man is lord	'The Son of man is lord	'The Son of man is lord
of the sabbath.'	*even* of the sabbath.'	even of the sabbath'.

separate texts of Luke and one of Mark, or one called Luke and two of Mark, or three separate texts? Or are they all one text? Of course, we have taken only half a dozen verses, and the question needs answering on a larger scale. But it must be answered. This is a matter of the utmost importance in our understanding of the Gospels. It should be kept in mind as we examine more material in the following chapters.

Leaving this sample behind, we turn in the following chapters to explore a series of passages which pose particularly interesting or representative problems. It is important to approach them with two thoughts in mind. The first is that the way of studying them will not be uniform, for that would be to ignore the peculiar characteristics of each; the second is that, for the same reason, we must not expect to reach similar conclusions at the end of each chapter. Some of them may appear more dramatic than others. It must be remembered at all points that some of the arguments which will be presented in the final chapters are based upon cumulative evidence.

CHAPTER 4

'As our Saviour taught us . . .': the Lord's Prayer

St. Paul's whole teaching on liberty has to be applied to
prayer.   Hans Urs von Balthazar, *Prayer*

Modern services often preface the saying of the Lord's Prayer with
an invitation, for example, 'As our Saviour taught us, so we pray.'
While we may accept that the words and the use are in harmony
with the early tradition of Jesus, we shall certainly be mistaken if we
believe ourselves to be uttering Jesus' words *verbatim*. As a matter of
fact, this prayer contains within its short compass every conceivable problem that could afflict a Gospel saying: it exists in widely
divergent forms, it includes a word otherwise unattested whose
meaning is unknown, it contains an ambiguity, and its text was
altered in the course of its transmission. For good measure, it is
used in liturgical forms which draw on different Gospels.

To explain the last point first: in England, we use the word
'trespasses' or 'sins', which is from Luke, in an otherwise Matthaean form. In Scotland, the Matthaean word 'debts' is used.

The prayer is found twice in the Gospels: in the Sermon on the
Mount in Matthew, as a part of teaching about prayer; and in Luke
when Jesus has been praying, and his disciples ask 'Lord, teach us
to pray, as John taught his disciples.' Let us begin by setting
alongside each other these two forms of the prayer, as they are
found in the Revised Standard Version:

Matthew 6.9–13	Luke 11.2–4
Our Father who art in heaven,	Father,
Hallowed be thy name.	hallowed be thy name.
Thy kingdom come,	Thy kingdom come.
Thy will be done,	
On earth as it is in heaven.	
Give us this day our daily bread;	Give us each day our daily bread;
And forgive us our debts,	and forgive us our sins,
As we also have forgiven our debtors;	for we ourselves forgive every one who is indebted to us;
and lead us not into temptation.	
But deliver us from evil.	

It is only since 1881 that a Protestant English Bible has given two texts which differ so much from each other. The first printed English New Testament, Tyndale's 1534 translation, has this version of Luke:

O oure father which arte in heaven,
halowed be thy name.
Thy kyngdome come.
Thy will be fulfilled,
even in erth as it is in heaven.
Oure dayly breed geve vs evermore.
And forgeve vs oure synnes:
For even we forgeve every man that treaspaseth vs.
And ledde vs not into temptacion.
But deliver vs from evill.

The substance and shape of this prayer are identical to the form found in Matthew. Tyndale's example was followed by his successors. We note amongst them the Geneva Bible (1560) and the Authorised Version (1611). But not every English Bible had this form of Luke. The Douai New Testament, published at Rheims in 1582 for English Roman Catholics, reads

Father,
sanctified be thy name.
Thy kingdom come,
Our daily bread give vs this day,
and forgiue vs our sinnes,

for because our selues also doe forgiue every one that is in debt to vs.
And lead vs not into temptation.

This denominational difference in text continued for three
centuries until a major new English version was brought out. The
Revised Version, which was published in 1881, adopted the text
found in Westcott and Hort's edition *The New Testament in the
Original Greek* (published in the same year). In substance it agrees
with the Douai Bible. Textual scholarship had bridged a gap
between the versions used in different churches. There is considerable agreement among the churches today, and there are many
shared translation projects; the RSV, in the guise of the Common
Bible, is itself accepted by all the major denominations. But we
should not underestimate the way in which separate versions have
contributed to the fragmentation of the church. The text of the
Lukan Lord's Prayer is a good example, because the difference had
an ideological basis: the respective authority of the Greek text and
the Latin Vulgate.

Tyndale's translation was made from a printed Greek New
Testament. The tradition that included the Geneva Bible and the
Authorised Version was also made from the Greek (and from
Hebrew for the Old Testament). The Douai Bible, on the other
hand, was translated from the Latin Bible.[1] In Luke 11.2–4, the
manuscripts on which sixteenth-century Greek New Testaments
were based differ dramatically from the Vulgate. The reasons for
this lie as much with the chances surrounding sixteenth-century
scholarship as with the history of the Greek and Latin texts of the
passage.

The first Greek New Testament to be published was, as we
already know, edited by the great Dutch humanist Desiderius
Erasmus. He got his edition out in something of a hurry, because he
wanted to beat a competitor on to the market: the first *printed*
edition, the Complutensian Polyglot, had gone through the press
and was awaiting publication. Of course, Erasmus had to get his
printed text from manuscripts, and he turned to the manuscripts
that lay most conveniently to hand in Basle, the city where he was

---

[1] Although the title page reads *The New Testament of Jesus Christ, translated faithfully . . . out of the
authentical Latin, according to the best corrected copies of the same, diligently conferred with the Greeke and
other editions in diverse tongues.*

living. Scholars of the time had two great handicaps in work of this kind. The first was that the science of palaeography, the study of ancient hands leading to their classification and dating, was not to receive its first scientific formulations until the end of the next century. The second was that scholars had only begun to realise just how much the text of the New Testament had changed in the process of copying. Almost all copies of the New Testament that were available to Erasmus were medieval, and presented the Byzantine text. The great achievement of Erasmus and his contemporaries was that they studied the original Greek ('original' as opposed to the Latin Vulgate derived from it), and made it available to others. Within a short time commentators and preachers were taking it for granted that they should work from the Greek Testament. But what the humanists printed was a very late form of the text. Erasmus based his Gospels on one manuscript (Gregory–Aland number 2), and compared it with a couple more; 2 is, as it happens, a manuscript of Byzantine text dating from the late eleventh or early twelfth century.[2]

The Byzantine textual tradition received and accepted a form of the Lord's Prayer in Luke that harmonised it to the text of Matthew. Thus it is that Tyndale, who translated from Erasmus' Greek Testament, has the long version of Luke.

It has already been shown that the origins of the Latin Vulgate are complicated and sometimes obscure, and that its subsequent history was chequered. But there is no doubt that the Gospels were edited by Jerome, on papal commission, in 382, and that Jerome produced his version by revising existing translations, and by comparing them with Greek manuscripts. It should not surprise us (for he is amongst the handful of the best Christian scholars to have lived) that the Greek manuscripts which he consulted were of excellent quality, and that they had at this point a text of Luke quite different from that of Matthew.

This accounts for the differences between Tyndale and Douai. But what led to the change of heart represented by the Revised Version? Seventeenth-century scholarship began to find and to

---

[2] C. C. Tarelli, 'Erasmus' manuscripts of the Gospels', *JTS* 44 (1943), 155–62.

compare many new witnesses, and to see that the Byzantine text differed from early materials. The *De Re Diplomatica* of Jean Mabillon (1681) and the *Palaeographia Graeca* of Bernard Montfaucon (1708) laid the foundations of Latin and of Greek palaeography respectively.[3] With these aids, it began to be possible to date manuscripts scientifically. Discovering and studying ever-increasing amounts of evidence,[4] eighteenth- and nineteenth-century scholarship found manuscripts of that fourth-century Greek text which Jerome had used for his Vulgate, and decided that it was superior to the Byzantine form. Every critical edition of modern times has published the shorter text of Luke. We learn from this story that the humanists were not always right when they preferred the Greek manuscripts they studied, and that traditionalists were not always wrong in favouring the Latin Vulgate.

There continue to be those who believe that the Byzantine text most accurately represents the original text, essentially on the grounds that God would not have allowed the original text to perish, and that it is preserved in the majority of manuscripts (which are Byzantine). There is perhaps a certain irony in the fact that today's traditionalists favour the text rejected by their predecessors of four hundred years ago.

Today everyone, except the supporter of the Majority Text, agrees that shorter Luke is better. This is because of a sound rule discussed in the previous chapter: that in textual criticism of the Gospels, the forms of sayings which increase their dissimilarity are more likely to be original than those which harmonise them.

We have now reached the point of beginning to face the larger historical problem raised by study of the text: the existence of the prayer in such divergent forms. When we look at this in a little more detail, we find that there is one large textual problem in

---

[3] For a brief account of the sciences of palaeography and papyrology, and their application to the New Testament, see my article 'Was Matthew Written before 50 CE? The Magdalen Papyrus of Matthew', *Expository Times* 107 (1995), 40–3. See further B. M. Metzger, *Manuscripts of the Greek Bible: An Introduction to Palaeography* (New York and Oxford, 1981).

[4] The growth in the number of manuscripts known may be illustrated by the number of majuscule manuscripts listed at various times: 8 in 1704, 22 in 1751, 88 in 1884, 166 in 1909. Their recovery was at first largely due to the systematic exploration of libraries throughout Europe and then Asia. More recent discoveries and the advent of the papyri are principally due to Egyptian excavations (see Chapter 2).

Matthew, and that in Luke the text exists in three main forms, with a couple of other smaller but very interesting variations. We shall deal first with Matthew.

The main variant in Matthew concerns the Doxology. There are eight possibilities. In addition, we have the text of the Didache (which will be discussed separately). We shall first list the readings, and then describe the support for them.

1 the shortest text (there is no Doxology, and the text ends with 'evil')
2 'Amen' after 'evil'
3 the Doxology in the form 'Because thine is the kingdom and the power and the glory for ever. Amen.'

Readings 4–7 are all variants on 3:

4 the Doxology, adding 'of the Father and of the Son and of the Holy Spirit' after 'glory'
5 the Doxology, omitting 'the kingdom and'
6 the Doxology, omitting the Amen
7 the Doxology, omitting 'for thine is the power for ever and ever'.

1. The shortest text. Here for the first time we meet a wide range of support for a reading. It is customary to give evidence in the order Greek manuscripts, versions (in the order Syriac, Latin, Coptic, then others) and patristic quotations.

> Greek manuscripts: five majuscules – Codex Sinaiticus (ℵ), Codex Vaticanus (B), Codex Bezae (D), Codex Dublinensis (Z), 0170; several minuscules – Family 13, 1582
> Versions: most Old Latin manuscripts, the Vulgate, a middle Coptic manuscript and some Bohairic manuscripts
> Patristic citations: Cyril, Origen and Cyprian knew a text without the Doxology.

Two of the Greek manuscripts, B and D, have already been described. The symbol given to Codex Sinaiticus (numbered 01) is a Hebrew *aleph*. The story of its discovery is one of the best known, and will not be repeated here. Suffice it to say that it was first studied by a modern scholar at the monastery of St Catherine on

Mount Sinai in 1844. Most of the codex (including all of the New Testament) was taken thence to St Petersburg, and was removed to the British Museum in 1933. Some portions of the Old Testament are in Leipzig, and more leaves were found in St Catherine's monastery some years ago. Like B, it is a manuscript of the entire Bible, copied at about the same time, by three scribes, one of whom was responsible for the entire New Testament. It was also compared at an early stage against a much older manuscript itself corrected by Pamphilus, a scholar of Caesarea who was martyred in 309. These corrections are of particular interest. Its text in the Gospels is less consistent than that of B. In John, at least, it appears to have blocks in which it follows different types of text.[5] The copyist was prone to miss out text – words, lines, and even longer blocks. Many of these omissions were replenished by the *diorthotes*, the official corrector, before it left the scriptorium. In spite of these difficulties, Codex Sinaiticus remains one of the witnesses to be taken most seriously.

Z (035) is a palimpsest now preserved in Dublin. It was reused to produce a patristic text. It was first written in the early sixth century; all that survives of it is parts of Matthew. Its text is very close to that of Codex Sinaiticus. Although it is the Book of Kells that attracts the visitors to the library of Trinity College in Dublin, it is this drab ruin which affords the more interest to the textual critic. 0170 is another sixth-century manuscript of Matthew. Very little of it remains – just parts of verses 5–6, 8–10, 13–15 and 17 in Matthew 6. What of the Lord's Prayer it contains is identical with the text of Codex Vaticanus. Family 13 is a group of a dozen manuscripts that is also known as the Ferrar Group. They were all copied from the eleventh century on, and are descended from a single manuscript, now lost, which had been produced in either southern Italy or Sicily. It has been argued that the group is related to what is known as the Caesarean text.

There are several other minuscule manuscripts supporting this form of the prayer – at least three, including 1582. This interesting manuscript will be described when we look at the Lukan text.

[5] See G. D. Fee, 'Codex Sinaiticus in the Gospel of John: A Contribution to Methodology in Establishing Textual Relationships', *NTS* 15 (1968–9), 23–44; also *Papyrus Bodmer II (P66): Its Textual Relationships and Scribal Characteristics*, SD 34 (Salt Lake City, 1968).

These are the Greek witnesses. The versional evidence is quite striking: most of the pre-Jerome manuscripts as well as the Vulgate. It should be explained that the pre-Jerome manuscripts are nearly all pre-Jerome in the sense that they represent the multiplicity of texts that came into being before the end of the fourth century, not because they were actually copied so early. One or two of them may have been, but the rest are later, and several are actually medieval. There are two Coptic versions. The one in a Middle Egyptian dialect, the Glazier Codex, is a fourth-century copy of an early form of the text. It has striking affinities with the text also represented by Codex Bezae.

The support of Origen and Cyprian is especially valuable. The former, writing in Alexandria and then in Caesarea in the first half of the third century, was a shrewd exegete who quite often commented on textual matters. We shall return to him in the course of this chapter. Cyprian, Bishop of Carthage, was martyred in 258. His writings (in Latin) are the oldest witness to the African text, and to the Greek text on which it was based. Cyril of Jerusalem, writing in the middle of the fourth century, used a Caesarean form of the text.[6]

2.   One Greek minuscule manuscript (17, copied in the fifteenth century) and a few Vulgate witnesses (a thirteenth-century annotated copy and the authoritative printed version) add 'Amen' after 'evil'.

3.   This is both the best-known and the best-attested form of the Doxology ('Because thine is the kingdom and the power and the glory for ever. Amen'). It is supported by the majority of manuscripts, of which the oldest is W, known as the Freer Gospels and (less commonly) as the Codex Washingtonianus, which was copied in the late fourth century. It was found at the very beginning of this century. One of the most remarkable features of this important witness is that its text differs so markedly in different books. The whole of Matthew and most of Luke are Byzantine; other parts are variously akin to Alexandrian, Caesarean and the

[6] J. H. Greenlee, *The Gospel Text of Cyril of Jerusalem*, Studies and Documents 17 (Copenhagen, 1955).

Old Latin, while some parts contain a mixture.[7] Its value, and the way in which we appraise it, will therefore vary. Here its value is as the earliest Byzantine witness.

This ending is also the text of the Apostolic Constitutions 3.18. This was a collection of writings on liturgy and matters of church law and governance, which was probably compiled in about 380 in Syria (very possibly Antioch). As a compilation of older materials, it varies greatly in value. We shall see shortly that it is interesting here.

4. This extended version of the Doxology is found in the twelfth-century minuscule manuscript 157. This is another manuscript whose comparative youth hides its significance. Far from being a representative of the Byzantine text, it is based on independent and old materials. Its frequent agreements with Codex Bezae have long been known. But its reading here may be not ancient but an aberration, an automatic response from tired hand or inattentive mind.

5. Some Bohairic and Sahidic manuscripts omit 'the kingdom and'.

6. Most Old Latin manuscripts, the Syriac Peshitta and other Bohairic manuscripts contain the Doxology (3) but omit the Amen.

7. This shorter version of the Doxology is found in the late fourth-century African Latin manuscript Codex Bobbiensis. This is one of the oldest Old Latin witnesses. It was copied in north Africa in the late fourth century, and was throughout the Middle Ages in Bobbio, the monastery in north Italy founded by Columbanus. When the house closed at the end of the sixteenth century, the manuscript was brought to Turin. It contains most of the Gospels of Matthew and Mark. With Cyprian, it is a major witness to the African Old Latin version.

Besides these witnesses, the Didache requires special mention.

---

[7] Mark 1.1–5.30: Old Latin; Mark 5.31–16.20: Caesarean; Luke 1.1–8.12: Alexandrian; Luke 8.13–24.53: Byzantine; John 1.1–5.11: Alexandrian plus some western readings; John 5.12–22.25: Alexandrian. The first editor suggested that it was descended from a copy made up of fragments of books destroyed in the Diocletianic persecution.

Although this document is of great antiquity (it is generally considered to have been written in Syria at a time between 100 and 150), it survives in its original Greek only in one manuscript, copied in 1056. There are fragments of translations, including two in Latin, but none of them covers the section including the Lord's Prayer (8.2). The text of these verses, then, survives only in the Greek manuscript. It has two variants not found in any Gospel manuscript: it has the singular instead of the plural form for 'heaven' in the first clause;[8] and it has a different word for 'debt', again in the singular. It has the form of the Doxology listed above as No. 5 – it omits 'the kingdom and'.

Although it is clear that the Didache must give us the text of the Lord's Prayer as it was known in the time and place at which it was composed, it is far less certain that our single copy, written almost a millennium later, preserves the original text of it. There is some justification for this scepticism when we turn to the Apostolic Constitutions. Book 7 of this compilation draws heavily on the Didache; indeed, to the extent that it largely *is* the Didache. The text it gives of the Lord's Prayer differs from that in our manuscript of the Didache in four respects: it does not have the two unique readings (singular 'heaven' in the first clause and 'debt'), it omits the definite article before 'earth', and its Doxology runs 'For thine is the kingdom, for ever. Amen.' It could of course be that it is the Apostolic Constitutions that have suffered corruption, and the fact that two of the Didache's singular readings are missing could be taken as evidence for that. On the other hand, it has its own distinctive form of the Doxology. In addition, we can compare it with the text of Apostolic Constitutions 3.18 (see above). This part of the work is dependent on the Didascalia Apostolorum. The Didascalia is also a compilation, of ethical and legal regulations. It was written in northern Syria in the first part of the third century, and here is also modelled on the Didache. The text is the same as that at 7.24, except that 'on' is missing before 'earth', and the Doxology reads 'for thine is the kingdom and the power and the glory for ever. Amen.' It goes without saying that there are textual questions about this writing also. The original Greek is wholly lost.

---

[8] Matthew regularly uses the plural 'heavens'.

There is a complete Syriac version and an incomplete Latin one.

The upshot of this is that we cannot be certain of the precise original wording of the prayer in the Didache. We can only say that the extant manuscript presents the text known to us from the manuscripts of Matthew, with minor variations.

The evidence is overwhelmingly that the Doxology is an interpolation into Matthew. In the first place, the manuscripts which do contain one are by no means unanimous in the form given. Such variation is frequently an indication that the text without the words is the oldest form. That is, readers felt that the absence of a Doxology was a gap that needed to be filled, and filled it as well as they could. In the second place, some important early witnesses to the text (and ones that do not always agree together) have no Doxology. The agreement of D with B and ℵ and related manuscripts is of some significance. The strength of the two points together is overwhelming. It allows us to recreate the story of the text, thus meeting the textual critic's fundamental principle that the reading which best explains the origin of all the others is most likely to be original. That is, the history of the text must be explained. The lack of a doxology is recognised by a number of manuscripts. Some copyists feel that it is appropriate to supply so obvious a lack, and a variety of doxologies is introduced. The emergence of the Byzantine text, with its reluctance to lose anything, leads to one form (the longest, excepting manuscript 157) becoming standard.

The fact that the textual evidence indicates that written doxologies were absent in the earliest period has little bearing on the question of the appropriateness of such a conclusion to the prayer. It may be that the user was expected to supply a suitable doxology *ad lib.*, rather as collects (for example, in the 1549 Book of Common Prayer) sometimes end 'through Jesus Christ &c', so that the appropriate formula could be used. There is support for this in the Didache. It has a doxology at the end of its post-communion prayer (10.5) that is identical to that used by it for the Lord's Prayer.

The slightly strange wording of the line 'Give us this day our daily bread' is due to uncertainty with regard to the meaning of the Greek word represented by 'daily'. The word is *epiousion*, and it comes nowhere in literature but here in Matthew and Luke, and in texts dependent on them. It has been regarded as a problem at least since the time of Origen in the third century. It is beyond the scope of this study to discuss the problem and the various solutions that have been proposed, except to record that the weight of modern scholarship is in favour of the meaning 'the day that is coming' – signifying either today, if one prays in the morning, or the next day when one is praying at night. But we do note that, difficult though the word is, every Greek manuscript reproduces it. There is no attempt to provide an easier synonym. It is different with the versions, of course, where the task of translation has led to a number of interpretations. As for the Greek, the point is that, although we shall not find it hard to find places where difficult words and phrases have been replaced with easier ones, there are also plenty of substantial problems which the copyists left untouched. Perhaps the very peculiarity of such a word as *epiousion* was an attraction. Beyond the general meaning of something from God for which one waits daily, a sense of mystery in the unknown word may have been perceived to enhance the feeling of waiting on the Giver.

We turn now to Luke. There are three main text forms:

1 the short text
2 the long form in Codex Bezae
3 the long Byzantine form
4 a different form of the clause 'Thy kingdom come.'

Let us look first at the short form.

The oldest witness to this is P[75]. Although I gave the text of the Revised Standard Version at the beginning, let us put P[75] into our own words here:

> Father
> Hallowed be thy name
> Thy kingdom come
> Give us each day our daily bread
> And forgive us our sins
> For we ourselves also forgive each one in debt to us
> And do not bring us into temptation.

Codex Vaticanus is absolutely identical, except for one spelling error that was later corrected. P75 is new to us, and so requires a description.

This papyrus copy of Luke and John was found in 1952, acquired by the Bodmer Library, Geneva, and published in 1961. It is extremely important, for two reasons: like Vaticanus, it is carefully copied; it is also very early, and is generally dated to a period between 175 and 225. Thus, it pre-dates Vaticanus by at least a century. A careful comparison between P75 and Vaticanus in Luke by C. M. Martini demonstrated that P75 was an earlier copy of the same careful Alexandrian text. It is sometimes called proto-Alexandrian.[9] It is our earliest example of a controlled text, one which was not intentionally or extensively changed in successive copyings. Its discovery and study has provided proof that the Alexandrian text had already come into existence in the third century. It has been suggested that, along with the other manuscripts with which it was found, it was part of the library of a community of Pachomian monks.

Three other manuscripts, all minuscules, have the same text as P75 and B: 1192 and 1210, both copied in the eleventh century, and the thirteenth-/fourteenth-century manuscript 1342. 1192 and 1210 are both in the monastery of Saint Catherine on Mount Sinai, and it is possible on this evidence that they are somehow related. 1342 is a manuscript that has an interesting text in Mark; I do not know that its text of Luke has ever been studied.[10]

The twelfth-century minuscule manuscript 1 is also identical to P75 B, except that it has a different word for 'sins' (it reads *hamartēmata*). It is a member of the group known as Family 1. The relationship between the members of this group is very complicated. Suffice it to say that the family is a representative of the Caesarean text. Most other members of Family 1 (118 205 209) have a longer form of the prayer, but they agree with 1 in reading *hamartēmata*. But one other member of the family, 1582, has exactly

9 C. M. Martini, *Il problema della recensionalità de codice B alla luce del papiro Bodmer XIV*, Analecta Biblica 26 (Rome, 1966).

10 See Silva New in K. Lake and S. New, *Six Collations of New Testament Manuscripts*, Harvard Theological Studies 17 (Cambridge, Mass. and London, 1932), pp. 77ff.

the same wording as 1; it is a particularly interesting manuscript, so let us pause to learn more about it.

Completed in 949, it was copied by a monk of Constantinople called Ephraim, almost certainly the same Ephraim who copied several other significant manuscripts.[11] These include an important copy of Aristotle, and the New Testament manuscript 1739, which contains Acts and the Catholic and Pauline epistles. According to information in its colophon, 1739 is derived from a codex written not earlier than the end of the fourth century, which itself depended on a very ancient manuscript containing a text very close to that known to Origen. A colophon at the end of Mark in 1582 (identical to one in Codex 1) provides textual information that prompts one to presume similar antecedents for this other copy from Ephraim's pen. It has even been conjectured that 1582 represents the first twelve gatherings of 1739, which begins at Quaternion 13.[12] Kim studied the text of Matthew in 1582, and concluded that the text is very similar to that found in Origen's citations. This strengthens the connection of Family 1 with Caesarea, since Origen taught there in the later part of his life. The existence of a Caesarean text – that is, a text distinctive to that city – has been questioned.[13] But even those who do not believe that there ever was such a text will grant that there is, in 1739 and 1582, an Origenian form of text, and one that is associated with Pamphilus and Eusebius, both Caesarean scholars. We should note here that Caesarean readings have been found in Mark in minuscule 1342.[14]

This is the place to record the important fact that Origen knew the short text of Luke. He gives us both Matthew and Luke *verbatim*:

The verses of Matthew have it in the following form: 'Our Father in heaven, hallowed be your name, your kingdom come, your will be done, on earth as in heaven. Give us today our daily bread. Forgive us our sins, as we forgive our debtors. And lead us not into temptation, but deliver us from the evil one.' Luke's version reads, 'Father hallowed be your name, your kingdom come. Give us day by day our daily bread. And forgive us

[11] K. and S. Lake, 'The Scribe Ephraim', *JBL* 62 (1943), 263–8.
[12] K. W. Kim, 'Codices 1582, 1739, and Origen', *JBL* 69 (1950), 167–75. But, against this, the two volumes have different dimensions, and different numbers of lines to the page (according to Aland, *Liste*).   [13] See Alands, *Text*, pp. 66f.
[14] In the study by Silva New already cited.

our sins, for we ourselves forgive everyone who is indebted to us. And lead us not into temptation.'[15]

There is also a small amount of versional support for the short text. First there is the Sinaitic Syriac. This is one of the two manuscripts containing the so-called Old Syriac Gospels, the oldest known Syriac version. The manuscript, which is in St Catherine's Monastery on Mount Sinai, was copied either at about the same time as Jerome produced his Latin Gospels or slightly later. It is a text that often agrees with Codex Bezae. The origins of the version it represents are obscure, but the majority of scholars favour a date in the second half of the second century. If they are right, and if the extant manuscript accurately reproduces the earliest form of the text here, then the Sinaitic Syriac is the oldest evidence for the short form of the Lord's Prayer. This is an interesting point, to which we shall return. The other supporter is, as has already been made clear, the Latin Vulgate.[16] Where Jerome altered the Old Latin texts he knew, he generally did so on good grounds: we have seen that he knew Greek texts similar to manuscripts like Vaticanus. So his testimony bears witness to a Greek text such as that of B current in the 380s.

The story of 1582 is an unusual example of the preservation of ancient material along with information about its provenance. Generally instructive is the precarious survival in Greek manuscripts of the short Lukan text: one papyrus of the early third century; one parchment manuscript of the fourth century; one minuscule manuscript produced in 949; two eleventh-century manuscripts from Sinai; one twelfth- or thirteenth-century manuscript. Of these, the papyrus has been recovered from the sands of Egypt only in the last half-century, and the minuscules have become known only in the course of this century and still await thorough examination. Only the fourth-century copy has been known for any length of time. The editorial activity that produced P75 and B kept this divergent form alive, and a few witnesses of later centuries testify to its continued, though weak, persistence. It would have taken only a little more ill-fortune for the Greek of this

---

[15] Origen, *On Prayer* 18.2 (tr. R. A. Greer, The Classics of Western Spirituality (New York and London, 1979), p. 118).

[16] There is also one manuscript that is sometimes listed among the Old Latin witnesses, g[1], which has the reading. But it generally has a Vulgate text, and so cannot be counted here. See p. 164 below.

text to have been lost to us for ever. Yet it appears to have been the only form of Luke known to Origen. At least, he does not mention any disagreement over the Lukan text. Origen regularly discusses differences between manuscripts when he knows of them.[17] Here he mentions only one, the Marcionite reading 'Your bread' instead of 'Our bread' discussed below. That he refers only to this small variant indicates that he was unaware of any other. His silence is strong evidence that short Luke was the dominant reading of Origen's generation.

As it is, the short text has survived. And in a very firmly fixed form. These manuscripts differ only over the word for 'sins' – *hamartias* against *hamartēmata*. There is no difference in meaning here, and very little reason to prefer one or the other (both are ancient readings) except – for what it is worth – that *hamartēmata* does not appear elsewhere in Luke.

The second form of text is found in Codex Bezae. I provide my own translation, keeping the rather inconsequential lines which the manuscript's 'sense lines' have become at this point:

> Our Father who art in heaven
> Hallowed be thy name upon us
> Thy kingdom come Thy will
> be done As in heaven so on earth
> Our daily bread
> give us today And forgive us
> our debts as we also
> forgive our debtors
> And do not bring us into temptation
> But deliver us from evil.

This is the text of Matthew's version of the prayer, though not the text of Matthew as it is contained in Codex Bezae – there are six differences between the two. The most noteworthy is the presence of 'upon us' in the second line, to which we shall return. This manuscript also makes the context of the prayer more Matthaean, by importing a version of Matthew 6.7 into the introduction to the prayer: while other manuscripts read 'When you pray, say "Father..."', it reads

---

[17] See B. M. Metzger, 'Explicit References in the Works of Origen to Variant Readings in New Testament Manuscripts', in *Historical and Literary Studies: Pagan, Jewish and Christian*, NTTS 8 (Grand Rapids and Leiden), pp. 88–103.

When you pray, do not heap up empty phrases like the others do. For some think that they will be heard for their many words, But praying say 'Our Father...'.

For 'others', all manuscripts of Matthew 6.7 have either 'gentiles' or 'hypocrites'. This is a skilful addition of Lukan colour: *hoi loipoi*, 'the others', is used in a similar way at 8.10 and 18.9. It may also indicate either a non-Jewish readership which did not understand the reference of 'gentiles' or an anti-Jewish bias. This is also presumably the reason for 'hypocrites' in some manuscripts of Matthew (including the Vaticanus). Admittedly, Codex Bezae in Matthew has 'gentiles', but manuscripts are as generally inconsistent as people.

Third, we have the longer text of the Byzantine witnesses. The oldest support for this is Codex Ephraemi Rescriptus, C (04). This manuscript was produced in the fifth century, and palimpsested in the twelfth to take a copy of writings by Ephraem the Syrian. It originally contained the entire Bible, but a great deal is either lost or illegible. Its text represents, in different places, all the major text types. The text of the fifth-century Codex Alexandrinus, A (03) is identical, except for one detail that has no effect on the sense.[18] This codex is one of the oldest surviving examples of the Byzantine text, and one of the earliest majuscule examples of it to be studied.[19] Presented to Charles I in 1627, it is now to be seen next to Codex Sinaiticus in the British Library. It is the fourth of the complete Bibles to have survived from the early church.

A and C follow Matthew as far as 'earth', and then revert to Luke as it is found in P75 B, with the addition of 'but deliver us from evil' at the end. Surprisingly, neither they nor any other extant manuscript adds a doxology to Luke. Does this indicate that the text of Luke was influenced by Matthew at a point before Matthew was 'improved' by doxologies?

This is the text of the vast majority of witnesses, with occasional variations in the second part under Matthaean influence.

The Curetonian Syriac has some Matthaean additions, but not all. It runs:

Our Father which *art* in heaven, Hallowed be thy name. And come thy

---

[18] A reads *eltheto* instead of C's *elthato* in 'Thy kingdom come.' This variant is also present in the Matthaean text.   [19] Its text in the rest of the New Testament is Alexandrian.

kingdom. And give to us bread continual of every day. And forgive us our sins; and may we also forgive every *one* that is indebted to us. And bring us not into temptation; but deliver us from evil.[20]

So far, the history of Luke's text seems to be quite straightforward: an original short version has been expanded into a more Matthaean form by two separate processes of revision. But we come now to a problem which suggests a much more complicated development. The first hint of this is another interesting reading in Codex Bezae – the presence of 'upon us' after 'name'. This may have some connection with a remarkable discussion by the famous theologian Gregory, Bishop of Nyssa in central Asia Minor from about 371. His treatise on the Lord's Prayer contains this passage:

Luke . . . when he desires the Kingdom to come, implores the help of the Holy Spirit. For so he says in his Gospel; instead of Thy Kingdom come it reads 'May Thy Holy Spirit come upon us and purify us.'[21]

Maximus Confessor, writing in the seventh century, quotes this reading. It is also found in 700, an eleventh-century minuscule manuscript that has many unique readings (the figure 270 has been given);[22] 162, copied in 1153, also has this text, with the omission of 'upon us'. Besides this evidence, it is possible that the reading was known by the end of the second century, in the African writer Tertullian (the first theologian to write in Latin). Tertullian wrote a large treatise against Marcion. Marcion had produced his idiosyncratic version of Luke, and in Book 3 Tertullian goes through this text, criticising it. It is our chief source for recovering Marcion's text, difficult though it often is to know whether Tertullian is quoting precisely or not. The uncertainty in the present instance is a typical example. Tertullian says at this point

Whom shall I ask for the Holy Spirit? . . . Shall I pray for the kingdom to come?[23]

[20] Translation from *Remains of a Very Antient Recension of the Four Gospels in Syriac, Hitherto Unknown in Europe; Discovered, edited, and translated by William Cureton* (London, 1858), p. 61.
[21] *The Lord's Prayer. The Beatitudes*, tr. H. C. Graef, Ancient Christian Writers 18 (Westminster, Md. and London, 1954), p. 52.
[22] A plate of the page with this reading is given by Metzger, *Manuscripts of the Greek Bible*, Plate 37.   [23] Tertullian, *Against Marcion* 4.26.

It is not clear whether this is the text known to Marcion, or to Tertullian, or to both of them. It is also somewhat unclear in what order Tertullian read the clauses. In his work *On Prayer*, he places them in the order 'Hallowed be thy name, Thy will be done on earth as it is in heaven, Thy kingdom come.' It is the opinion of Chase that both Marcion and Tertullian knew the clause referring to the Spirit, but that it is not clear which of the two clauses Tertullian considered it to replace.[24] If it *is* Marcionite, then this form of Luke is attested by an older witness than any of the others.

Although the surviving support for it (popping up briefly every couple of hundred years as it does) is even slighter than that for the shorter form of the prayer, it was probably once quite well known. A number of scholars have even argued that it is the original form of Luke, and that 'Thy kingdom come' is a harmonisation to Matthew. It will be recalled that Luke in his writings frequently emphasises the activity of the Spirit. What more natural than that he should show the meaning of Jesus' words in this way? The matter deserves serious consideration, and a number of scholars have argued for its authenticity.[25] But an at least equally cogent theory is that this form is a liturgical adaptation, perhaps for baptism or a service including the laying on of hands. There is a close parallel in the Acts of Thomas 27:

Come Holy Ghost and cleanse their mind and their heart, and confirm them in the name of the Father and of the Son and of the Holy Ghost.

The fact that it is a striking and distinctive reading does not mean that it is original. As we saw in studying Luke 6, a reading is not preferable simply on the grounds that the alternative might be a harmonisation.

The form of the clause in Gregory may be the origin of the rather strange phrase in Codex Bezae. The synoptic texts speak of the kingdom coming, or even of its being in the midst, but not of its

---

[24] F. H. Chase, *The Lord's Prayer in the Early Church*, Texts and Studies 1.3 (Cambridge, 1891), pp. 27f.

[25] The views of scholars who have supported and rejected the reading are conveniently listed in Shawn Carruth and Albrecht Garsky, *The Database of the International Q Project: Q 11:2b–4*, ed. S. D. Anderson, Documenta Q, (Leuven, 1996), pp. 4–18. Eighteen scholars who prefer the reading are cited. For the problems inherent in the use of textual material in the reconstruction of hypothetical documents, see Chapter 7 below.

coming upon people. It is likely that, either intentionally or out of some kind of confusion such as a half-preserved marginal note or a half-memory, it has an echo of Gregory's text. Or it may be that the phrase is an echo of what became a commonplace of patristic interpretation. Cyprian of Carthage, in his treatise *On the Lord's Prayer*, expresses it clearly:

It is not that we pray God that He be hallowed by our prayers, but that we ask of Him that His name be hallowed in us.[26]

Thus the reading in Codex Bezae may, rather than directly due to the clause invoking the Spirit, be a parallel development to it.[27]

There are several other interesting variations in the Lukan text: Four Old Latin and two Latin Vulgate manuscripts have a strange reading in Luke 11.2. Instead of *Pater Noster*, they begin the prayer *Pater Sancte*, 'Holy Father'. This reading may be an allusion to John 17.11. The phrase 'Holy Father' is found in the eucharistic liturgy as early as Didache 10.2: 'We give you thanks, Holy Father, for your holy name.' Closer to home for our Latin manuscripts, it is found in the preface to the Lord's Prayer in the Gallican Rite (the non-Roman rite of Gaul that was used until the time of Charlemagne). The Old Latin manuscripts are a c ff² i, and the Vulgate are D E. The last two are Irish manuscripts. The explanation for their containing the Old Latin reading is that they are derived from the same north Italian text-type as the four Old Latin manuscripts.

A catena preserves an interesting note by Origen: 'The Marcionites have the following reading: "Give us each day your daily bread."'[28] The point of this variant is subtle. Origen himself said something similar in *On Prayer* when he wrote 'If we pursue our inquiry deeper and ask about "ours" in the latter book [Luke] where it is not said "give us today our daily bread" but "give us day by day our daily bread", then it becomes a question of how this bread can be ours.'[29] The reading of Marcion is probably an over-sophisticated revision on the grounds of a similar line of reasoning.

---

[26] Section 12.   [27] See Chase, *The Lord's Prayer*, pp. 35f.
[28] *Die Homilien zu Lukas*, ed. M. Rauer, GCS 49 (35); *Origenes Werke* IX (Berlin, 1959), Fragment 180, p. 302.   [29] pp. 146f.

There is one final area for investigation. The question arises as to the number of independent sources on which our texts depend. Setting aside the patristic writings, and the Apostolic Constitutions and the Didascalia Apostolorum (which we have seen to depend on the Didache), we have three books containing versions of the prayer: Matthew, Luke and the Didache. Does the Didache depend on Matthew? Scholars have generally answered this question by comparing what we have – the tenth-century text – with that of Matthew. Not surprisingly, the majority have decided in favour of dependence. However, all that we can really say is that the text of our own extant manuscript of the Didache seems to be so close to that of Matthew as to justify our concluding that it is dependent on Matthew. But the possibility that the text has been harmonised to Matthew is too strong for us to claim more. However, it should be added that Massaux, in his study of the use of Matthew in the early church, concluded that the wider context of the passage in the Didache showed the writer to be dependent on Matthew.[30]

The time has come to sum up the findings of this chapter. They may be divided between historical conclusions, and the wider significance of those conclusions for our exploration. First, the historical conclusions:

1. We have found the following main forms of the Lord's Prayer:

1 Matthew finishing at 'evil'
2 Matthew with a Doxology (and several variations)
3 Luke in a short form
4 Luke in a form supplemented from Matthew (Byzantine text)
5 Luke in a form supplemented from Matthew (Codex Bezae)
6 Luke with the clause 'Thy Holy Spirit come upon us and cleanse us.'

If I were editing the Greek New Testament, I would print numbers 1 and 3. But all six forms contribute to our overall understanding of the tradition: the Doxology in Matthew, because the intention to end with one is likely to be authentic even if the wording is spurious; the two longer forms in Luke, because they state strongly a belief in the unity of Jesus' teaching; and the last because it deserves serious

---

[30] E. Massaux, *Influence de l'Evangile de saint Matthieu sur la littérature chrétienne avant saint Irénée* (repr. Louvain, 1986 (1950)), pp. 615ff., p. 640.

consideration as authentically Lukan, and because it is Lukan in spirit if not in fact.

2. All these forms are likely to have had a wide circulation at different times, even though several of them are now known only in a very few witnesses. And the evidence indicates that all of them came into existence at a very early point. Matthew without a Doxology was known to Origen and Cyprian, and was therefore in existence in the first part of the third century. Matthew with a short Doxology (Codex Bobbiensis) and a longer one (Freer Gospels) is fourth century. Short Luke is in the Sinaitic Syriac and P75, and so known by the early third century at the very latest. The version of Luke with the reference to the Holy Spirit may be in Marcion, and therefore second century. With that goes the possibility (no more) that the long text of Luke in Codex Bezae is of a similar age. The most recent text is the Byzantine form of Luke, which cannot be traced before the fifth century, although the process of expansion is certainly older.

3. Although the texts of the Gospels continued to develop, it seems that the most dramatic change took place in the first 150 years of their transmission. This is true of many other textual traditions – initial fluidity followed by stability. The consequence is that many of the variants which occur in quite late manuscripts had their origins at an early date. The evidence of P75 has demonstrated this for the text of two medieval manuscripts (1192 and 1210) in the Lukan Lord's Prayer. The testimony of 1 and 1582 underlines the fact that it is not the date of a witness but the age of the text which it presents that matters.

4. As in Luke 6, we find that some witnesses to Luke 11.2–4 are actually closer to Matthew 6.9-13 than to some other Lukan forms.

5. The haphazard nature of scribal activity is clear. It is striking that the harmonisation to Matthew is not precise, and never includes the Doxology. Some difficulties in the text are resolved, while some (such as *epiousion*) are left untouched.

6. Our evidence demonstrates the tenacity with which early independent Lukan forms of the Lord's Prayer survived.

7. Finally, we have seen how narrowly some forms of the text have escaped oblivion. We are justified in wondering how much more variation there was of which we know nothing; and, if the variation occurred at an early stage, how often it is the oldest text form that has been lost. Short Luke just survived and almost no trace survives of the Holy Spirit clause. How many similar readings have been lost where P[75] is deficient, B is at fault, and no father comments on the text?

We turn now to our more general conclusions.

First, it may have been noticed that the various forms of text are not preserved coherently in various groups of witnesses. Thus, for example, Codex Bezae preserves an echo of the clause 'Thy Holy Spirit come upon us and cleanse us', but in other ways it harmonises. This is because all the manuscripts of the New Testament contain mixed texts. This baffling fact, even more than the numbers involved, is what has made them so difficult to categorise. Let us look at the matter in a way that is traditional to the discipline: genealogically. The idea of manuscripts being copied from other manuscripts may be expressed as a family tree. So long as a manuscript is simply copied from one other, it is possible to trace the line of descent. But once a copy has been corrected by comparison with a manuscript other than its parent, has been in the technical phrase conflated, it becomes much harder to establish the parentage of a manuscript then copied from it. For that new manuscript will contain features of two grandparents. Repeat this for each copy, when most of the links in the chain have been lost, and the difficulties may easily be imagined. The most that can be established is groupings of manuscripts, and even when placed in their groups manuscripts are often capricious enough to lend occasional support to a rival group or to disagree with every one.

The second of these more theoretical conclusions takes up a matter raised at the end of the last chapter, where we asked how many texts there were of Luke 6.1-10. If we return to the question now, we find that this is a problem which has been resolved in different ways at different times. The harmonising process of introducing Matthew into Luke is a declaration that there is a single text. But there are, running alongside this, a number of traditions which keep Luke separate. The manuscript variations bear witness that the problem has been recognised, and different solutions have been provided, since as far back as can be traced.

Behind the question 'How many texts?' is the question 'Is there a single original prayer?' We find that, among modern writers, there is a strong determination to find a single original form of the prayer. It is generally agreed that Jesus will have delivered his teaching, or at least some of it, in Aramaic.[31] And both Matthew and Luke will go into Aramaic fairly readily. For example, Matthew's 'debts' and Luke's 'trespasses' are often explained as alternative translations of the one Aramaic word *hôbā*. This feature could lead one to suppose that they are independent versions of a single Aramaic original. However, the fact that there are clauses in which they have identical wording suggests the conclusion that they are both dependent on an earlier Greek form of the prayer, which Luke has altered so as to make the word 'debt' clear for readers further removed from the Aramaic milieu of Jesus.

If there is an earlier form, Greek or Aramaic, on which both depend, then how do we explain the differences between them? Is Luke a simplified version? Is Matthew an expansion to clarify what he felt to be obscure? Does Matthew represent liturgical development of the prayer and, if so, is Luke free from such influence? Nor should one overlook the degree to which the prayer finds conscious literary parallels in the evangelists' accounts of Jesus' life, and may thus be influenced by Matthew's or Luke's creativity.

But our aim is not to discuss the matter exegetically, but to get our bearings on it by studying the character of the prayer as a tradition preserved in manuscripts. Let us attempt this by trying to look at it through the eyes of someone to whom a written tradition could only be a manuscript tradition. We return to Origen's treatise *On Prayer*. In the passage already quoted, he tells us where Matthew and Luke differ:

---

[31] Matthew Black, *An Aramaic Approach to the Gospels and Acts*, 3rd edn (Oxford, 1967); J. Fitzmyer, 'The Languages of Palestine in the First Century AD', *CBQ* 32 (1970), 501–31; reprinted in *A Wandering Aramaean: Collected Aramaic Essays* (Missoula, Mont., 1979), pp. 29–56; and again in S. E. Porter (ed.), *The Language of the New Testament: Classic Essays*, JSNTSS 60 (Sheffield, 1991), pp. 126–62.

First of all, it must be observed that Matthew and Luke seem to many to have written down the same prayer, sketched out to show how we ought to pray. The verses of Matthew have it in the following form . . . Luke's version reads . . .

Now it must be said to those who hold the opinion I have mentioned that first, the words, even if they have a close resemblance to one another, nevertheless appear to differ in the two versions, as I shall explain when I examine them carefully. Second, it is impossible that the same prayer should be spoken in two places. The first is on the mountain . . . in the context of the beatitudes and of the commandments that follow. The second is in 'a certain place' in which 'he was praying' and 'when he ceased' he spoke the prayer to one of the disciples who asked to be taught to pray 'as John taught his disciples'. For how can we admit that the same words were spoken in a prolonged speech without a prior request and also proclaimed at the request of a disciple? Yet perhaps someone will say in reply that the prayers have the same force as a single prayer spoken one time in a prolonged speech and another time in answer to the request of a disciple, who was apparently absent when he spoke the prayer in Matthew's version or failed to understand what was said then. On the whole, it is better to suppose that the prayers are different, even though they have certain parts in common.[32]

He ends with a comment that is very revealing: 'We sought also in Mark, in case a similar passage there had escaped our notice, but found nothing.'[33] That the Lord's Prayer is found in Matthew and Luke, but not in Mark, is today the kind of thing that every student knows. Origen in his day was innovative to have thought of looking. The point is that he has concluded that comparison is the best means of searching out Jesus' words and purposes, that the Gospels are the bearings which will allow him to fix the position of Jesus, the co-ordinates which he may plot on the map.[34] Origen is obviously not working with a purely literary theory of synoptic relationships in which similarity indicates dependence or a shared source. He can assume that the evangelists are recording separate events where their accounts differ, and the same one when they agree.

The passage contains two points which are of particular interest for us. The first is that Origen's sharp awareness of the distinctness

---

[32] *On Prayer* 18.3.   [33] *Ibid.*
[34] We find the same technique in the surviving fragments of his Homilies on Luke: GCS 49.299–302, Fragments 172–81.

of Matthew, Luke and Mark is in marked contrast to the harmonising tendencies which we have already so regularly observed. The acuteness of his scholarly perceptions is paralleled in the manuscript tradition of Alexandria as it is represented in P[75] and B. The second may, to us, appear to be quite contrary. There is for Origen no gap between the narrative and the events described. If there are two narratives which differ significantly from each other, then there are two events. Such an approach today could seem to be apologetic. This is because we have grown accustomed to a critical approach that is focussed on the recovery of a single point in the history of a text, an approach that studies a multitude of manuscripts in order to recover the single original text of Matthew, Mark and Luke. It then compares these three in order to arrive at the core tradition. For Origen, in a world where each manuscript copy was unique, and had at least the potential to come up with something very unexpected, life could never be so simple. He knows that all manuscripts are faulty. Nothing would be easier than to fly from imperfect manuscripts to the pure text which they represent. But he does not. His business is with the truth *in* the text rather than the truth behind the text. And this text is – of course – a manuscript text. It therefore follows that the truth is also not behind the individual manuscripts. To understand this point, we shall need to understand properly how different a manuscript tradition is from a printed tradition. Further investigations will be necessary before we have achieved that understanding.

Third, the history of the Lukan form of the prayer illustrates a point which is easily forgotten: that we cannot read one form of the text as though we did not know other forms. We may supply additions to the short version of the Lord's Prayer, or subtract expansions from the long form. But we are unable to read either as though the other did not exist.

Finally, a brief but certainly not a small point. What we have established in this chapter is the extent of substantial variation in a passage which might be supposed to be so popular as to be well established in a single form. It may be that the reader will consider the theological significance of the text of the variants to be slight. It must be stressed that the significance rests not in the character of the variants, but simply in the fact that the variants exist.

CHAPTER 5

The sayings on marriage and divorce

Jesus said 'I am the way, the truth and the life', not 'I am the
way, the social convention and the life.'   Gregory the Great

It has sometimes been claimed that words of Jesus were reproduced
particularly carefully and reverently by scribes. This claim is based
on the belief that his words were regarded as so sacred that, while
errors of all kinds might be found in less important passages,
sentences and phrases, *they* were handled as reverently as the
Massoretic tradition preserved the oracles received by Moses. The
claim owes everything to piety, and nothing to the study of the
manuscript evidence. Examine any edition of the Gospels that
extensively details the manuscript evidence, and you will find that
the number of variant readings in a narrative is small. Come to a
block of sayings, and the number rises dramatically. The complexity of interpreting Jesus' sayings led to an increase in variant
readings. We have encountered this already in the Lord's Prayer,
which one might expect to exist in a single form if anything did. But
we come now to a problem more thorny and to a situation more
tangled than those we have studied so far.

The basic reason for the complexity in the passages we are to
study and in many others of Jesus' sayings is precisely the
importance accorded them. A recent major study (whose title
neatly makes the point) has illustrated how much copyists might
change the text in order to bring out the meaning which they
believed to be correct.[1] Orthodox scribes literally rewrote the text
in order to make it say what they knew it meant. Such changes
sometimes arose from theological controversy. It is these, and

[1] B. D. Ehrman, *The Orthodox Corruption of Scripture* (New York and Oxford, 1993).

especially those due to Christological debate, that are the subject of Ehrman's study. Others were the consequence of changing presuppositions about Jesus and his disciples: just as the painter clothes the biblical subject in contemporary dress, so the copyist and reader will assume what is true in their day to have been the case in Jesus' time. Other changes arose out of changing interpretations of the way in which sayings of Jesus moulded the Christian life. It is with a group of such sayings that we deal now.

It is necessary to recognise at the outset how much higher the text-critical stakes have become. The assumption that Jesus issued specific, verbally precise commandments on certain matters is deeply seated. And this assumption has demanded that textual critics deliver the original specific, precise wording spoken by Jesus and recorded by the evangelists. But this is to prejudge the issue. First the evidence must be collected and scrutinised. Then conclusions will be drawn, and the legislators will have to make what they can of what they are given.

In no area of contemporary concern is the teaching of Jesus more debated than that regarding the nature of marriage, the problem of divorce, and the possibility of remarriage. These have been pressing theological and pastoral concerns in the modern churches. It is inevitable that the sayings of Jesus have been claimed as support in what has been said and done. It is perhaps equally inevitable that the text-critical questions have been either ignored or misunderstood. Yet the fact that there *are* textual problems is the first and most important fact about Jesus' sayings.

Generally, debate has centred on the meaning of a single authoritative text. But it will soon become plain that such a text does not exist today, and never has existed, and that therefore the theological arguments built on such a text are castles in the air. The consequence of the belief that there is a single text has meant that study of the sayings about divorce in the Gospels has almost invariably followed a standard pattern. First, the text of each evangelist is described, using a modern printed Greek or English text. Then the differences between them are discussed, and certain of them shown to be secondary. Finally, one form or another is declared authentic, and by implication authoritative. But there are two massive problems with this approach: the first is that, as we should by now have come to suspect, there are also variations within the manuscript traditions of each Gospel passage. Sometimes, yet again, the differences between the manuscripts of one passage are greater than those between our printed Gospels. The problem is not simply one of explaining the differences between Matthew, Mark and Luke. As we shall see, we are in fact discussing a score of different forms of words of Jesus. The second problem is that in general an equivalence has been assumed in the meaning of words such as 'divorce' and 'adultery' between our culture and those of early Christianity. A study of the manuscripts shows this set of presuppositions to be gravely mistaken.

In addition to the principal ancient evidence for each variation, I shall also indicate which of the major English versions support it, and which is preferred by Nestle–Aland and by the synopsis of Greeven.[2] This will indicate with just what diverse authoritative texts people are working.

The passages are Matthew 5.27–32; 19.3–9; Mark 10.2–12; Luke 16.18. We shall also discuss John 7.53–8.11, the story of the woman taken in adultery. But, because the problems are quite different in nature, so that different issues arise, we shall look at that story in a separate chapter. One could also include 1 Corinthians 7.12–16. But the textual variation in this passage is less remarkable and, since the problems of Paul's letters are of a different character, and this book is in any case dealing with the Gospels, we shall set the passage aside. We begin with the oldest Gospel, that of Mark.

MARK 10.2–12

In this episode, Pharisees ask Jesus the question 'Is it lawful for a man to divorce his wife?' In reply, Jesus quotes Genesis 2.24. When they are alone, his disciples ask him for clarification. It is in his explanation that most of the textual problems are found. We have the following forms:

---

[2] A. Huck, *Synopsis of the First Three Gospels*, 13th edn, fundamentally revised by Heinrich Greeven (Tübingen, 1981). The abbreviations of English Bibles are as follows: AV – Authorised Version; GNB – Good News Bible; JB – Jerusalem Bible; NEB – New English Bible; NIV – New International Version; NJB – New Jerusalem Bible; NRSV – New Revised Standard Version; REB – Revised English Bible; RSV – Revised Standard Version.

1. The Freer Gospels (W):

If a woman divorces her husband and marry another, she commits adultery; and if a man divorces his wife, he commits adultery.

In this part of Mark, W has a Caesarean text.

2. Two members of Family 1 (1 209) and the Sinaitic Syriac:

If a woman divorces her husband and marry another, she commits adultery; and if a man divorces his wife and marry another, he commits adultery.

Not all members of Family 1 agree. In fact, only one of them, 1 itself, has the text given above, while 209 omits the second half ('and if a man . . .'). This error is probably mechanical, caused by the recurrence of the word translated as 'commits adultery'. The other member of the group attested in the chief edition of the family has our Text 5.[3]

3. (‭א‬ B C; N.–A. RSV NEB NIV NRSV REB)

Whoever divorces his wife and marries another commits adultery against her; and if she, divorcing her husband marries another, she commits adultery.

This, from the witness of ‭א‬ B, is the Alexandrian text.

4. Codex Bezae (D) and (with minor variations) the Latin manuscript Codex Brixianus (f):

Whoever divorces his wife and marries another commits adultery against her; and if a woman goes out from her husband and marry another, she commits adultery.

Codex Brixianus, of the sixth century, contains an Old Latin text that appears to have been influenced by the Gothic version. It has also been extensively revised to be brought into agreement with the Vulgate. It is not identical with the Vulgate here, although there is no difference in sense.

5. (A Byz; AV):

Whoever divorces his wife and marries another commits adultery against her; and if a woman divorces her husband and be married to another, she commits adultery.

[3] Kirsopp Lake, *Codex 1 of the Gospels and its Allies*, Texts and Studies 7.3 (Cambridge, 1902).

The abbreviation *Byz* indicates the Byzantine text. Its oldest witness here is Codex Alexandrinus.

6.   (Greeven JB GNB NJB):

Whoever divorces his wife and marries another commits adultery against her (GNB 'his wife'); and if a woman divorces her husband and marries another, she commits adultery.

7.   (Three Old Latin manuscripts, with small differences between them):

If a man divorce his wife and marry another, he commits adultery against her; and if a woman separate from her husband and marry another, she commits adultery against him; likewise also he who marries a woman divorced from her husband commits adultery.

The double prohibition that is distinctive to all the forms of the Markan version presupposes that a woman divorce her husband. This was possible in the pagan world, but not in Judaism. It is generally argued that the clause referring to the woman divorcing a man is therefore a formulation by the Roman community, in which Mark's Gospel is likely to have originated. It is the first clear instance in our survey of a saying of Jesus being adapted to new circumstances. In Jesus' culture, a woman could not divorce her husband. Therefore, it was not an issue which Jesus could have addressed; therefore, the clause cannot be from Jesus' lips. The Roman church was faced with handling a completely different set of circumstances: are women still permitted to divorce their husbands? The words of Jesus are adapted to comprehend these new circumstances.

We note that the text of No. 6, although it is widely accepted today, is not attested by any surviving manuscript. It combines elements from Nos. 3 (active 'marry' instead of passive 'be married') and 5 ('a woman' instead of 'she').

No. 5 has the mark of ecclesiastical sanction. The potentially confusing 'she' has been replaced with the clear 'a woman', and we have a simple prohibition of remarriage (not divorce, but remarriage) applied to both sexes. Nos. 7 and 8 also recognise the potential confusions, and in addition try to reconcile differences between this passage and the Matthaean parallel.

Forms 1 and 2 are unusual. They seem to take the behaviour of women as the more serious matter for concern. There also appears to be a difference in the act that 'constitutes' adultery. For a woman it is remarriage; for a man it is the prior step of divorce. Is there any possible sense to this? The text might represent a reinterpretation of the tradition in the light of concern over the status of single, formerly married women in the Christian community. But the form of the saying in the Sinaitic Syriac (No. 2) suggests that W has omitted 'marries another' by mistake. The second prohibition has also the effect of protecting a wife. This is the least 'rigorist' form of the text.

No. 4 may reflect a situation where formal divorce is not possible for a woman. She can only 'go out' from her husband.

Before moving on to the next passage, two points should be underlined. The first is that although Mark is the oldest Gospel, it already presents a form of the saying that has been adapted to new circumstances – the right of a Roman woman to divorce her husband. We shall have to be alert to the possibility that a younger Gospel may present an older form of the saying. The second is that in this passage Jesus is speaking about the status of divorces by describing second marriages as adultery. That is, the reference to remarriage is intended to condemn divorce, not remarriage. This is not the same as to condemn remarriage *per se*.

MATTHEW 5.27–32

The second passage is one that is unique to Matthew. But the situation is complicated. Matthew 19.3–9 is parallel to Mark 10.2–12. The passage Matthew 5.27–32 does not, as a passage, have a parallel in either Mark or Luke. But the saying in verse 32 does have similarities with the other passages. It is because of such complications that it is important to look at all the passages together and in full.[4]

The event is not, as in the parallel story, one of debate. But it is still in a context of controversy. It is the third of the antitheses of the Sermon on the Mount: 'You have heard it said . . . But I say to you that . . .'. The antithesis here is between a summary of Deuteronomy 24.1–4 and the saying of Jesus to be discussed. There is a

---

[4] See M. W. Holmes, 'The Text of the Matthaean Divorce Passages: A Comment on the Appeal to Harmonization in Textual Decisions', *JBL* 109 (1990), 651–64.

connection with the previous antithesis which has often been overlooked. Verses 27–8 are on the definition of adultery ('Every one who looks at a woman lustfully has already committed adultery with her in his heart'). There is also a thematic link between verses 29–30 and the section following the passage in Matthew 19. In the former passage it is stressed, with references to the right eye and the right hand, that 'it is better that you lose one of your members than that your whole body go into hell'; in the latter there is a catalogue of different kinds of eunuchs.

There are two major variations within these verses. The first is that D, along with a few other witnesses (including the Sinaitic Syriac), omits the whole of verse 30. This may be an accidental copying error, in which the scribe's eye jumped from the end of verse 29 (which he made more like the end of verse 30) to the end of verse 30. Such error, known as *homoeoteleuton* or *parablepsis* or *saut du même au même*, is easy enough. The long sequence of letters *kai mē holon to sōma sou apelthē eis geennan* occurred twice, and the scribe's eye will have gone back to the second after he had copied the first, and then picked up the following letters. (We encountered a similar error in the reading of 209 at Mark 10.12.) The support of the Sinaitic Syriac for the reading shows it to be at least late second century. The other alteration is to verse 32. This is found in the manuscripts in four forms:

1.   (D and three Old Latin witnesses (d accidentally omits the last four words)):

Whoever divorces his wife, except for the cause of *porneia*, makes her an adulteress.

The Greek word *porneia*, whose meaning constitutes a separate important problem, will be left untranslated for the present.

The three Old Latin witnesses are all very early. Two represent the European Old Latin text. The first is Codex Vercellensis, produced perhaps as early as the third quarter of the fourth century. It is a most important witness to the north Italian textual traditions of the time, for it pre-dates Jerome's activity, and therefore its text cannot have been affected by it. According to tradition, it was copied by Eusebius, Bishop of Vercelli, in the 360s.

There is no evidence to render this implausible. The manuscript is still in Vercelli. The second is another north Italian manuscript, Codex Veronensis, a fifth-century codex perhaps close to the type used by Jerome as the foundation for his edition. The third manuscript is Bobbiensis, the African witness. But there is a fourth Old Latin witness, which we have hitherto neglected. It will be remembered that Codex Bezae has both a Greek and a Latin column. The latter is a representative of the Old Latin text. And the Greek column is often the only Greek witness to support an Old Latin reading. We have such a case here. There are two possible reasons for this special relationship. One is that the Greek text of Codex Bezae has been systematically revised to agree with the Latin. There have been supporters of this view in the past. But close study has led to the conclusion that, while there are certainly individual passages where the Greek appears to have been modified into agreement with the Latin, there has been no large-scale or systematic revision. We are left with the conclusion that Codex Bezae often happens to be the sole survivor of that type of Greek text from which the oldest Latin versions were derived. This is perhaps an over-simplified explanation, but let it suffice at present.

2. (B):

Everyone divorcing his wife, except for the cause of *porneia*, makes her an adulteress, and the person marrying a divorced woman commits adultery.

This is the reading of one or two other manuscripts as well Vaticanus, and possibly of the Sahidic version.

3. (ℵ W f¹ N.–A. Greeven AV RSV JB NJB):

Everyone divorcing his wife, except for the cause of *porneia*, makes her an adulteress, and whoever should marry a divorced woman commits adultery.

In Matthew it is an early witness to the Byzantine type, although here it differs from other Byzantine manuscripts. That Codex Sinaiticus shares this reading illustrates how the Byzantine text was constructed out of a variety of materials.

4. The majority of witnesses, including the Byzantine text; NEB

NIV NRSV REB:

Whoever divorces his wife, except for the cause of *porneia*, makes her an adulteress, and whoever should marry a divorced woman (her REB) commits adultery.

This is the reading of the Byzantine text. The witnesses include Codex Regius (L 019), an eighth-century manuscript written with many mistakes, but generally following (or attempting to follow) the Alexandrian text. It seems here, however, to follow the Byzantine text.

5. (GNB):

If a man divorces his wife, even though she has not been unfaithful, then he is guilty of making her commit adultery if she marries again; and the man who marries her commits adultery also.

The form of the rendering in the GNB is so free as to demonstrate that variant readings are still coming into existence. It is clearly the first four which concern us. We could present the variants in a different manner, so as to show the points of variation (x indicates an omission):

Whoever divorces
                    his wife, except for the cause of *porneia*
Everyone divorcing
Anyone who divorces

_____

                    x   x   x   x   x   x   x
          an adulteress   the one marrying
makes her   and   a divorced woman
          an adulteress   whoever marries

_____

        x   x
commits adultery

The second, third and fourth forms do not differ significantly from each other (the beginning 'Whoever divorces' is a harmonisation of

Matthew to Mark 10 that does not affect the sense). Our interest is
therefore in comparing two forms of the text. In the first, D keeps
the concern of the logion clearly focussed on divorce, without
including any discussion on the further vexed question of remarriage. This is at least an old text, since it appears to have been the
form known to Origen. A catena fragment quotes his comment on
this verse that

in many manuscripts we do not find 'the man marrying a divorced
woman commits adultery'.[5]

In the context, this short text makes much simpler and better sense
than the longer form. For the logion's concern is essentially with
'hardness of heart'. And it is the cruelty of putting off the wife that
Jesus is criticising – divorce makes the wife into an adulteress, one
guilty of *porneia*, even though she is not. The second part in the
longer text could appear to return to preoccupation with the man
as the centre of attention – don't marry a divorced woman. But it
could also be aimed at protecting a rejected wife from further
ignominy, by establishing her right to remain single: her loyalty to
her husband has not, from her side, been broken. From her point of
view, it is as though she were married still, and this is to be
respected. She is not disposable property. We can see that this is
consonant with the practice recommended by Paul (1 Corinthians
7.10–11) and elsewhere in the early church.

The text of the Good News Bible highlights for us that there
continue to be widely divergent presuppositions about the content
of the key words in this passage. What constitutes the adultery: the
divorcing or the remarrying?

The point of all these sayings is quite different from that in Mark.
There, divorce was condemned by the statement that remarriage
amounts to adultery. Here, the point is that divorcing one's wife is
to treat her as though she were an adulteress. It can at once be seen
that the saying is driven by different motives from that in Mark. For
one thing, the circumstances under which divorce is possible are

---

[5] Origen, *Matthäuserklärung*, ed. E. Klostermann, GCS 41; *Origenes Werke* 12 (Leipzig, 1941),
p. 59 (Fragment 104). The quotation is found in a manuscript from Mount Athos, the
Laura Monastery. It is a copy of the Gospels (Gregory–Aland number 1507) with
commentary. It is dated to the tenth–eleventh centuries.

quite different. And the question of the 'Matthaean exception' – 'except for the cause of *porneia*' – is crucial. We saw that the application of the principle to the woman in Mark was likely to be secondary. Thus, the simple rule about a man divorcing his wife here in Matthew is likely to be closer to the original circumstances in which Jesus might have spoken on the subject. But what are we to make of the exception? The answer to that question must wait. But its presence here (and not in Mark) makes the whole situation very complicated. Provisionally we have to say that the two sayings in Matthew and Mark are dealing with two completely separate issues.

MATTHEW 19.3–9

This, the parallel passage to Mark, is extremely complex in its final verse.

1. Codex Sinaiticus (ℵ), the third hand of Codex Ephraemi Rescriptus (C³) and Codex Regius (L); N.–A. RSV NIV JB NJB NRSV:

Whoever divorces his wife, except for *porneia*, and marries another commits adultery.

The hand of Codex Ephraemi Rescriptus designated 3 consists of corrections made in the ninth century.

2. Codex Bezae (D) and an Old Latin manuscript (Codex Corbeiensis, ff¹); NEB GNB REB): The text is identical with 1, except that it reads 'except for the cause of *porneia*' instead of 'except for *porneia*'.

3. Codex Purpureus Petropolitanus (N) and a few other witnesses:

Whoever divorces his wife, except for *porneia*, makes her an adulteress; and the person marrying a divorced woman commits adultery.

N is, by and large, a representative of the Byzantine text. It is a fairly early one, for it was copied in the sixth century. It is also a splendid one for, as its name indicates, it is written on parchment that had been dyed purple, using silver ink (and gold for the divine names). It is scattered across a number of libraries, besides that of St Petersburg which is contained in its name.

4.   Family 1, the Bohairic version and B (with a minor difference in the second 'marrying') have the same text as 3, but read 'except for the cause of *porneia*' instead of 'except for *porneia*'.

5.   The Freer Gospels (W), the Koridethi Codex (Θ), 078, Family 13 and, with a minor difference in the second 'marrying', the Byzantine text and the Syriac versions; Greeven AV):

Whoever divorces his wife, except for *porneia*, and marries another commits adultery; and whoever marries a divorced woman commits adultery.

The Koridethi Codex is a ninth-century manuscript whose Greek characters have the appearance of having been penned by a scribe better acquainted with the Georgian alphabet. In Mark it is an important witness to the Caesarean text, and in the other Gospels to the Byzantine text.

6.   The first hand of Codex Ephraemi Rescriptus (C*):

Whoever divorces his wife, except for *porneia*, and marries another makes her an adulteress; and whoever marries a divorced woman commits adultery.

This is the first hand of Codex Ephraemi Rescriptus. The correction given under (1) above supplies additional wording.

7.   (P):

Whoever divorces his wife, except for *porneia*, and marries another commits adultery; and likewise also he who marries a divorced woman commits adultery.

P (024) is a sixth-century witness to the Byzantine text. It is a palimpsest, used the second time in the eighth century for a copy of texts by the Latin writer Isidore of Seville (c. 560–636). A Latin marginal note had already been added to the Greek as early as the seventh century.

8.   The Middle Egyptian Coptic version (mae):

= 7, but reads 'except for the cause of *porneia*' instead of 'except for *porneia*'.

This Middle Egyptian text has been the subject of much discussion since the announcement of its discovery in 1961. There are two manuscripts, found together; the other contains Acts as far as 15.2, and has many similarities with the longer text of that book.

As we look at these, we have to remember the tendency to harmonise, both within a Gospel and between Gospels. Thus we must be prepared for the influence of both Matthew 5.32 and Mark 10.11–12. And we immediately find that in 2, 4 and 8 'except for the cause of' from Matthew 5.32 has displaced 'except for'.

Nos. 3, 4 and 6 give the D text of Matthew 5.32 for the first clause, though only 4 has the exact wording 'except for the cause of'. Here, they seem to assume a situation where a man cannot commit adultery in the sense of stepping over a personal boundary. It is the second wife who is in an adulterous state (assuming that 'her' refers to the second and not to the first wife; this may be a very large assumption, affecting our understanding of Mark 10 as well). These, 5 and 7 all add the extension of adultery to a man who marries a divorced woman. The wording is a mixture of the second clause forms in Matthew 5 and Luke 16.

Almost all these Matthaean forms put it differently from Mark. There, adultery is described as divorcing one's spouse and remarrying. Here it consists in marrying a divorced person. Exceptions to this are Nos. 1 and 2. Both of these present, in the form of their statement, the same words as form 3 of Mark without the words 'against her', except for the 'Matthaean exception', which, in the case of No. 2, is derived from Matthew 5. Here we have a conflict of interests. Source criticism has generally maintained that Matthew here takes over Mark, adding the exception clause. Textual criticism is aware of the tendency to harmonise the text. And D is, as we have seen, especially prone to this – less so in Matthew than elsewhere, it is true. But prone none the less. ℵ, it is also known, has a more mixed text than B, preserving a number of readings that are typical of D. Here, ℵ D agree, except that D has a secondary harmonisation to Matthew 5.

If Matthew is to be expected to show consistency, then we may propose that the most Matthaean form of the saying must be one clause, addressing the divorce of a wife rather than the remarriage. Such a saying can be found enshrined in 3 and 4: 'Whoever divorces his wife, except for *porneia*, makes her an adulteress.' Let us for a moment assume that this is the oldest form of saying here, and trace its subsequent history. This saying, identical in form to the D version of Matthew 5.32, and in principle to all versions of that saying, was later changed in three ways. The first was by the addition at least partly taken from Luke 16.18 that is found in forms 3 and 4: 'and whoever marries a divorced woman commits adultery'. The second was by harmonisation to Mark, found in 1 and 2, introducing the reference to remarriage in the first clause and making the adultery the man's: 'Whoever divorces his wife, except for *porneia*, and marries another commits adultery.'

A third text conflates these two options, giving us the harmonisation to Mark and also additions from Luke 16; this is forms 5, 7 and 8: 'Whoever divorces his wife, except for *porneia*, and marries another commits adultery; and whoever marries a divorced woman commits adultery.'

There are a few other combinations; some forms harmonise the exception clause to Matthew 5. Form 6 gives us the double harmonisation (Mark 19 and Luke 16), but keeps the wording 'makes her an adulteress' found in 2 and 3.

These various developments can all be dated fairly early. Indeed, they may reflect the claim that all significant variants had come into being by the end of the second century.

But other cases could be argued. For example, is there any need for Matthew to be consistent, given the differing themes of the two passages? If he maintains the exception clause, then that may be sufficient consistency. And then we need to remember that he is also here trying to follow Mark. The clause about a woman divorcing her husband will immediately be meaningless to him, in his Jewish setting. We have now to ask simply whether Matthew could in Chapter 5 have condemned divorce because it makes the wife as though she were an adulteress, and in Chapter 19 have condemned it because it was not so from the beginning. Certainly there is a difficulty here, and it was spotted by Origen. If Jesus condemns divorce as being due to hardness of heart, does he then not go on to give voice to such hardness by permitting divorce on grounds of *porneia*?[6] We begin to sense that Mark's story does not fit

---

[6] Origen, *Matthäuserklärung*, ed. E. Klostermann GCS 40; *Origenes Werke* 10, (Leipzig, 1935), 19.24, p. 341. To be sure, Origen attributes such an objection to a supposed 'audacious Judaizer', and goes on to reject it. But he *does* want to discuss it.

very easily with Matthew's way of looking at the matter. It is because the shoe pinches that we have the degree of manuscript variation that there is.

A different solution was proposed by Jean Duplacy. In his view, the original text of the first half of the verse was 'Whoever divorces his wife, except for *porneia*, and marries another commits adultery.' He states that it cannot be decided whether or not there was a second part to the verse (as in Nos. 5–8), although a mechanical explanation for the shorter form is feasible: that the clause could have dropped out by *homoioteleuton*. The fact that he felt the original text to be beyond our reach is significant.

Before we turn to Luke, it is worth recalling an observation made by Holmes: the clause 'except for *porneia* does not find its way into any copy of Mark or of Luke, and is absent from no manuscript of Matthew'.[7] There is only the minor variation where the precise wording of the clause in Matthew 5 finds its way into Matthew 19. As with the Lord's Prayer, the pattern of change and preservation is unpredictable.

LUKE 16.18

The text is here found in one form, with only slight variations:

1.   (nearly all witnesses and all English versions cited):

Whoever divorces his wife and marries another commits adultery, and whoever marries a woman divorced from her husband commits adultery.

2.   (D, a few medieval manuscripts, syr (s p) and some other early versions):

The words 'from her husband' are absent. The fact that they are not found in the addition to Matthew 19.9 in text forms 5, 6 and 7 suggests that it was not part of the second-century text.

3.   (One fourth-century Old Latin manuscript, one Latin Vulgate manuscript, and four medieval Greek manuscripts):

Whoever divorces his wife and marries another commits adultery.

The emphasis in this text is again on the adultery of the man.

The complexity of text, particularly in Matthew 19, provides a

---

[7] Holmes, 'The Text', p. 659.

valuable insight into the tradition. The first point is that 'hard sayings' were hard from the beginning. It is certainly not the case that they are made hard by an over-sophistication on the part of modern society. Passages which were the focus of contentious issues were particularly prone to change.

Further, the differences in emphasis, not only between Matthew 5, Mark 10, Matthew 19 and Luke 16, but also between different versions of those Gospels, show the oral period and the first centuries of the written period to have been a continuum of reinterpretation. Even after the development of 'standard', 'ecclesiastical' texts – such as the Greek Byzantine text and the Syriac Peshitta – variant forms survived.

This question of emphasis and interpretation is, in Matthew's context for the saying in Chapter 5, said to stem from Jesus' own interpretation of the tradition. For the saying at Matthew 5.27–8 about the nature of adultery changes the content and nature of the language being used. The question can no longer be 'Who is guilty?' It is now 'Who is innocent?'

It seems that the early church took *porneia* to mean 'adultery'. This is the important point so far as our understanding of the manuscript tradition is concerned. But we shall have missed the purpose of Matthew's saying if we assume anything about the meaning of the word 'adultery'. The point is that if one gives 'except for the cause of *porneia*' a meaning such as 'even though she has not been unfaithful' (GNB) or 'for any cause other than unchastity' (REB) or 'except for the case of an illicit marriage' (New JB), then the link with verse 28 is lost, and the absurdity of the paradox sinks in the legal verbiage. A clear account of the reasons why *porneia* should be translated as 'adultery' is provided by the latest major commentary.[8] We are left with a saying that condemns the cruel and arbitrary dismissal of a faithful wife. We can see that such a saying is devoid of the casuistry and problematical exceptions of the modern versions. We can also see that the problem addressed is the opposite of the use to which the passage is often put. It is employed to hinder divorced people who wish to remarry. It

[8] W. D. Davies and D. C. Allison, *A Critical and Exegetical Commentary on the Gospel According to Saint Matthew*, Vol. 1 (Edinburgh, 1988), pp. 529–31.

was intended to protect vulnerable people who wished not to remarry.

Let us return to the variations in the manuscript tradition; in particular, to the difficulty of establishing a fixed point in the tradition that has any unique 'authority'. We have seen that to compare the Gospels with a view to establishing the priority of one form is to presuppose that each Gospel has a definitive form. The investigations of this chapter have found no evidence that either the evangelists or their successors believed such a form to exist. The recovery of a definitive 'original' text that is consequently 'authoritative' cannot be presumed to be an attainable target. The concept of such a text, essentially the 'ecclesiastical text' of a modern printed book, is present to modern minds, but was foreign to those of the early Christians.

That claims for an authoritative text are significant in modern debate about divorce and remarriage has already been emphasised. The matter is not academic. These texts have repeatedly been cited for the purpose of telling people how to behave in some of the most important decisions of their lives, to censure and to commend.[9] And the differences are not small. To condemn divorce and to condemn remarriage are two very different things. There are many differences in social context that need also to be considered before the meaning of the words can be understood.

In fact, the formulation of decisions with regard to divorce and remarriage has generally used several texts together. This is marked in, for example, two of Jerome's letters. The first is a response to a question whether a woman was permitted to divorce her husband after he had been unfaithful with both women and men, and whether having remarried she might be permitted to be in communion with the church without first doing penance.[10] Here he works together a series of texts – Romans 7.1–3, 1 Corinthians 7.39 and Matthew 5.32. He insists that ' "whosoever shall marry her that is divorced committeth adultery". Whether she has put away her husband or her husband her, the man who marries her is still an adulterer.' He then refers to Matthew 19.10–12. In a letter

[9] I have examined the use of the texts in modern reports commissioned by English churches in 'The Early Tradition of Jesus' Sayings on Divorce', *Theology* 96 (1993), 372–83.
[10] Letter 55.3.

written about five years later, in 399, on the death of Fabiola (who may have been the woman whose case he discussed in the earlier letter – the circumstances are certainly very similar) he exculpates her behaviour. Here he argues that

The Lord has given commandment that a wife must not be put away 'except for fornication, and that, if put away, she must remain unmarried'. Now a commandment which is given to men logically applies to women also.[11]

He goes on to deal with the further question of her remarriage, and condones it by saying that

I readily admit it to have been a fault, but at the same time declare that it may have been a case of necessity. 'It is better', the apostle tells us, 'to marry than to burn.'[12]

In this quite different treatment of her marital life, he combines Matthew 19 with 1 Corinthians 7.9, interpreting both in the spirit of the double saying of Mark 10, which is useless to him directly because it has no exception clause.

In practice, most customs in this matter contain some influence from Paul as well as from the Gospels. Without that, some strange possibilities arise. For example, the two Matthaean sayings exclude *porneia* from the forbidding of divorce. It could therefore follow that today Christians forebade divorce and remarriage for mental cruelty, but permitted it when a partner was adulterous. This has not been proposed. Instead, the Matthaean exception has been ignored so as to evade the problem. Thus the claim that the texts are authoritative is tacitly denied by those who claim to pay most attention to it. For to ignore the exception clause is already to accept that the saying has no absolute authority within itself.

The importance of the manuscript evidence has been demonstrated. To what conclusion does this evidence lead? The main result of this survey is to show that the recovery of a single original saying of Jesus is impossible. We have been able to show that some forms of text were developments. But it does not follow that one of those with which we are left is more original than the others. The

---

[11] Letter 77.3.   [12] *Ibid.*

differences between the four passages in Matthew (twice), Mark and Luke are already great. But the development of the tradition goes beyond that, both in time and in extent. We can see the tradition being developed right through to the formation of the Byzantine text. And well beyond then, manuscripts were being produced which preserved non-Byzantine versions.

The quest for a Law in the teaching of Jesus cannot be pursued in the face of the evidence that, for those early Christians who passed the tradition to us, there was – no law, but a tradition whose meaning had to be kept alive by reflection and reinterpretation. What we have is a collection of interpretative rewritings of a tradition. It would be unscientific to claim, on the basis of these few passages, that there was no such thing as a Gospel in the sense of a recension, an attempt to produce a fixed form. But any writer who crystallises a point in a changing tradition (which he thereby also changes) must accept that his writing may also be liable to alteration by somebody else. And once this is acknowledged, then the concept of a Gospel that is fixed in shape, authoritative, and final as a piece of literature has to be abandoned. The invitation to pay heed to the words of Jesus is then freed from the demand to accept the authority of that shaped and final text. Just as we saw in the previous chapter that Origen looked for truth in the (manuscript) text and not behind it, so we may say here that the words of Jesus can be found only in the tradition and not behind or beyond it. They are available to us *only* in the manuscript continuum in which they were written down.

In one respect we are well placed today. We are better able to see the variant forms and to compare them. Who before in the history of theological thought has had access to the text of dozens of early manuscripts? More than at any other time, we are able to see how the tradition developed. We have no excuse for claiming simplicity where there is confusion.

Because of contemporary debate on the issues surrounding divorce and remarriage, we can see very clearly the problems that arise when textual criticism is not practised. First, to ignore the textual variation leads to pious fictions rather than to realities. Honesty requires that we begin with the manuscript tradition, and with it the history of the text in the early Christian communities from whom we have received it. Second, we can see that textual criticism permits several gains. There will be a gain ecumenically, for we shall all be working with the same material (that is, *all* the forms of the text), rather than with the divergent forms of our favourite versions. This already became apparent in the previous chapter.

We have found that if we abandon the *a priori* of single original texts, then we find that the saying(s) of Jesus on this subject had, as one might say, a life of their own. Thus, the study of the text-critical evidence has not reinforced an existing way of thinking. It has led to a new way of handling the material. Textual criticism is more than an essential tool for theology. It is an essential theological tool.

What, in retrospect, is marked is the degree to which textual criticism has for long accepted the role that has been demanded of it as provider of authoritative text. The reason for this is not hard to seek. When large collections of variant readings first began to be made, in works such as John Mill's *Novum Testamentum Graece* of 1704, the very act was considered by some to be impugning the inspiration and authority of Scripture. Given the anxiety to which the very existence of their stock in trade gave rise, it is small wonder that textual critics sought to avoid the further obloquy that might arise from the alarming disclosure that their findings gave reason to believe that copyists had tampered with the sense of the text. Thus it was that Richard Bentley could write that

the real text of the sacred writers is competently exact . . . nor is one article of faith or moral precept either perverted or lost . . . choose as awkwardly as you will, choose the worst by design, out of the whole lump of readings.

Thus it is that even Westcott and Hort declared that there were no theologically motivated variants to the New Testament. G. D. Kilpatrick offered the same disclaimer in discussing the passages which have occupied this chapter's attention.[13] But damage has been done by such excessive caution. It is not merely that too much confidence has been expressed in the reconstructed text of certain passages. It is that it has encouraged an attitude to the whole manuscript tradition which is based on a misunderstanding of its nature.

[13] Appendix 7 (pp. 61–3) of *The Church and the Law of Nullity of Marriage* (London, 1955).

CHAPTER 6

The story of the woman taken in adultery

Treat each according to his deserts, and who shall 'scape a
whipping?   Hamlet

The passages covered so far have all been teaching firmly
embedded in the canonical Gospels. That to which we now turn
has had a different history. It poses a particular problem for those
who believe that there is a single authoritative text, a problem that
they generally ignore. For this passage is demonstrably spurious to
that text. Read in the lectionaries of most denominations, it attests
a tradition about Jesus received into several places in the Gospels at
a later date. It is not part of the supposed authoritative and original
text.

The story of the woman taken in adultery is one of the
best-known examples of expansion to the Gospel text. It is
generally known as the passage John 7.53–8.11, although it is found
elsewhere in some witnesses. Present in the Authorised Version, it
has been excised from most modern versions. But it has not gone
out of use, nor has attachment to it diminished. It continues a part
of the lectionary. This allows us to expand a point made at the end
of Chapter 4. There we saw that our reading of one form of the text
will be influenced by other forms. Here we learn that passages do
not lose their influence once they have been declared and
acknowledged to be spurious.

As with the story of the man working on the sabbath, there are
two questions to be kept separate: is the story authentic to the life of
Jesus? And is it a part of one of the canonical Gospels?

The study of the evidence has two parts to it. The first concerns
the passage's location, the second the form of its text.

LOCATION

1 After John 7.52
   This is the reading of D and the Byzantine text. Versional
   evidence includes some Old Latin manuscripts (including the
   African manuscript Palatinus (e)) and the Vulgate.
2 A few copies of the Byzantine text use symbols taken from
   Alexandrian classical scholarship to indicate that a passage is
   probably an interpolation. Some of these manuscripts place the
   first marker not at verse 53 but at 8.2 or 8.3, showing that they
   regarded the first couple of verses as genuine. Many of these also
   contain a note indicating that not all copies have the passage.
3 After John 7.36
   One manuscript has this reading. It is 225, a copy of the Gospels
   written in 1192.
4 After John 21.25
   Placing it at the end of the Gospel, as a kind of appendix, is the
   solution of Family 1.
5 After Luke 21.38
   Family 13 (except a couple of its members) copy the passage as an
   authentic part of Luke's Gospel.
6 After Luke 24.53
   Even more baffling is the corrector of one manuscript, who
   copied it in at the end of Luke. The manuscript is 1333, an
   eleventh-century copy of the Gospels.
7 Some witnesses have a blank space after 7.53.
8 Finally, the section is omitted completely by all other manuscripts. Amongst them we may single out P^{66} P^{75} ℵ B L N T Θ,
   the entire Syriac tradition, some Old Latin manuscripts (including Vercellensis) and the majority of the Coptic versions. A and
   C both have missing pages at this place in the Gospel, but the
   missing space was clearly too short to contain the section. The
   scribe of 565 (see p. 113 below) notes that although the passage
   was present in the manuscript from which he was copying, he
   has omitted it as spurious.

THE TEXT FORM

One of the most full and accurate editions of the Greek New
Testament is that produced by Constantin von Tischendorf and

published in the years 1869–72. In printing the text of this passage he followed a course of action which he adopted nowhere else. He printed the text of Codex Bezae on the left-hand page, and that of the Byzantine text on the right. There thus appear to be two forms of the passage. When another scholar, Hermann von Soden, was conducting his exhaustive investigations into the relationship between Byzantine manuscripts, it was in the text of this passage that he compared them. There is therefore unusually extensive information available. We shall now follow Tischendorf's example in placing the D and the Byzantine text side by side. The form of Byzantine text which Tischendorf presented was not scientifically constructed, for that had not yet been attempted. It is the Textus Receptus (Received Text), the printed edition descended from Erasmus through the French printer Robert Stephanus, which held sway as the Greek New Testament until the last century. As before, several typefaces are used to highlight the differences. Bold indicates wording unique to that column, and underlining a change in word order.

D	Received Text
And **they** went each to his house. But Jesus went to the Mount of Olives. Again **he went** early into the temple, and all the people came to him.	And each went to his own house. But Jesus went to the Mount of Olives. Again **he went** early into the temple, and all the people came to him. **And sitting down he taught them**.
But the scribes and Pharisees bring a woman **taken** in sin, and placing her in the midst the priests say to him <u>**testing** him, so that they should have a case against him,</u> Teacher, this woman **was caught** in the very act of adultery. <u>Now Moses **commanded** in the law **to stone** such women.</u>	But the scribes and Pharisees bring **to him** a woman **taken** in sin, and placing her in the midst, the priests say to him Teacher, this woman **was caught** in the very act of adultery. <u>Now Moses **ordered** in the law **that** such women **should be stoned**.</u>

(D)

But what do you say?

But Jesus bending down, **wrote**
on the ground with his finger.
As the people questioning him
remained,
he straightened up and
said to them
The sinless one of you, let him
first <u>throw a stone at her.</u>
And bending down again,
he **wrote** with his finger
on the ground.

Each of the Jews went out,
beginning with the oldest,

so that they all went out.
And **he** was left alone,
and the woman **being**
in the middle.

Jesus straightening up

said to the woman
Where **are they**?
Does nobody condemn you?
And she said **to him**,
Nobody, Lord.
He said,
Nor do I condemn you.
Go, **from now on** sin no
longer.

(Received Text)

So what do you say?
But this they said testing
<u>him, so that they should have a</u>
<u>case against him.</u>
But Jesus bending down, **wrote**
on the ground with his finger.
As the people questioning him
remained,
straightening up he
said to them
The sinless one of you, let him
first <u>throw **the** stone at her.</u>
And bending down again,
he **wrote** with his finger
on the ground.
But they hearing,
condemned by their
conscience,
went out **one by one**,
beginning with the oldest
down to the youngest.

And **Jesus** was left alone,
and the woman **standing**
in the middle.
Jesus straightening up
and seeing nobody except
the woman
said to **her**
Woman, where **are those who**
accuse you;
Does nobody condemn you?
She said,
Nobody, Lord.
Jesus said **to her**
Nor do I condemn you.
Go **and** sin no longer.

The Received Text may be seen to have in general one chief
characteristic of the Byzantine text: its tendency to include
everything. It is clearly a full text, with various phrases expanded,

such as 'Jesus said to her' for 'He said' in D. There are, in this narrative, no differences between the two versions that have a large impact on the meaning, even though the variants are valuable for the history of the text.

Another version of the story is found, after John 7.52, in an Armenian Gospel manuscript. This witness was produced in Edschmiadzin, the ancient principal see of Armenia. It is dated 989:

A certain woman was taken in sins, against whom all bore witness that she was deserving of death. They brought her to Jesus (to see) what he would command, in order that they might malign him. Jesus made answer and said, 'Come ye, who are without sin, cast stones and stone her to death.' But he himself, bowing his head was writing with his finger on the earth, to declare their sins; and they were seeing their several sins on the stones. And filled with shame they departed, and no one remained, but only the woman. Saith Jesus, 'Go in peace, and present the offering for sins, as in their law is written.'[1]

What can we say about this story? First, its age must be noted. It seems that it was known in the early second century. The evidence is from Papias. Bishop of the church of Hierapolis, a town in Phrygia in Asia Minor, he wrote a long work (five books) called *Exegesis of the Sayings of the Lord*. This is now lost in its entirety; a copy of a Latin translation was in existence as late as the end of the sixteenth century – how much we could learn from it had it only survived a little longer and been edited![2] However, there are a few quotations extant, most of them in Eusebius' *Church History*. In them, we read that

He [Papias] has set forth as well, another story about a woman accused falsely of many sins before the Lord, which the Gospel of the Hebrews contains.[3]

---

[1] F. C. Conybeare, *Expositor* (December 1895), 406; also cited in F. C. Burkitt, *Two Lectures on the Gospels* (London and New York, 1901), p. 88.

[2] See C. H. Turner, *Studies in Early Church History: Collected Papers* (Oxford, 1912), pp. 247–8n: 'That the Oracles of Papias were at some time translated is not impossible, for a mediaeval catalogue of the Chapter Library at Nîmes – destroyed by the Huguenots in the sixteenth century – contains among the Biblical books the notice *librum Papie; librum de verbis Domini* ("a book by Papius; a book about the oracles of the Lord").'

[3] Eusebius, *The Ecclesiastical History and the Martyrs of Palestine*, tr. by H. J. Lawlor and J. E. L. Oulton (2 vols., London, 1927–8), 3.39, p. 101.

It is thus pretty certain that our story was known as early as the beginning of the second century, a time scarcely later than the formation of the canonical Gospels.[4] It is also certain that Papias' source need not have been written. He makes it quite clear (in another quotation in Eusebius) that he considered oral sources to be more authentic than written ones. But here, as Eusebius also tells us, there is a second written source, the Gospel according to the Hebrews. This was a Jewish-Christian Gospel, which like Papias has survived only in a handful of quotations by others. It probably originated in Egypt in the first half of the second century.

The version of the story in the Edschmiadzin codex has some affinities with the story as Eusebius reports it of Papias and the Gospel of the Hebrews: that she was found 'in (many) sins' and that she was brought 'to Jesus'. These similarities, and its greater brevity and consequent simplicity, led Conybeare to conclude that it is the oldest original form of the text. One feature that is unlikely to be so old is that we are told what Jesus wrote on the ground, since a reader would be more likely to solve such a mystery than to create it. But the argument is in many ways strong. The strange point about her accusers' departure in order of seniority is absent. The ending is markedly different. 'Nor do I condemn you. Go and sin no longer' is replaced by a phrase with a blend of synoptic (Mark 1.44 and Matthew 8.4) and Johannine (15.24) parallels. This is evidently secondary.

If we apply text-critical criteria to the passage, then the fact that it is omitted by some of our oldest and most reliable witnesses suggests that it is unlikely to have been always a part of the Fourth Gospel. The fact that it appears in a number of other places supports this conclusion. For it is regularly the case that passages whose inclusion is in doubt come at different places in different groups of witnesses. Thus, the fact that 1 Corinthians 14.34–5 is placed after verse 40 in some witnesses has been taken by G. D. Fee to indicate that it is not an authentic part of the letter.[5] But the

---

[4] It is the thesis of B. D. Ehrman in 'Jesus and the Adulteress', *NTS* 34 (1988), 24–44, p. 25, that two separate stories, one of an attempt to trap Jesus (found in Papias) and one of Jesus intervening in a stoning (found in the Gospel according to the Hebrews and in the fourth-century commentary of the Alexandrian writer Didymus the Blind), were conflated to make the composite story found in some copies of John.

[5] G. D. Fee, 'Excursus: On the Text of 1 Corinthians 14:34–35', in *God's Empowering Presence: The Holy Spirit in the Letters of Paul* (Peabody, Mass., 1994), pp. 272–81.

distance between the places of insertion in this example is almost unprecedented. Here other techniques of examination come to our aid. It has been pointed out that the story fits into Luke 21 much better than it does into John 7. Jesus is already going in and out between the Mount of Olives and the temple. If we study the vocabulary and style of the passage, we shall quickly find a number of un-Johannine characteristics, and some Lukanisms. In all, a better case can be made for this having been an authentic piece of Luke which dropped out than for its having been original to John.

It has been suggested that a possible reason for its excision is that it might seem to condone adultery.[6] But one might not even have to assume that it was at one time in all copies of Luke, and then became so generally offensive as to be almost universally excised. Perhaps Luke himself revised his Gospel and removed it. There have, after all, been quite strong arguments advanced in favour of Luke's having had two attempts at writing the Gospel, and the existence of two very different versions of Acts has led some to suppose the same of his second volume.

However, if it was original to Luke, and then excised, there is the difficulty of accounting for its inclusion in John's Gospel.

The textual conclusion must be that this story should not form part of the printed text of either Luke or John.

The question of its authenticity has not yet been broached. As with the story of the man working on the sabbath, the issues are separate.

It seems clear that we have here a piece of oral tradition. Although the sub-apostolic age still valued such traditions more highly than they did the written texts, it was inevitable that the passage of time would bring a change in emphasis, and that floating stories would be put into books for safe keeping. Of course, the questions about the authenticity of this passage are not different in form from those that have been asked about much that is indisputably a part of the written Gospels. It is tempting to whittle away various apparently legendary accretions – the writing on the ground, the order of departure – in order to recover the most primitive form. Whether such an original form is likely to be an

---

[6] But this is very dubious. See Tertullian's robust rejection of the claim that the woman who washed Jesus' feet provided an analogy for Christian conduct: 'there were no Christians before the Ascension'.

authentic account of an event in the life of Jesus has to be doubted. The story has all the marks of an illustrative story, for its purpose is to describe Jesus' interpretation of the law in a given (hypothetical) situation. Thus its presence in the text of the Gospels is significant, not for the factual information that it might contain but for the interpretation of Jesus' teaching of the law that it conveys. That this continues to be its appeal is shown by the extreme reluctance which readers of the Gospels show in accepting that the story is inauthentic. It is beautiful; it tells us so much about Jesus' true intentions that it must be true. This is not logic. It is a proof of the story's power. And we may use this to illustrate an important point.

We noted at the end of examining the Lord's Prayer that all six forms contribute to our understanding. Once we have discovered their existence, they will be a part of the way in which we read and interpret the Lord's Prayer. We shall not be able to erase them from our minds, and to read a single original text as though the others had never existed. So it is with this pericope. We may make the decision that it is not a part of the canonical Gospels; we may even decide that it is not an account of an incident in the life of Jesus. But, however we read the Gospels or think about the historical Jesus, this story will have influenced our views, and we cannot read or think as we would had it never existed. The oral tradition is thus not something which ended at some point in the second or third or fourth century. The way in which we read the written text is a part of the whole tradition which has been passed on from generation to generation. This can sometimes be chronicled in details such as the number of magi or the presence of animals in the infancy narratives. But it is more pervasive and more important than that. The sum total of all that we have received from the tradition, written and oral (not even to mention such possible curiosities as inherited memory), is a part of the way in which we build up our interpretations, regardless of our decisions about the historical value of particular items.

CHAPTER 7

Secrets and hypotheses

> It is still a current oddity that many a literary critic has in-
> vestigated the past ownership and mechanical condition of
> his second-hand automobile, or the pedigree and training of
> his dog, more thoroughly than he has looked into the
> qualifications of the text on which his critical theories rest.
>
> Fredson Bowers, *Textual and Literary Criticism*

The phrase 'To you has been given the secret of the kingdom of
God' (Mark 4.11) has been one of the most significant for the
twentieth-century study of Mark's Gospel, for two reasons. The
one concerns its theological interpretation, the other its relationship to the Gospels of Matthew and Luke.

In his book *The Messianic Secret*, published in 1901, the German
scholar William Wrede argued that the key theological theme in
Mark's Gospel is what he called the Messianic Secret, the idea that
Jesus kept his messiahship hidden. There was, he claimed, a very
good historical reason for this: that the earliest Christians believed
God to have made Jesus the Messiah only after the resurrection (see
Acts 2.36). The idea that he had already been the Messiah during
his ministry was a later development and, to explain why it had not
always been known, Mark developed the idea of a Messianic
Secret. Jesus had indeed always been the Messiah, but he had told
his disciples that only after the resurrection were they to speak
about it (Mark 8.30; 9.9). You can come at Wrede's idea another
way, by considering the gap between Jesus as Messiah and the
reality of the crucifixion. To bridge it, Mark develops his idea of
Jesus as a hidden and suffering Messiah, whose true identity can be
known only in the light of the crucifixion and resurrection. The
significance of Simon Peter's 'confession' at Caesarea Philippi is

that although he acclaims Jesus as the Messiah, he totally fails to understand the truth of that messiahship, when Jesus goes on to predict his betrayal and death.

According to Mark's account Jesus strictly and of set purpose kept his messianic dignity secret even after the disciples' confession, into his very last period.[1]

Also secret in a pre-eminent sense is the necessity of Jesus' suffering, dying and rising... In 9.30 Mark says that Jesus finally wanted to hide his presence in Galilee, and adds in verse 31 '*for* he was teaching his disciples, saying to them, "The Son of man will be delivered into the hands of men, and they will kill him; and when he is killed, after three days he will rise"'.[2]

If we place Mark 4.11 in this context, then it presents a startling view of the parables. Rather than simple stories intended to explain difficult ideas and to make recollection easy, they are intentionally unintelligible. They are spoken to those outside, so that (in a quotation from Isaiah 6.9f.), 'they may indeed see but not perceive, and may indeed hear but not understand; lest they should turn again, and be forgiven'. The embracing story of the Sower emphasises the same point. The preacher is like a sower, for the word is spread liberally about for all around to hear, but only those who are predetermined towards it (the already fertile soil) bear fruit. The secret of which we read is, then, to be taken as the 'Messianic Secret', and the verse central to Mark's Christology. Much more could (and has) been said on this, but enough should have been said to show the importance of the *precise* wording: 'the secret'.

The attempt to resolve the relationship between the Synoptic Gospels has been another significant enterprise of modern times. Given the acceptance of Markan Priority, the dominant 'solution' to the Synoptic Problem of the century has been the one variously known as the 'Two Document', 'Four Document' and 'Streeter' Hypothesis, or (more commonly today) the Two Source Hypothesis: that Matthew and Luke each and independently used both Mark and a now lost document which is named Q. The indepen-

[1] W. Wrede, *The Messianic Secret*, tr. J. C. G. Grieg (Cambridge and London, 1971), p. 24.
[2] *Ibid.*, pp. 8of.

dence requires that they never agree together in changing Mark in the same way except by coincidence. But there are, in the commonly accepted printings of the Greek New Testament, not a few places in which they do agree in making the same change to Mark. It is the number of these 'Minor Agreements', with the significance of some of them, which has led some scholars to argue that Q never existed, and that Matthew used Mark, and Luke used both of them: thus the agreements between Matthew and Luke against Mark are simply places where Luke copies a change made to Mark by Matthew. All of this paragraph will be familiar to anyone who has ever sat in a set of introductory lectures on the New Testament, or who has read an introductory book on the subject. It is the Minor Agreements that are the matter for our present examination.

Some of these readings are found in the parallels to the verse from Mark with which we began. Matthew 13.11 (RSV) reads

To you it has been given *to know* the *secrets* of the kingdom of heaven.

And Luke 8.10 (RSV) has

To you it has been given *to know* the *secrets* of the kingdom of God.

The word 'secrets' is the Minor Agreement which concerns us most. But it is not the only one. There are three more. The first of these is the wording of the introduction of the saying, 'And he said', though Matthew reads 'And answering he said'. The other is itself as it were a double Minor Agreement. While Mark reads 'to you the secret is given', both Matthew and Luke have 'to you is given to know the secrets'. Both in the word order and in the addition of '*to know*', they agree against Mark. There is a risk, both in textual criticism and in the study of the synoptic problem, of atomising the units (nothing wrong with that) and then failing to put them together again to look at the whole unit.[3] So let us note that the variation *secret/secrets* is only a part of a larger Minor Agreement.

Various explanations have been offered for the Minor Agreements by defenders of the Two Document Hypothesis. One is that they are in the main coincidental, the kind of small changes and stylistic improvements that might have occurred to Matthew and

---

[3] See, e.g., M. D. Goulder, *Luke: A New Paradigm* (Sheffield, 1989), p. 50.

Luke independently. Another is the suggestion of an overlap between Mark and Q so that, where we suppose Matthew and Luke to be independently altering Mark, they are in fact both reproducing Q *verbatim*.[4] Even when these techniques have been used, there remains a hard core of Agreements not explained. It is here that the study of the manuscripts is brought into the operation.

In our passage, the possibility of coincidence in the word 'secrets' is not impossible. Neither Matthew nor Luke seems to have been aware of anything like a Messianic Secret in Mark. Or, if they were, they made no strong use of it in their own work. It is therefore possible that they might have independently preferred to portray Jesus' preaching as disclosing a number of mysteries. That they should both also have added *to know* perhaps stretches coincidence a little far. So instead of pursuing this line of speculation, let us look at the ways in which the manuscript evidence is significant.

It is one of the enduring qualities of Streeter's study *The Four Gospels* that in presenting his solution to the Synoptic Problem he combined a study of the manuscripts and the earliest history of the text with a comparison of the Gospels. In one volume he managed to combine the classic presentation of the Two Document Hypothesis, a ground-breaking study of the local texts of the great sees of early Christianity, a strengthening of the evidence for a Caesarean text and a study of the relationship of John's Gospel to the synoptists. His approach to the most intransigent of the Minor Agreements was to adopt this argument: almost all the evidence points overwhelmingly to the conclusion that Matthew and Luke independently used Mark and a document called Q. There is a small body of readings which do not fit this hypothesis. Given the very strong propensity for manuscripts to be harmonised, the best explanation is that the Minor Agreements are places where in one Gospel all or nearly all manuscripts have been changed to be more like the text of the other Gospel.

Is there any manuscript evidence for his argument? In each Gospel there is support for both the singular *secret* and the plural *secrets*:

---

[4] But some defenders of the Two Source Theory treat Mark–Q overlaps and the Minor Agreements as quite separate phenomena.

In Matthew, the singular is read by both the Old Syriac manuscripts, the Old Latin, Clement of Alexandria, and the Latin translation of Irenaeus of Lyons.

In Mark, the plural is found in Family 1, Family 13 and some other minuscule manuscripts.

In Luke, the singular is again attested in Latin witnesses.

Of this, Streeter adduces the evidence for Matthew.[5] It is his contention that 'secret' was the original text of that Gospel.

A startling variation on this argument is advanced by the North American scholar Helmut Koester in his book *Early Christian Gospels*. He is a devotee of the Streeter Hypothesis. For him also there cannot be a genuine Minor Agreement, so the text of one of the three Gospels must be corrupt. He points out that it is clear that both Matthew and Luke are dependent on Mark in the passage Mark 4.1–20, and not on another common source. Because they agree against Mark in reading 'secrets', 'It is difficult to avoid the conclusion that they preserved the original Markan text.'[6] This is not all of Koester's argument.[7] But it is the part of his argument that concerns us here. Koester takes two other passages where he argues that Matthew and Luke preserve the original wording of Mark. These are Matthew 16.21‖Mark 8.31‖ Luke 9.22, in which they have the wording 'on the third day' against 'after three days', and Matthew 17.18–20‖Mark 9.25–29‖ Luke 9.42–3.[8] In this second passage, Matthew and Luke present a much shorter version of the story of the healing of the possessed boy that comes after the transfiguration. This shorter version, in Koester's view, is substantially the original text of Mark, which was later and rather clumsily expanded. This block is not (so far as I am aware) classed as a Minor Agreement by anyone (though

---

[5] B. H. Streeter, *The Four Gospels: A Study of Origins Treating of the Manuscript Tradition, Sources, Authorship, and Dates*, 4th impression, revised (London, 1930 (1924)), p. 313.

[6] Helmut Koester, *Ancient Christian Gospels: Their History and Development* (London and Philadelphia, 1990), p. 279.

[7] He also suggests that the characterisation of the Gospel as a 'mystery' is a later idea, first found in Ephesians – which he presumably assumes to be post-Pauline.

[8] Besides these three passages, Koester's evidence is of two other types: 'common omissions', in which Matthew and Luke both omit Markan passages; and differences between the document known as 'Secret Mark' and canonical Mark.

there is one within it in verse 19 with the addition of 'and perverse' after 'faithless'[9]).

Intrinsically, there is nothing historically impossible about Koester's proposal. That there are readings in which all extant manuscripts of Mark are occasionally corrupt may be regarded as by no means improbable; we shall see when we study the end of this Gospel that there are those who believe the original ending to have been lost at an early stage.

Koester does not discuss the Minor Agreements, nor does he take any of the present three passages under that head. By taking these three passages together he attempts a quite different kind of argument. It is based simply on the premiss that Matthew and Luke in agreement against Mark are the earliest witnesses to his text. Under what circumstances might such an argument be reasonable? The answer is, when a writer sets out faithfully to reproduce the text of an earlier writer. The emphasis must be on 'faithfully'. There are two reasons for such faithfulness. One is a commentary. Where, for example, Origen or Jerome is discussing the *precise* wording of a biblical text, they will need to make sure that the reader knows the words which they are discussing. Granted all the difficulties with patristic citations that arise, the general point may still be taken. The other reason will be that a writer is lifting blocks from a source into his own text and reproducing them *verbatim*.

Does either of these scenarios apply to Matthew and Luke's use of Mark? A little study suggests that neither does. With regard to the first, there can be no sense in which either of them is a commentary. The use of a source is quite different from the conventions of exegesis. With regard to the second possibility, there are a number of objections. In the first place, both Matthew and Luke are capable of altering Mark even where they are following him quite closely. For example, in the same passage they both make a number of other changes. In the following transcription, which is that of the RSV with a few minor changes, the bold type indicates the precise wording in common between all three of the synoptic evangelists, the italic indicates where Matthew preserves Mark, the underlining where Luke preserves him, and

---

[9] Streeter, *Four Gospels*, p. 317.

double underlining the Minor Agreements. It should also be noted that I have followed the rules of the Greek precisely. It is an inflected language, so that although the word 'parables' appears in both Matthew and Mark near the beginning, each evangelist has the word in a different case so that Matthew does not follow Mark *precisely*. There can be no doubt that both Matthew and Luke are following Mark, yet how little of Mark do they *both* use! And how little of Mark is preserved in its exact form by the other two! On this evidence, neither of them is incorporating unassimilated blocks of Markan material. We cannot, therefore, in general treat Matthew or Luke as witnesses to the earliest form of the Markan text. But the places where they *agree together* against Mark appear to be in a separate category. For here we have cross-bearings from two sources.

Matthew 13.10–13	Mark 4.10–12	Luke 8.9–10
Then	And when he was alone,	But
the disciples came and said	those who were about him	when his disciples asked
to him, 'Why do you speak	with the twelve asked him	him what this parable
to them in parables?'	concerning the parables.	meant,
And he answering said that	And he said to them,	And he said
'To you it **has been**	**'To you has been**	**'To you** it **has been**
given to know	**given** the secret	**given** to know
the secrets **of the**	**of the**	the secrets **of the**
kingdom of heaven	**kingdom of** God,	**kingdom of** God;
but for *those* it has not	**but for** *those* outside	**but for** others they are
been given.	everything is	
For to him who has will		
more be given, and he will	[= 4.25]	[= 8.18]
have abundance;		
but from him who has not,		
even what he has will be		
taken away.		
This is why I speak to		
them **in parables**	**in parables**;	**in parables**,
because **seeing**	so that **seeing** they may	so that **seeing**
	indeed see	
they do not see,	but not perceive,	they may not see,
and hearing	**and hearing**	**and hearing**
they do not hear,	may indeed hear but not	
nor do they understand.	understand;	they may not understand.'
	lest they should turn again,	
	and be forgiven.'	

Second, there is a textual problem. Koester assumes that here
the manuscripts of Mark are of no use in recovering his original
text, while those of Matthew and Luke are so reliable that we can
be certain that they both wrote 'secrets'. But we are relying on the
same manuscripts for all three Gospel passages. So, until we have
demonstrated by thorough analysis that these particular manuscripts are less reliable in Mark than they are in Matthew, we shall
have to give them equal weight as either accurate in both or
corrupt in both.

The corruption is no more likely to be in Mark than in one of the
others. That is, we have here a reading where Matthew and Luke
agree against Mark. According to the Two Document Hypothesis,
which we may for the sake of following the argument accept, this is
impossible. It follows that the text of one of the evangelists is
corrupt. But because Matthew and Luke agree against Mark, *it does
not therefore follow that it is Mark which is corrupt.* Although Koester
advances other more specific arguments in each of the three
passages which he discusses, it is this appeal to the agreement of
Matthew and Luke that gives credibility to his case. And, attractive
though the case is, the flaw appears to be fatal. Instead we must
ignore all parallel passages, set aside the Synoptic Problem, and set
out to establish the text of each Gospel separately.

I have described Koester's argument as a variant on Streeter's.
But although his way of arguing uses the language of textual
criticism, the drift of his case is towards another documentary
hypothesis. If I understand the matter aright, his proposal is similar
to the case for what is called Ur-Markus. This theory is that the
version of Mark used by Matthew and Luke was itself revised, and
that this revision is our canonical Mark. Thus the Minor Agreements are places where Matthew and Luke preserve the text of
Mark's first version. The theory seeks to preserve both the independent use of Mark by Matthew and Luke and the existence of
Q.

Another theory which makes use of the same double-formed
Mark is that which alleges Deutero-Markus. Here it is our Mark
which is older, and Matthew and Luke used the second, now lost,
form. I forbear to discuss either of these theories further here. But
their character is noted, and to that we shall return.

Can we decide which reading was original to each Gospel? Since the strongest support is for the plural in Mark, we should start there. Is it conceivable that the witnesses which support 'secrets' are correct? We repeat the canon of criticism (and one quite independent of the study of the Synoptic Problem) that one should adopt the reading which makes a passage less like its parallels. The reason for this is that the tendency to harmonise was so strong. The initial step is therefore to accept the singular 'secret', on the supposition that the plural is harmonising. But this must be provisional, while we check several other things. First, we need to be sure that the reading we adopt for Mark really does avoid harmonising. If we were to decide that the original text of Matthew and Luke is 'secret', then we shall have to go back to Mark and ask whether 'secrets' is not more probably original. Thus, it is in the nature of the problem that we always have to weigh the evidence for every passage in a set of parallels when we are scrutinising one of them. Second, regardless of what we think was original, we have to be sure that the harmonising reading was available to the witnesses which we are examining. That is, for the witnesses reading the plural in Mark to be harmonising, they would have to be dependent on a text of Matthew or Luke that had the plural. There can be no doubt here that such was the case. Third, we have to be sure that the proposed tendency to harmonise is credible. Most often it is Mark that is harmonised to Matthew, and Luke to Mark. Thus, the plural in Mark is best understood as a harmonisation to Matthew.

The evidence for the singular in Matthew and Luke is more perplexing. For in these readings Matthew and Mark are harmonised to follow Mark. Harmonisation in this direction is unusual. The most obvious line to follow here would be an enquiry into the history of the text. For, with the exception of Clement, the support is all from Latin witnesses.

Our study of this passage leads us to the conclusion that there are no adequate grounds for abandoning the texts with which we began. On textual grounds, taking each Gospel on its own, we have 'secret' in Mark and 'secrets' in Matthew and Luke.

Our discussion has still some way to go. But it begins to become apparent that an underlying problem is one of recognising that textual evidence has a place in the study of the Synoptic Problem, yet avoiding hybrid arguments. In particular, suspicion must arise when the text is emended to conform with a particular solution to the Synoptic Problem. We shall return to this. But let us now turn to another passage.

One of the most striking problems in a Minor Agreement is found in the story of Jesus' trial before the High Priest, at the point where Jesus is mocked by bystanders. The passage in Mark (14.65) runs thus:

And some began to spit on him and to blindfold his face and to strike him and to say to him 'Prophesy.'

Matthew 26.67 has a few changes to make to this:

Then they spat in his face and struck him, and some slapped him saying 'Prophesy to us, Christ, who is it who struck you?'

Luke, who has the passage in a different place, before the trial (22.63–5), reads

And the men who were holding Jesus mocked and beat him, and blindfolding him asked him saying 'Prophesy, who is it who struck you?' And they spoke many other things against him, reviling him.

In these three translations I have followed the most widely accepted text. The Minor Agreement is the phrase 'Who is it who struck you?' The words are found in some manuscripts of Mark, including N W X Θ f¹³ 33 565. The earliest of these witnesses is fourth century, and a number of them are valuable and not to be quickly dismissed. The two last named manuscripts deserve mention. 33 is an early minuscule (ninth century) of all the New Testament except Revelation. It is a good representative of the Alexandrian text in the Gospels, and has rather more Byzantine readings elsewhere. 565 is a purple manuscript, written in gold letters. It too is of the ninth century. It has an unusual text, particularly in Mark, where it is closest to the Caesarean text of Θ.

The easiest solution would be to conclude that these words were authentic to Mark. But they are far likelier to have been added by harmonisation to Matthew and Luke than to have been removed. What purpose could their excision serve?

A far more subtle explanation is offered by Streeter. He suggests that the veiling and 'Who is it who struck you?' are both original only to Luke. The one found its way into Mark and the other into Matthew. There is some textual evidence for the former, since D and some versional witnesses omit 'and to blindfold his face'. This part of Streeter's argument has been generally ignored, and we will follow suit, for it is not essential to his argument. The second idea draws on an idea first formulated by C. H. Turner.[10] It arises out of a problem with the version presented in Matthew. Here, there is no record of Jesus having been blindfolded. So the mocking call for Jesus to name his persecutor appears meaningless. Excise the words 'Who is it who struck you?', and you are left with the demand 'Prophesy!', a mocking demand for Jesus to demonstrate his messianic ('Prophesy to us, *Christ*') gifts. The words 'Who is it who struck you?' are then found only in Luke, as his expansion of Mark's typically concise 'Prophesy!' The boldness of this proposal lies in the fact that *every* manuscript of Matthew contains the words 'Who is it who struck you?' Streeter is suggesting that all the manuscripts are wrong, and that we should abandon them and follow our own wit and omit the words. The act of ignoring all manuscripts and providing our own alternative is known as conjectural emendation.

The Turner/Streeter solution to the problem causes scholars some anxiety, because the use of conjectural emendation in the restoration of the New Testament text has been much debated. Widely practised in classical studies, the elegant conjecture has always been the mark of the outstanding critic. The conjecture which is confirmed by the discovery of a new manuscript which supports it is the highest vindication of a scholar's abilities. Thus much in classical studies. But, it has often been said, that kind of thing is necessary only for texts whose manuscripts are few and late. We are justified in emending the Roman poet Catullus, whose works survive only in three fourteenth-century manuscripts, all dependent upon one lost manuscript of the tenth century.[11] But, where the manuscript has so many witnesses, the earliest so close in

---

[10] *Ibid.*, pp. 325–8.
[11] See, for some sample Catullan problems, J. Willis, *Latin Textual Criticism*, Illinois Studies in Language and Literature 61 (Illinois, 1972), pp. 158–61.

time to the autographs, the original reading will always have survived somewhere. Why go to the trouble of dreaming up new variant readings, when there are already too many to choose from? Moreover, emendation is often a matter of discovering a false measure in verse or a stylistic feature at odds with the author's habits, and then of determining what wording might better serve the metre or the prose. It is surely particularly of this that A. E. Housman was thinking when he called textual criticism 'the science of discovering error in texts and the art of removing it'.[12] The New Testament, on the other hand, nowhere contains elegiacs or pentameters; and for a large part of it, there is little attempt at elevated or perfectly constructed prose following consistent habits.

Thus, the pursuit of conjectural emendation is viewed by contemporary scholars in much the same way as liberal opinion looks upon fox hunting.[13]

An ingenious challenge to this was proposed in conversation by G. D. Kilpatrick. There are, let us say, six places in Acts where Codex Bezae stands alone in preserving the original text. Codex Bezae is extant in only about twenty-one of the twenty-eight chapters of Acts. We may therefore suppose that Codex Bezae was the only correct manuscript in a couple of places where it is now lost. So, there are a couple of places in seven chapters of Acts where

[12] 'The Application of Thought to Textual Criticism', *PBA* 18 (1922), 67–84; reprinted in *The Classical Papers of A. E. Housman*, collected and edited by J. Diggle and F. R. D. Goodyear, Vol. III, 1915–36 (Cambridge, 1972), 1058–69.

[13] I found a series of conjectural emendations jotted down by a reader in the margins of a novel I took out of the library the other day. The reader might like to practise the art of criticism by deciding whether any of them is worth consideration:

I must *emend** the point I was trying to make. You are now the only person who can possibly tell whether the Osprey Collection still exists in its *integrity*‡.
   *Emended to *amend*
   ‡Emended to *entirety*
He had to confess that he hadn't a clue as to *whom** it might have been.
   *Emended to *who*
Allow me to *recur* to the incident in the library.
   *Emended to *refer*
They are now resigned to *spend** another night in the place.
   *Emended to *spending*

It should be apparent that these corrections to the prose of Michael Innes are a warning against hasty emendation, and underline the importance of a thorough knowledge of vocabulary, grammar and style.

Another novel yields a case of emendation by two readers. The Dornford Yates text reads *shoot*. Corrector A wrote *shute* in the margin every time. Corrector B crossed out *shute* and wrote *chute or shoot*.

the right reading can be recovered only by emendation. We can certainly see how highly the skilled conjecture ought to be regarded. To read the last six chapters of Acts, detect error and hit on what Luke is more likely to have written would be an impressive achievement.

Conjectural emendation is a weapon that, even if it need not be used, should not be surrendered. The possibility that there are places where no manuscript preserves the original reading must continue to be entertained. That errors were made so early as to affect all our surviving copies may even be taken as more probable than possible. So, we do not deny that conjecture may be required.

But the present case is somewhat unusual. Its opponents feel that conjectural emendation is such a *deus ex machina* as to be beyond all logic. In claiming that all extant witnesses are corrupt, Streeter is breaking the rules, because the study of the Synoptic Problem as normally conducted includes the agreement between practitioners that the text of Nestle–Aland is, to all intents and purposes, what Matthew, Mark and Luke originally wrote. Once claim that conjecture is necessary, and the entire enterprise is under threat. To put it differently, the student of synoptic relationships will assume that the textual critics have done their work on the printed text that is most commonly available, and that it is based on a thorough study of the surviving manuscripts. But here is Streeter, in full flow on the Minor Agreements, suddenly plucking a convenient conjecture out of the air. The conjecture may well seem to be conceived more out of loyalty to his solution to the Synoptic Problem than to the prior task of restoring the text. We must try to look at the matter under another aspect.[14]

There is one set of circumstances under which conjecture may be required: when all the manuscripts present texts which do not make sense. Of course, we shall have to be very careful to be sure that what is nonsense to us must have been nonsense to the author. But the requirement that the writer be allowed to make sense is

---

[14] We must also do justice to Streeter. To the charge that he has 'taken the liberty to pick and choose from any out-of-the-way MS. any reading that happens to fit in with my argument', he replies that 'I have purposely limited my citations to a very few MSS., selected because on other grounds they can be proved to represent local texts current at the beginning of the third century' (*Four Gospels*, p. 329).

paramount. The nineteenth-century editor Haupt went so far as to
claim that 'If the sense requires it, I am prepared to write Constan-
tinopolitanus where the MSS have the monosyllabic interjection
o.'[15] The force of this can hardly be denied. If we read the sentence
'The Nicene Creed is also known as the Niceno-O! Creed', we
would quickly begin to cast around for another reading, and a little
research would come up with an emendation. The text-critical
approach to 'Who is it who struck you?' must be to set aside the
Synoptic Problem, and to deal with the question whether or no the
commonly printed text of Matthew makes sense. To quote Housman quoting Haupt again, 'The prime requisite of a good emendation is that it should start from the thought; it is only afterwards that
other considerations are taken into account.'[16] The decision in this
place should be made without reference to the decision which we
have made with regard to the other Minor Agreements; for we are
not treating the reading as a Minor Agreement, we are not even
comparing Matthew with the other Gospels.

We are thus back with the question whether 'Who is it who
struck you?' makes sense without Jesus having first been blindfolded. One possibility is that Matthew rather carelessly took the blindfolding as read. This is the suggestion of Goulder. He draws our
attention to other passages in which Matthew makes a muddle out
of improving Mark. Here, the confusion is caused by his desire to
emphasise Jesus' ill-treatment. In Mark, we read that 'they began
to spit upon him and to blindfold his face and to strike him'; the first
element is heightened by Matthew, who writes 'they spat in his
face'. Jesus' face is now mentioned, and Matthew forgets that he
has to mention it to make sense of the demand for a prophecy,
which he goes on to expand.[17] According to Streeter, no manuscript of Matthew makes sense here; the text must therefore be
emended. In terms of some sort of absolute sense, Streeter has a
strong case. But the issue of sense in conjectural emendation is
always one of relative sense: whether the text could have made
sense to the author. And here we have to admit the force of

[15] Housman, 'The Application of Thought', p. 77 (1065). Housman's thoughts on the matter
should be carefully considered.   [16] *Ibid.*
[17] M. D. Goulder, 'Luke's Knowledge of Matthew', in Georg Strecker (ed.), *Minor Agreements: Symposium Göttingen 1991*, Göttinger Theologische Arbeiten 50 (Göttingen: Vandenhoeck & Ruprecht, 1993), pp. 143–62, pp. 153–5.

Goulder's argument. Matthew knows Mark's story, and very likely his readers do as well. Matthew is developing Mark's story. There are reasonable grounds for concluding that Matthew believed himself to be writing sense. The text is difficult, but not impossible.

To summarise, we defend the right to offer conjectural emendation, but consider it unnecessary here.

In our examination of both these parallels we conclude that the textual evidence leaves us where we began. The Secret is intact, and we still have Minor Agreements of Matthew and Luke against Mark. Before moving to a conclusion, we should note that we have clear evidence that editors of the Greek New Testament do not seem to be influenced in their choice of reading by their preferred solution to the Synoptic Problem. So far as I am aware, the editors responsible for the United Bible Societies' text support the Two Document Hypothesis. But they certainly do not adopt Streeter's readings in order to remove Minor Agreements, and print those readings which, while best to them on text critical grounds, pose the most serious threat to the Two Document Hypothesis.[18]

But while we have been unable to offer any new wisdom on the text of the passages which we have studied, we have found some serious methodological problems. We examined Koester's suggestion that Matthew and Luke can be used as primary manuscript evidence for the recovery of the text of Mark, and were not convinced. We studied Streeter's solution to the problem of the Minor Agreements and, while defending his right to emend, found his solution to be unsatisfactory. We could also have studied writers who conduct their source criticism from printed editions with no reference whatever to the manuscript evidence. The basic problem in all these hypotheses is the use of a model which separates the process of creating Gospels and the process of copying them. In the study of the Synoptic Problem, the production of each Synoptic Gospel is often treated as though it were identical with the publishing of a printed book today: the author prepares the text, the

---

[18] But a spectacular example of editors solving textual problems with the Synoptic Problem may be found in the NEB of Luke 22.62, where the words 'He went outside and wept bitterly', which are found in Matthew but not Mark, are rejected on the grounds that Luke did not know Matthew, and so could not have written them. The support for the omission is one majuscule (0171) and the Old Latin. Manuscript 0171 has considerable affinities to D (given the brevity of the surviving fragments). I owe this example to my colleague Dr Mark Goodacre.

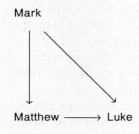

Figure 1

printer prints it, the publisher publishes it, the booksellers sell it, and we have in our hands Matthew, Mark or Luke. All that we have to do is to buy all three, take them home, lay them out on our desk and compare them. Then we can come up with our solutions.

This model might be described as two-dimensional. The diagrams of the Synoptic Problem such as are shown in Figure 1, and (Streeter's version) Figure 2, are of this kind.

The right ordering of the world has often been seen to be as follows. The source critic wants to establish the relationship between the Gospels – which was written first, who used what parts of the others, and so forth. To do this, the original text of each Gospel is required. The textual critic's task is to recover those first texts. This assumption has been studied in relation to the Minor Agreements by C. M. Tuckett.[19] After studying passages which include 'Who is it who struck you?', he concludes that the use of textual criticism to solve this problem 'is not changing the facts to fit the theory. It is rather an attempt to combine two facets of developing tradition – source-critical and text-critical – to explain the one set of facts which we have, viz. the later witnesses of the texts of our three gospels.'[20] The separation of textual criticism from source theory is to be resisted because the textual critic uses exegetical work in order to determine the original text; source theory is one part of this exegetical work.[21] There is nothing in Tuckett's argu-

---

[19] 'The Minor Agreements and Textual Criticism', in Strecker, *Minor Agreements*, pp. 119–42.
[20] *Ibid.*, p. 138.
[21] Tuckett discusses an unpublished dissertation by F. Wheeler, 'Textual Criticism and the Synoptic Problem: A Textual Commentary on the Minor Agreements of Matthew and Luke against Mark', Waco, Texas, 1985. Wheeler argues that source criticism has no place in the establishing of the text. I have not seen the thesis, so cannot compare his views with my own.

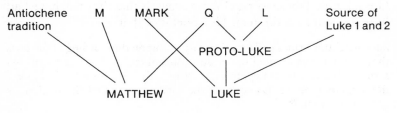

Figure 2

ment which is not reasonable. It is his premiss I question, for he assumes that textual criticism contributes towards a documentary solution to the source question.

Against this and similar theories, I propose a model which attempts to do away more thoroughly with the idea of published editions. There are two kinds of evidence demonstrating that our idea of a published edition is incorrect. The one is the general evidence of antiquity.[22] The second is the nature of the synoptic texts. With them, we are dealing with a manuscript tradition which in each copying differed, not only through the chance errors of the copyist but also through his intention. In this and the two previous chapters we have seen two kinds of intentional change. One arises out of the belief that the Gospels were not archives of traditions but living texts. We saw this in studying the sayings on divorce. The other arises particularly from the present chapter. The Gospels were harmonised to each other, not just because the copyist knew them all and tended to add in bits he remembered, but because they all told the same story and needed to be cross-referenced, to be supplemented from one another. It would be going too far to deny that there were no scholarly attempts to improve the text. For example, it was suggested above that the Alexandrian text may have followed Origen's interest in the distinctive character of each

---

[22] See Harry Y. Gamble, *Books and Readers in the Early Church: A History of Early Christian Texts* (New Haven and London, 1995), 82–143. See also M. W. Holmes, 'Early Editorial Activity and the Text of Codex Bezae in Matthew', in D. C. Parker and C.-B. Amphoux (eds.), *Codex Bezae: Studies from the Lunel Colloquium June 1994*, NTTS 22 (Leiden, 1996), pp. 123–60. Holmes draws our attention to J. E. G. Zetzel, *Latin Textual Criticism in Antiquity* (New York, 1981), who illustrates just how unhelpful (to us) ancient textual work can be. For a study with regard to the two texts of Acts, see W. Strange, *The Problem of the Text of Acts*, SNTSMS 71 (Cambridge, 1992).

Gospel. But, if there were, Holmes suggests that they will have had little influence on the text. He concludes that

> ancient textual critics had a *much smaller effect* upon the wording of the texts they studied, commented upon, and transmitted than we generally assume . . . If the present hypothesis is correct, then we must begin to view the scholars more as *transmitters* of the various textual traditions than as creators of them.[23]

Instead, he suggests that

> well-intentioned but unsupervised and largely undisciplined amateurs, not professionals, will have been the most frequent transmitters of the text of the New Testament.[24]

In studying the Lord's Prayer, we saw how nearly the shorter Lukan text was lost. We have seen also how widespread and extensive harmonisation was. It is beyond doubt the most frequent kind of corruption in the Gospels. I have already suggested in this chapter that there are likely to be corruptions in Mark which are unknown to us because no manuscript preserves the original text. I return to this point now, to look back into the period from which no manuscript survives. The second half of the second century saw two developments. With Irenaeus, there came the recognition of the four-Gospel canon. But also, with first Justin and then Tatian came harmonisation on the largest possible scale, with the blending of all the written sources into a single narrative. While such harmonies may have left their mark on subsequent copyings of the separated Gospels, it is the attitude to the tradition that is important. It is an attitude which assumes the essential unity of the separate Gospels which, as I have already said, treats them as *needing* harmonisation.

While source criticism requires the separation of the several strands into their constituent threads, the harmony weaves them together into a cord.

With regard to the period between the activity of the evangelists and the period of Justin and Tatian, our evidence is extremely slight. But the possibility that the separated Gospels were harmonised as extensively in this period as they were by later copyists in this for us pre-history of the Gospels (for no manuscript survived) is one to be taken very seriously. The answer that we do not know what happened is almost as damaging to the quest for a documentary solution to the Synoptic Problem as the conclusion that harmonisation was rife.

I am proposing that the evidence does not permit us to attempt a documentary solution. I am not thereby denying the existence of documents. I do not attempt to deny the substantial reality of Mark. His style alone is a sufficient criterion for us to know him in bulk from Matthew or Luke. But a documentary solution requires more than the degree of detail needed to know Mark from Matthew. It requires published editions, in which every last word, syllable and letter is known. It is this discernible, published precision which is lacking. The reason for the lack is not – as it might seem I was about to conclude – that we do not have the evidence to recover *precisely* what the evangelists wrote. It is that the comparison of published editions assumes, in its two-dimensional diagrams, that there is a single point of contact between two texts, for example, the single contact when Matthew copied Mark, and there was an end of the matter. I am proposing a three-dimensional diagram, in which the third dimension represents a series of contacts between texts each of which may have changed since the previous contact. For example, Matthew copies bits out of Mark in reproducing a tradition; then a later copy of Mark is enriched by some of Matthew's alterations; and next a copy of Matthew (already different from the one we began with) is influenced by something from the also changed Mark. Add in Luke, and oral tradition, and any other sources that might have been available, at any points in the development that you please, and you have a process a good deal less recoverable than any documentary hypothesis. It is not at all the orderly business we had hoped, and looks instead like molecules bouncing around and off each other in bewildering fashion.

It may be that I will be considered to be offering what has been called a complex solution, in distinction to the simple solutions such as those of Streeter and Farrer. Such a solution is presented by Boismard, who discerns over a dozen documents, some existing in earlier and later forms. But there is a major difference. I am not attempting to identify and to name sources or to recover layers. I am suggesting that the evidence is not of a kind to permit one to demonstrate the existence of the many documents posited by such theories. Thus, while Boismard's solution, like Streeter's argument for Proto-Luke, along with other theories, may be close to mine in recognising more than one point of contact between the Gospels, we differ more than we agree.

The same must be said after comparing my suggestion with the Deutero-Markus theory. I agree that the copy of Mark used by Matthew will not have been identical to the copies available to us. I would add that Matthew's copy will have been different also from Mark's autograph (unless he used the autograph, which must be regarded as improbable), and that Luke's copy will have been different again. But Deutero-Mark is a document, an edition. In contrast to that, I am proposing that we should be thinking of a process, and that the solid blocks of the documentary hypotheses prove to be at best soft and crumbling rock, at worst slowly shifting sand. Let us suppose, for example, that somebody who has read newly written Matthew copies Mark from a manuscript already different from the version known to Matthew, and introduces (intentionally or inadvertently) a few Matthaeanisms, and that Luke worked with such a copy. Who is to say that such a thing is impossible? That such confusing things occurred at a later date may be demonstrated from the manuscripts. A manuscript may harmonise a passage in Luke to Matthew; when we look at the Matthaean parallel in that manuscript, we find that it has a quite different form of the text from that taken into the Lukan version. This phenomenon may be found many times in Codex Bezae, one of the most frequently harmonising manuscripts. At its most extreme, we might say that every copying of a Gospel is, in the sense required by source criticism, a separate document, for it will to a greater or lesser extent be different from any other copy.

What are we left with? Is any attempt at source criticism a futile enterprise? The study of material in bulk seems safe enough. That the emergence (to use a colourless word) of Mark came before that of Matthew and Luke and that they both initially made use of it can hardly be questioned on the grounds which I have set out. For the discovery of the derivation of Matthew and Luke from Mark is based on the study of the *differences* between them, such as the many improvements of Markan style and vocabulary. It appears to me to be in the further and vexed question of the relationship between Matthew and Luke that source criticism goes beyond the evidence and is mistaken by treating traditions as though they were documents. Here the argument concerns not the differences between the Gospels but their similarities, and it is precisely this area which our knowledge of the surviving manuscript tradition shows us to be problematical.

I have not discussed the arguments concerning order, the debates which compare the order of pericopae in each Gospel with a view to determining who is dependent upon whom. Since the manuscripts rarely differ from one another in this regard, textual criticism has little enough to offer on the matter.

The material constituting this chapter is intended to enforce the importance of keeping textual criticism in mind when studying other approaches to the Gospels. E. M. Forster's 'Only connect' is not a bad motto for what is proposed. We started with the fact that the Gospels came into existence as manuscripts and for most of their existence have been preserved as manuscripts. We are discovering that this simple truth should be kept in mind even when studying apparently quite unrelated matters.

CHAPTER 8

The endings of Mark's Gospel

Is this the promised end?
William Shakespeare, *The History of King Lear* and
The Tragedy of King Lear

We might suppose it to be invariably the case that a story has an ending, and that is that. But some recollection will suggest that we are familiar from various sources with the possibility of multiple endings. The fairy stories of the brothers Grimm often have variants. Is Red Riding Hood eaten by the wolf or does she live happily ever after? Greek myths are told and retold with different endings. In Gluck's opera, Eurydice is finally restored to Orfeo, even though he has looked back at her as he leads her out of Hades. Modern novels have extended the possibilities. John Fowles' *The French Lieutenant's Woman* gives us a choice of endings. Other books avoid telling us the ending, avoid closure.

Armed with the knowledge that there are more options than the so-called fairy-tale ending, let us turn to one of the most fought-over extensive variant readings, the ending of Mark's Gospel. There are six different endings attested.

1. The Short Ending. This consists of the first eight verses of the last chapter. Their authenticity is undisputed.

And when the sabbath was past, Mary Magdalene, and Mary the mother of James, and Salome, brought spices, so that they might go and anoint him. And very early on the first day of the week they went to the tomb when the sun had risen. And they were saying to one another, 'Who will roll away the stone for us from the door of the tomb?' And looking up, they saw that the stone was rolled back – it was very large. And entering the tomb, they saw a young man sitting on the right side, dressed in a white robe; and they were amazed. And he said to them, 'Do not be amazed; you seek Jesus of Nazareth, who was crucified. He has risen, he is not here; see the place where they laid him. But go, tell his disciples and Peter that he is going before you to Galilee; there you will see him, as he told you.' And they went out and fled from the tomb; for trembling and astonishment had come upon them; and they said nothing to any one, for they were afraid. (Mark 16.1–8, RSV)

This dramatic and abrupt ending is found in only a few witnesses: in Codices Sinaiticus and Vaticanus; in 304, a twelfth-century commentary manuscript of Matthew and Mark. These are the only three Greek witnesses. The versions supporting them are the Sinaitic Syriac, one manuscript of the Sahidic, and some Armenian manuscripts. The Armenian text of Mark is of considerable interest. It is a secondary translation, being derived from a Syriac version of a type no longer extant. The Greek text which it represents at this remove is of the Caesarean type and the Armenian version is, in spite of the complications arising out of its comparative remoteness from the Greek, a principal witness to that text. In addition, we have the testimony of four fathers: Clement of Alexandria, Origen, Eusebius and Jerome. Both of the latter refer to manuscripts with this ending. A different kind of evidence which should be mentioned here is that the last division of the text in the oldest form of the Ammonian sections was at verse 8. The text so divided must, therefore, have ended here.

This form is known as the Short Ending.

2.   The second ending, known as the Intermediate, is translated by the RSV as follows:

And when the sabbath was past … and they said nothing to any one, for they were afraid [verses 1–8]. But they reported briefly to Peter and those with him all that they had been told. And after this, Jesus himself sent out by means of them, from east to west, the sacred and imperishable proclamation of eternal salvation.

This on its own is read by only one witness, the African Old Latin witness Codex Bobbiensis. It should also be noted that this manuscript has a unique addition between verses 3 and 4:

But suddenly at the third hour of the day it became dark throughout the world, and angels descended from heaven and rising in the glory of the living God at once ascended with him, and immediately it became light.

3. The third alternative is verses 9–20, called the Long Ending. This is the Received Text, and thus the one known from the Authorised Version, whose translation I present:

And when the sabbath was past ... neither said they any thing to any *man*; for they were afraid [verses 1–8].

9¶ Now when *Jesus* was risen early the first *day* of the week, he appeared first to Mary Magdalene, out of whom he had cast seven devils.

10*And* she went and told them that had been with him, as they mourned and wept.

11And they, when they had heard that he was alive, and had been seen of her, believed not.

12¶ After that he appeared in another form unto two of them, as they walked, and went into the country.

13And they went and told *it* unto the residue: neither believed they them.

14¶ Afterward he appeared unto the eleven as they sat at meat, and upbraided them with their unbelief and hardness of heart, because they believed not them which had seen him after he was risen.

15And he said unto them, Go ye into all the world, and preach the gospel to every creature.

16He that believeth and is baptized shall be saved; but he that believeth not shall be damned.

17And these signs shall follow them that believe; In my name shall they cast out devils; they shall speak with new tongues;

18They shall take up serpents; and if they drink any deadly thing, it shall not hurt them; they shall lay hands on the sick, and they shall recover.

19¶ So then after the Lord had spoken unto them, he was received up into heaven, and sat on the right hand of God.

20And they went forth, and preached every where, the Lord working with *them*, and confirming the word with signs following. Amen.

This is found in A C D W Θ fam[13], the majority of Greek manuscripts, the rest of the Latin tradition, syr[cph] cop[bo]. Fathers who quote from these verses include Irenaeus, and possibly Justin. These references will be discussed below.

4. The fourth alternative is to include verses 9–20, but with either a critical symbol or a note on the problem between verses 8 and 9.

(a) In some copies the evangelist ended here, as also Eusebius Pamphili considered canonical. But in many this also is in circulation.

This is found in 1 209^mg 1582. Since these manuscripts all belong to Family 1, it may be considered to be the family reading.

(b) The end. * In some copies the evangelist ended here, but in many this also.

This is found in 22.

(c) From here to the end is not present in some copies. But in old ones everything remaining is present.

This is the note to be found in 20.

(d) Asterisks: 137 138.

5. The fifth alternative consists of *everything* so far recorded:

verses 1–8 – But they reported ... eternal salvation – verses 9–20.

It has to be subdivided into three groups.
(a) The first consists only of L, the eighth-century witness which (it will be recalled) is badly copied, but attempts to reproduce an Alexandrian text. It has the following text:
verses 1–8
[decoration]
This also is in circulation
But they reported ... eternal salvation
This also is in circulation after 'For they were afraid'
verses 9–20.[1]
(b) The second group contains the note between '... eternal salvation' and verses 9–20, but not the one between verse 8 and 'But they reported ...'. It consists of Ψ 0112 (099 *l*602 cop^sa mss bo mss). The bracketed witnesses show some further smaller variations, which we need not examine. The Sahidic version is the oldest supporter of this solution to the problem.
(c) The third group has this material without any comment. It consists of 274^mg 579 syr^h mg.

---

[1] A plate showing this page (f113r) is reproduced in J. W. Burgon, *The Last Twelve Verses of the Gospel According to S. Mark Vindicated against Recent Critical Objectors and Established* (Oxford and London, 1871). A copy of the next page but one (f114r), with verses 17ff., is given in Alands, *Text*, p. 112 (Plate 29).

6.   There is one final form to be recorded separately. It is an addition at the end of verse 14, which runs:

And they justified themselves saying that 'This age of lawlessness and unbelief is in the power of Satan, who does not allow the truth and power of God to prevail over the unclean things of the spirits. Therefore reveal your righteousness now.' Thus they spoke to Christ, and Christ replied to them that 'The measure of years of the authority of Satan is fulfilled, but other terrible things draw near. And I was handed over to death for the sake of those who have sinned, so that they might return to the truth and sin no more; so that they might inherit the spiritual and incorruptible glory of righteousness in heaven.'

This passage is found in only one manuscript, W. It has therefore been named the Freer Logion. It has thus been rediscovered only in the present century. But a partial version of it had always been known, from a comment of Jerome's in his polemical treatise *Against Pelagius* (2.15). He had written

In some exemplars and especially in Greek manuscripts of Mark in the end of his Gospel is written: Afterwards when the eleven had sat down at table, Jesus appeared to them and rebuked their unbelief and hardness of heart because they had not believed those who saw him risen. And they justified themselves saying that this age of iniquity and unbelief is under Satan,[2] who does not allow the truth and power of God to be grasped by unclean spirits. Therefore reveal your righteousness now.

Of course, within both the ending after verse 8 and verses 9–20 there are variants. There are also some other curious but less important notes relating to the passage in various places, which have not been listed here.

Nearly all these forms of text have been adopted in modern versions. The third is adopted by the RSV (with the Intermediate Ending supplied in a footnote). The fifth is the text printed in the New English Bible in 1961.

There are a number of ways in which we could discuss this material. One would be to follow a literary critical approach, in

---

[2] The text which I have followed is found in one manuscript. In others the phrase *sub Satana* is replaced by *substantia*, which is probably a corruption. *Sub Satana* presents the text found in W.

which the effect of the different endings on the whole shape of the story would be discussed. Another would be to discuss the history of the text, with a view to determining which form is likely to be original. A third would be to examine each form on its own merits, with the same purpose. We shall in fact follow each of these, beginning with the second and coming finally to the first. But before that, something needs to be said about some of the issues at stake in this debate.

My approach to the Received Text has regularly been to show how the scientific development of textual criticism, and the discovery of far older manuscripts, led to its replacement by texts based on older and better materials. But in reality the progress has not been so uniform. I have referred already to the fierce and instinctive opposition which any challenge to the Received Text incurred. We saw that even Mill's collection of variant readings led to his condemnation by some. Conservatism fought for the Received Text of the New Testament in the same way that it defended the Ptolemaic model of the solar system. Such opposition does not quickly fade and in this instance shows that the longevity of textual traditions so noted in the manuscript traditions of the New Testament is not a thing of the past. There are still supporters of the Received Text, and there is even a Majority Text Society, dedicated to furthering the claim that the majority of manuscripts (that is, of course, the representatives of the medieval Byzantine text) preserve the original text of the New Testament. That such a case should be made owes a great deal to the *a priori* claim that God would ensure the preservation of the original text in most manuscripts, rather than allow it to be almost lost and long unknown. It owes a good deal also to a kind of un-self-questioning conservatism. It owes very little indeed to either historical observation or self-critical scholarship.

We saw that the formation of the Received Text was due to accident, that it was based on the materials on which Erasmus happened to seize when preparing his first edition. Thus, the Received Text does not invariably present the Byzantine or Majority Text. Several editions have appeared in recent years that attempt to remedy this unfortunate state of affairs, by providing a text shown by the majority of manuscripts. It is on this that the claim is now based.[3]

Along with the story of the woman taken in adultery, the ending of Mark is one of the more substantial blocks of material where scientific textual criticism has produced a markedly different text from the Received Text. This bulk is perhaps one reason why it has been such a centre for debate on this issue. But there are two further reasons. One is historical. The conservative opposition to Westcott and Hort was most trenchantly, indeed unpleasantly, expressed by the Dean of Chichester, Burgon, in his book *The Last Twelve Verses of S. Mark*.[4] Burgon, who also supported the Authorised Version and the Received Text against the Revised Version and Westcott and Hort in *The Revision Revised*, collected all the evidence he could muster to support his case. The book has been reprinted, and the same case advanced by other writers.[5] The contents of Mark 16.9–20 provide another, theological, reason for the intensity of debate. We have in these verses a command to preach the gospel throughout the world; emphasis on the necessity of baptism for salvation; a list of signs that accompany belief – exorcisms, glossolalia, immunity to venom and poison, healing of the sick; the ascension and session of Jesus, and successful activity by the apostles. Most of these are found elsewhere. But the safe handling of venomous snakes (a popular subject for television programmes in search of the lurid) is not. It would be absurd as well as unjust to associate all supporters of the Majority Text with such activities, since the theory does not demand that particular practice. But the opposite works rather differently: those who do engage in such deeds are supporters of the Majority Text by their acceptance of the passage. This aside, the full contents of verses 9–20 provide a programme which, when interpreted in a certain way, is extremely congenial to a particular kind of conservative

---

[3] Since we are still far from having collated all the Gospel manuscripts in their entirety, we do not yet in sober truth know what the majority of manuscripts have in every variation. So for an account of how the edition was accomplished, see the introduction to *The New Testament in the Original Greek according to the Byzantine/Majority Textform*, ed. M. A. Robinson and W. G. Pierpont (Atlanta, 1991).

[4] Burgon, *The Last Twelve Verses*.

[5] See Metzger, *Text*, p. 136 n. 1. W. R. Farmer, *The Last Twelve Verses of Mark*, SNTSMS 25 (Cambridge, 1974).

Christianity. Conversely, those who argue that these verses are spurious might be charged by their opponents with a hidden 'liberalising' motive.

What has been outlined is a Majority Text case founded on the *a priori* supposition that the majority of manuscripts must be right. But another case has been advanced which attempts to use scientific textual criticism. This is the claim that Byzantine readings are original because they are found in the earliest evidence that is available to us.[6] There are a number of considerable difficulties with it. One is the simple fact that not all Byzantine readings are so old. Another is that, as we have seen, the text changed more in the first century and a half than at any subsequent time. A high proportion of all variant readings are thus very early, irrespective of the text-types supporting them. But, and this is a third (methodological) problem, that a text-type contains early readings does not make the text-type itself early. After all, where there is *no* variant reading *all* the text-types will contain an early text – the oldest that we have! – but they do not thereby lose their overall character as individual secondary text-types. If we look back to Luke 6.10 in Codex Ω, we can see that its version of the passage contains early readings shared with B and D. But the text-type itself is demonstrably, even in that brief passage, of a later and conflationary type. That is, we saw that its character was determined not by the fact that it shared ancient readings with both B and D, but by the fact that its text was based on the derivation of materials from both those text-types.

Enough should have been said above to indicate that the case for the Majority Text will not receive credence here. But before we leave the subject, something should be noted: that here there is as big a gap between the text received by different groups today as there was in the past between the various English versions of the Lukan Lord's Prayer. We shall be mistaken if we believe that absolutely everyone who reads the Bible is coming to a consensus on the text to be read.

There is another area of Gospel study in which the ending of Mark has become a centre of attention. The Griesbach solution to

[6] See Harry A. Sturtz, *The Byzantine Text-Type and New Testament Textual Criticism* (Nashville and New York, 1984).

the Synoptic Problem, which argues that Matthew was written first
and Mark last, has some difficulty with the idea that Mark should
have ended at 16.8. For it requires him to have rejected all the
material contained in Matthew 28 and Luke 24, and to have
decided to go against the tradition of recording resurrection
appearances. It is thus no surprise to find W. R. Farmer, a leading
contemporary 'neo-Griesbachian', claiming that we should consider the question 'still open', and in favour of the verses being
'redactional use of older material by the evangelist'.[7] The significance for the Synoptic Problem of the decision reached will not be
a major part of this study, though we shall need to consider it briefly
in due course.

We turn now to the history of the endings of Mark.

THE HISTORY OF THE TEXT

The framework within which Burgon and other supporters of the
Long Ending studied the problem was that provided by patristic
testimonies. We shall follow this initially.

We saw in Chapter 2 that it is often difficult to recover the text
which a father knew and used. But in such a case as this, of omission
against inclusion, the problems are fewer and less acute. For, if a
father quotes any words after verse 8, then he knew at least one of
the two endings. What we cannot do is to argue from silence. Thus,
that a writer never quotes this passage *might* be because he either
did not know or rejected it. But it might also be because he did not
need or did not choose to quote it. In addition, the patristic
testimony is valuable here because a considerable number of
important writers discuss the textual problem.

We begin with Justin, and a possible reference to verse 20 in his
Apology (1.45):

whom his apostles going out from Jerusalem proclaimed everywhere.

This might be no more than a general summary of the apostolic
activity. But three words, 'going out' – 'proclaimed' – 'everywhere', are identical, although the order of the second and third is
different. It cannot be regarded as certain, but only as more likely
than not, that Justin knew of the longer ending.

[7] Farmer, *The Last Twelve Verses of Mark*, pp. 109, 107.

Tatian is reported to have used the passage in the Diatessaron. In the resurrection narratives, Tatian was forced to abandon his usual way of combining the Gospels. We saw in Chapter 2 an example of a harmony produced in a similar way to Tatian's: by the weaving together of phrases from the four accounts into a single story. But in the last section, he had instead to insert longer blocks from each in turn. The Persian Gospel Harmony contains three pieces from the Long Ending: verse 14 (between the two halves of Luke 24.41); verse 16 (between Matthew 28.19 and 20); and verse 19 (between Luke 24.51 and 52).

Next is Irenaeus. He quotes verse 19, in a section of *Against Heresies* that is preserved only in Latin (3.10.6):

At the end of the Gospel Mark says And so the Lord Jesus after he had spoken to them, was taken into heaven, and sat down at the right hand of God.

Without the explicit reference to Mark, there would be nothing in the words that required us to suppose this to be a citation, for it seems a general enough credal statement. We should be grateful that he was explicit, for, after the general allusion of Justin, it is the first certain evidence for the Long Ending.

Hippolytus quotes from verses 17 and 18, in a fragment of a writing on spiritual gifts that is preserved in *Apostolic Constitutions* 8.1:

With good reason did he say to all of us together, when we were perfected concerning those gifts which were given from him by the Spirit: 'Now these signs shall follow them that have believed in my name: they shall cast out devils ... the sick, and they shall recover'.[8]

Hippolytus seems to identify the event with Pentecost.

The *Apostolic Constitutions* cites verse 16 in a section on baptism (6.15):

For the Lord says ... 'He that believeth and is baptised shall be saved; but he that believeth not shall be damned.'[9]

There is thus patristic evidence that verses 9–20 had come into existence by the end of the second century. The manuscript evidence is later. The oldest is versional, in the shape of the Old Syriac. All the extant Old Latin manuscripts except k contain the

[8] *The Apostolical Constitutions*, ed. James Donaldson, Ante-Nicene Christian Library (Edinburgh, 1870), p. 207.   [9] *Ibid.*, p. 159.

verses. The oldest of these is of the sixth century (but it is reasonable to assume that the Latin column of Codex Bezae, which is lacking from verse 6, followed the Greek in reading it). The oldest Greek witnesses are the Freer Gospels (W) and Codex Bezae (D). W is certainly a witness to the Long Ending, but aberrant in that it has a long Long Ending. D is somewhat unhelpful, since it is deficient from verse 15 (the missing verses were replaced in the ninth century). We note also that the verses are contained in the oldest Byzantine manuscripts. It is clear from this fact that it was part of the Byzantine text from its beginning.

It is in the fourth century that there is clear evidence of variation in the passage. From this date, with the Codices Sinaiticus and Vaticanus, comes the earliest evidence for the Short Ending.

From this period also, in Codex Bobbiensis, is the earliest evidence for the Intermediate Ending.

At this period we also encounter writers discussing the textual problems. Foremost among them are Eusebius of Caesarea and Jerome.

Eusebius was asked about the difference between Matthew 28.1 and Mark 16.9 on the timing of the resurrection. He replied

This can be solved in two ways. The person not wishing to accept this chapter [the passage under consideration] will say that it is not contained in all copies of the Gospel according to Mark. Indeed the accurate copies conclude the story according to Mark in the words of the young man seen by the women and saying to them Do not be afraid. You seek Jesus ... for they were afraid. For the end is here in nearly all the copies of Mark. What follows is found but seldom, in some copies but by no means in all. It could be considered superfluous, especially if it should turn out to contradict the witness of the other evangelists. This would be a response that avoided and altogether set aside an unnecessary question.[10]

Eusebius goes on to offer his own solution to the problem (to which we shall come in time). What is important to us here is his evidence about the manuscripts. It seems that the vast majority of manuscripts known to him end at 16.8. Since we only have a couple of manuscripts containing this part of Mark from the time of

[10] The comment comes from a lost work known to us as *Gospel Questions and Solutions Addressed to Marinus*. The excerpt is taken from an epitome found in the last century in a manuscript in the Vatican Library. See J. Quasten, *Patrology, Volume 3. The Golden Age of Greek Patristic Literature: From the Council of Nicaea to the Council of Chalcedon* (Utrecht, 1960; repr. Westminster, Md., 1983), p. 337.

Eusebius, we cannot evaluate the accuracy of this statement. But the fact is that both our survivors support his testimony. We find here, just as we did with Luke's Lord's Prayer, that a reading which was well known and even predominant in one period can later disappear almost totally.

Jerome twice commented on the matter. First, in a letter to Hedibia, who had asked the same question as Marinus.

Why is it that the evangelists narrate matters relating to the resurrection and appearance of the Lord differently? . . . There are two ways of solving this question. Either we do not receive the testimony of Mark because it is found in few Gospel books, nearly all Greek books lacking this final chapter – especially since it seems to narrate matters different from and contrary to the other Gospels – or we reply that both are true.[11]

The second passage is the reference to the Freer Logion which we have already quoted.

We thus seem to have Jerome supporting the claim made by Eusebius a generation or so earlier. But not so. For Jerome's work is simply a translation with some slight changes of what Eusebius had written. It is thus worthless for our purposes. Jerome, writing in Bethlehem, knew – as the reference to the Freer Logion shows – two forms of the Long Ending. And, as Burgon pointed out, the Vulgate contains a translation of verses 9–20. So Jerome is no evidence for the Short Ending.

The ending consisting of both the Intermediate and the Long Endings appears to come into being at a somewhat later date. Manuscript 0112 is the oldest Greek witness to it. This manuscript is of the sixth/seventh century. Thus equally old support is provided by the Harklean Syriac, which was produced in the year 616. The colophon tells us that the marginal notes were the result of comparing the text with three Greek manuscripts. It has been argued that one of these manuscripts contained a Caesarean text, and that the other two were Alexandrian.[12]

Such is the support for a double (or rather, triple) ending. The

---

[11] Letter 120.3. My translation, from the citation in Legg.
[12] K. Lake, R. P. Blake and S. New, 'The Caesarean Text of the Gospel of Mark', *HTR* 21 (1928), 207–404, pp. 376–95. They actually say of the two manuscripts that 'They may have been both Neutral, or both Alexandrian, or one may have been of each type' (p. 394). The word 'Neutral' was applied by Westcott and Hort to the text of Sinaiticus and (especially) Vaticanus, which they considered 'neutral' in the sense that it was usually the original one.

attitude which led to it can be charted from Eusebius, whose discussion we resume.

> But another [solution], on no account daring to reject anything whatever which is, under whatever circumstances, met with in the text of the Gospels, will say that here are two readings (as is so often the case elsewhere); and that *both* are to be received, – inasmuch as by the faithful and pious, *this* reading is not held to be genuine rather than *that*; nor *that* than *this*.[13]

Eusebius is arguing that the discrepancy between Matthew and Mark does not require that Mark 16.9 be rejected as spurious.

On the face of it, the history of the text appears to present a very clear picture. It yields these conclusions:

second century	evidence of the Long Ending
fourth century	awareness of a problem
	evidence of the Short Ending
	evidence of the Intermediate Ending
	evidence of the Short and the Intermediate and the Long Ending together
sixth century	evidence of the Intermediate and the Long Ending together.

But here we come up against a difficulty in the use of patristic evidence. How do we interpret the lack of evidence in Clement of Alexandria? Does it mean that he does not need or want to quote the passage? Or does it mean that it was unknown to him? It has been pointed out that he does not quote Matthew 28 either, yet nobody suggests that that chapter was absent from his copy of the Gospels. The case of Origen has occasioned debate. It has been argued that Mark 16.9–20 would have been useful to him in *Against Celsus* 2.56–70, where the resurrection appearances are discussed. But he does not cite it. This fact has been taken by some to indicate that he either did not know or did not accept it. Those who wish to argue for the originality of the Long Ending point to the weakness of this argument, and not unreasonably. It cannot be argued that the Long Ending was unknown to or rejected by Clement and Origen. But there is a more important point: neither can silence indicate that the Short Ending was unknown. The presence of evidence for the Long Ending is demonstrable. That there cannot

13 Burgon's translation, in *The Last Twelve Verses*, p. 45.

be similar evidence for an absence of text requires us to accept that there is no evidence *against* the existence of the Short Ending in the second century.

Here we need to turn to the manuscript evidence. It will be recalled that the study of B in Luke and John, where P75 is extant, has demonstrated the existence of an Alexandrian text in those books, which was in existence at the end of the second century. We have no reason to consider the text of B in Matthew and Mark to be inferior to that in Luke and John. We may therefore conclude that, according to our present knowledge, B in Mark preserves an Alexandrian text formed in the late second century. There is thus manuscript evidence that the Short Ending had been known earlier in the second century.

One other piece of evidence points to the age of the Short Ending: the existence of both the Intermediate and Long Endings. That two alternatives to it exist indicates that it was known early, and considered unsatisfactory. The reading which accounts for the others must be more primitive, and only the Short Ending accounts for both the others. For who would replace verses 9–20 with the Intermediate Ending, or excise it totally to end so baldly as verse 8 does?

In conclusion, the history of the text leads us to conclude that both the Short and the Long Ending are second century. The Intermediate Ending, as its language clearly shows, is later. Nowhere in the Gospels do we find such a phrase as 'the sacred and imperishable proclamation of eternal salvation', or anything like it.

Westcott and Hort divided the study of variant readings into the collection and assessment of two kinds of evidence. The first was external evidence, the manuscript support and its history. It is that which we have studied hitherto in this chapter. The second is internal evidence, the character of the variant. A variant so extensive as the present is a particularly good one for the study of internal evidence, to which we now turn.

THE INTERMEDIATE ENDING

This need not delay us long. It contains a brief statement that contradicts verse 8, followed by a summary of the apostolic preaching that by its wording proclaims it to have been written long after the rest of Mark. The phrase 'the sacred and imperishable message of eternal salvation' is from a later and oratund theologian.

THE LONG ENDING

We shall look at it in two ways: first, at its shape and (for this is inescapable) the ideas in it, and second at the language, syntax and style.

The formation and theology of the Long Ending

The Long Ending is best read as a cento or pastiche of material gathered from the other Gospels and from other sources, slanted towards a particular interpretation. This may be demonstrated by going through it verse by verse.

Verses 9–11: That the resurrection occurred early on the first day of the week is (except for Matthew 28.1) the universal tradition; it is found in Mark 16.2. That Jesus appeared first to Mary Magdalene is Johannine tradition (John 20.11–18), while in Matthew 28.9 he appears first to Mary Magdalene and the other Mary. Verses 10 and 11 are based on Luke 24.10b–11 (with John 20.18 as another parallel). The reference to mourning and weeping is an expansion of the tradition (and note that the oldest version, the Freer Gospels, lacks the second verb, so that this expansion can be shown to have grown by stages).

It has been pointed out that verse 9 sits very uneasily with verses 1–8. There is no resumption of the theme of fear and silence in verse 8, and Mary Magdalene is introduced afresh in verse 9, as though she were not already on stage.

Verses 12–13: This is a summary of the meeting in the journey to Emmaus (Luke 24.13–35), with the reference to unbelief added.

Verse 14: Stories of Jesus appearing to the eleven are found in Matthew, Luke and John. The closest parallel to this version, with Jesus reproaching their unbelief, is Luke 24.36ff.

Verses 15–16: In Matthew 28.19 the disciples are commanded 'Go therefore and make disciples of all nations, baptizing them in the name of the Father and of the Son and of the Holy Spirit.' The same pair of verbs, 'preach'/'baptise', is found here. The main idea here (belief–baptism–salvation) may be seen as a development of what is found in the New Testament (see Acts 16.31 and 33; 1 Peter 3.21).

Verse 17: The reference to signs accompanying believers is also found in Hebrews 2.4. In Acts 19.6 those who are baptised and receive the Holy Spirit at Paul's hands 'spoke with tongues and prophesied'. Both exorcism and glossolalia are attested in the New Testament and the early church.

Verse 18: The handling of dangerous snakes has its origins in Lukan material. In Luke 10.17f. with the return of the seventy(-two), Jesus replies to their statement that the demons have obeyed them 'I saw Satan falling as lightning from heaven, Behold I have given you authority to tread upon snakes and scorpions, and over all the power of the enemy, and nothing shall harm you.' This symbolic reference to Satan (the ancient serpent – Revelation 12.9) is acted out in Acts (28.1–6) in the famous incident when Paul accidentally picks up a viper in a pile of sticks, and to the astonishment of all bystanders suffers no ill effects. The apparent literalness of this reference in verse 18 is best understood as a failure to recognise the symbolic nature of Luke's references.

The reference to poison is perhaps not so easy to locate. The most similar biblical story is the near disaster suffered by Elisha and the sons of the prophets with a mismanaged vegetable soup (2 Kings 5.38–41). They are saved by Elisha's advice, and 'there was no harm in the pot'. Burgon claimed that a reference in Papias shows him to have known the Long Ending. The reference in Eusebius is

He [Papias] tells another marvellous thing about Justus surnamed Barsabas, how when he drank harmful poison he suffered no harmful consequences by the Lord's grace.[14]

There is no evidence here to sustain Burgon's case. One might as well suppose that the story of Paul and the viper proved Luke to have known verse 18. It is more probable that the proliferation of miraculous stories about the apostles led to such a passage being framed. The idea is probably suggested by the previous clause.

Verse 19: The ascension is narrated in Luke 24, and its place

---

[14] Eusebius, *Eccl. Hist.* 3.39.

there at the end of the last resurrection story is more likely than the version in Acts 1 to have led to its inclusion here. The presence of Christ at God's right hand is mentioned in Acts 7.55 and elsewhere. It soon became credal.

Verse 20: An analogy with Hebrews 2.3–4 is suggested.

The reader's own reflection may be able to add further parallels and influences. What has been supplied here appears to be sufficient for us to recognise that the verses are a summary of a number of events recorded at greater length in the other Gospels. The fact that each episode in Mark 16.9–20 is an abridgement is particularly telling. It is in contrast to parallels in 1.1–16.8, where Matthew and Luke abridge Markan material.

There is also a determined polemical slant, in that the conclusions of the first two stories are the same – that the disciples did not believe (neither source has such a reference), and that when Jesus does appear, he rebukes 'their unbelief and hardness of heart'. It is only when they see and speak with Jesus that they believe. This is in marked contrast to the Fourth Gospel, in which the superior quality of faith without sight is stressed. It is also in contrast to Mark, who emphasises that understanding for the disciples will come only after the resurrection. This is always implied and not stated – there is nothing like John 13.7 in Mark. See, for example, 9.9, where silence about the transfiguration is required of the three disciples until 'the Son of man should have risen from the dead'; or the previous scene, where Simon Peter's response to Jesus' first prediction of his passion shows him not to understand his own confession of Jesus' messiahship. This persistent unbelief and hardness of heart may seem to be in accord with the disciples' lack of belief (4.40) and particularly with the women's response to the announcement of the resurrection at 16.8. But this is not so. In the first place, as has just been said, it is an important theme of Mark that everything will make sense for the disciples only after the resurrection. In the second, the Markan disciples' problem is not that that they are unbelieving, but that they do not understand what it is they are to believe. Only with the suffering, death and resurrection of Jesus will his message and purpose be intelligible. In 16.8, there is no evidence that the women's silence is due to either hardness of heart or unbelief.

The polemic against the disciples in the Long Ending does, however, have one feature in common with Mark 1.1.–16.8, in that for Mark the disciples represent the contemporary experience of belief. That is, as is often pointed out, the reader or hearer of Mark is encouraged to identify with the disciples' experience as their own. The evangelist achieves this in the same way as a painter might do, by providing the scene with the background and the figures with the clothing of the viewers' own day. The theological use that Mark makes of this device will be discussed in the next section. The Long Ending adopts this device, to the extent of bringing out a theme of the disciples' unbelief which is found earlier, but uses it for completely different purposes. I suggest that in verses 9–20 the disciples represent a theology which, in the view of the writer, weakened true faith in the risen Jesus. The writer supplies an ending that both provides the Gospel with a physical resurrection of Jesus and condemns the disciples' hesitations as unbelief. The emphasis is firmly on the physical event. In verse 19 the narrator emphasises the physical character of the ascension.[15]

THE STYLE OF THE LONG ENDING

A full study of the evidence would require much Greek, and more space than we have available. This is therefore no more than a brief summary. As many as seventeen words in this short passage of twelve verses are either not found in Mark 1.1–16.8, or are used here in a non-Markan sense. The value of some of this evidence has been challenged by Farmer. For example, 'Afterward' in verse 14 is not found in Mark 1.1–16.8. But it only comes once each in Luke, John and Hebrews. So its presence only here in Mark is no argument. However, the argument about style and word usage is cumulative. It is that there are so many non-Markan points to be noted in these verses that is significant. Moreover, we need to be looking not only for non-Markan features, but also for Mark's favourite words and stylistic traits. This approach, adopted by Morton Smith in a chapter of his book *Clement of Alexandria and a*

---

[15] This is suggested by B. D. Ehrman, *The Orthodox Corruption of Scripture* (New York and Oxford, 1993), pp. 232f.

Secret Gospel of Mark,[16] should, for example, yield six or seven of Mark's 18 favourite words in every 175.[17] There are 170 words in the Nestle–Aland text of verses 9–20. Six favourites appear: 'to believe' (*pisteuein*) four times (verses 13, 14, 16, 17) and 'to preach' (*kērussein*) twice (verses 15, 20). We might add the reference to the eleven (verse 14), since 'the twelve' is another Markan favourite. The Freer Logion has another, 'unclean'. The problem with both 'believe' and 'preach' is that they are not distinctively Markan enough, and are so very likely to be a result of the pastiche formed from the other Gospel narratives. 'To believe' is much more a Johannine than a Markan word, and 'preach' is almost as common in Matthew as in Mark. This evidence does not, therefore, support the claims for authenticity.

THE SHORT ENDING

We come now to the Short Ending, and to the question whether Mark could have ended in this way. We deal first with theories that although the Intermediate and Long Endings are spurious, yet the ending of the Gospel at this place was not the evangelist's intention. Two kinds of reason are put forward. One was that the final verses were written, but then lost, so that the Gospel broke off in mid-sentence with 'For they were afraid.' The plausibility of this is somewhat lost in translation. For in the Greek it consists of two words; that translated as 'for' is one that by the rules of Greek comes second in the sentence. The Gospel thus ends with a particle. It has also been pointed out that the verb 'to fear' in Mark is more often followed by its object – 'they feared *something*' – than used without an object. But the usage which we have here does occur elsewhere in the Gospel, so this argument is of no force.

In this theory, it is supposed that the original ending was completely lost, because it was either the autograph which was damaged, or a very early copy, from which all our manuscripts are descended. The Intermediate and Long Endings are attempts to

---

[16] (Cambridge, Mass., 1973), pp. 123–35.
[17] The favourites are listed in R. Morgenthaler, *Statistik des neutestamentlichen Wortschatzes*, Zurich and Frankfurt-on-Main, 1958), p. 181. On p. 186, he lists the frequency of all the words in the Long Ending.

supply the deficiency. It was to this theory that Burkitt adhered ('That the Gospel was originally intended to finish at verse 8 is quite inconceivable'[18]). He believed that the original Markan account of a meeting between the eleven and the risen Jesus was used by Matthew and the Gospel of Peter. This is a good argument, once the premiss has been granted. But there is a great difficulty with the premiss. The difficulty is that if an early copy had been damaged, it could have been made good from either the autograph or another copy. If it was the autograph, then why did not the evangelist repair it? A second theory addresses the problem by suggesting that something happened to the evangelist to interrupt him. Either arrest or death overtook him in mid-sentence, and so we have in his Gospel an unfinished masterpiece.

One should treat such *dei ex machinis* with great caution. Idiosyncratic grammar is no proof of sudden death. The question is simply this. Since all our conclusions tend towards the originality of the Short Ending, is it impossible that it could have ended with a particle? The arguments on this matter have been protracted. The balance of them is that such an ending is strange (and would not be the only strange thing about Mark) but not impossible. We reach the conclusion, then, that the oldest form of the Gospel is the Short Ending.

The effect that the various endings have had on the understanding of Mark's Gospel can hardly be overestimated. For it almost goes without saying that a small alteration at the very end may have a momentous effect on the whole shape of a story. This passage beyond almost any other gives the lie to the idea that the variants of the manuscripts of the New Testament are insignificant and have no substantial effect on the text. The remainder of this chapter will therefore be devoted to considering the implications of the materials we have been studying.

The existence of the rival endings makes clear that the issue here is of a Gospel without a resurrection appearance. For if the story ends at verse 8 with ℵ B, there is no triumphal conclusion to the Gospel. The sequence of events is as follows. Jesus dies and is buried. The women go early to the tomb and find the stone rolled

---

[18] F. C. Burkitt, *Two Lectures on the Gospels* (London and New York, 1901), p. 28.

away and a young man in white. He announces that Jesus is risen, and tells them to go and tell the disciples about it, with the promise that they will see him. What then happens offers, as elsewhere in Mark, a bleak and realistic picture of the followers of Jesus: they flee in trembling and astonishment, and tell nobody anything, out of fear. End. They are *told* that Jesus is risen, and they receive a promise that they will see him. But no encounter is narrated. Instead, the story opens out into the present experience of the Gospel's first audience. Like the women at the tomb, they have received the news of the resurrection and must place their faith in that news; like the women, they are overcome with fear, with trembling and astonishment – not fright, but holy fear at the theophany. To speak about this is beyond their capability.

The way in which the evangelist's audience are invited to recognise themselves in his portrayal of the disciples has long been a matter for attention. The character of Simon Peter in particular has always been one with which readers have identified. But nowhere is this more true than in the experience of the resurrection as Mark tells the story. Nothing is offered which goes beyond the experience of an audience who have heard the Gospel from eye-witnesses: they are told that he is risen, they are given the promise that they will see him, and they are fearful. The demand for any more, for an encounter with the risen Jesus, is not accepted. It cannot be believed that the evangelist knew no accounts of resurrection appearances. But, remarkably, he decided that a Gospel did not need them.

The Intermediate and Long Endings are in marked contrast. A Gospel without resurrection appearances is incomplete, for the Gospel is about the resurrection and salvation. With these endings several things are changed about the whole story. For both are endings in a way that the Short Ending is not. In both, the reader's present is made secure as part of the ending's future. The preaching of the Gospel, through which belief comes, is the consequence of Jesus' command to the eleven. In the Long Ending, their baptism is declared to be the means of their salvation.

In addition, the Long Ending provides a credal formula which, with Jesus's ascension and session, establishes an ordered universe in which the limits are set. The same issue is addressed by the Freer

Logion, in its discussion of the limits of Satan's power and of the 'other terrible things'. By contrast, the Short Ending leaves all such issues unresolved. Where does Mark leave Jesus? His story does not give any chance of even beginning to address the question.

The fact that Tatian could not weave a single account out of the resurrection narratives may be taken as a parable of the difficulties posed for early Christianity by the different ways in which the evangelists dealt with the period after the burial of Jesus. Mark's version was the most problematic. In other ways also his Gospel presented ideas which were the source of continuing disagreement. One may see adoptionism in the way in which he began his Gospel with John the Baptist and Jesus' baptism. The words from heaven in 1.11 ('Thou art my beloved son; with thee I am well pleased') are particularly susceptible of the interpretation that only in this act does Jesus become God's son. These problems were dealt with by Matthew and Luke in their provision of prefatory material, and by later copyists in their inserting 'Son of God' in verse 1.[19] The dramatic and abrupt ending was a source of such uneasiness that several alternatives were fabricated. Does the tone of the Long Ending, with its censure of unbelief, even suggest that the lack of resurrection appearances in Mark had led to the claim that belief in them was not necessary to Christian faith?

The consequence of these different endings is that radically different, perhaps even incompatible, ways of reading Mark have emerged. Does the ending remove all uncertainty? How secure a business is it to believe today? Were the disciples and apostles in an easier position than the early Christians to believe in Jesus? What place does proclamation have in the church's life? Once we start reading a Gospel ending at 16.8, all manner of ambivalences become visible in the text. A Gospel ending at 16.20 is a different story altogether. The ending *is* resolved; the ground for faith is indisputable; the church's successful life of preaching, baptising and working wonders is in obedience to the commands of the risen Lord. An ending with the preaching from east to west of the sacred and imperishable proclamation of eternal salvation likewise is far from muted.

---

[19] See Ehrman, *The Orthodox Corruption of Scripture*, pp. 72ff.

One other interesting point emerges from this comparison. Both the Intermediate and the Long Ending, with their emphasis on proclamation, provide the Gospel with its own validation. By writing, Mark is obedient to this command, for he enshrines the command within his book. The Short Ending provides no such security for the book. Indeed, quite the reverse, for the women's *silence* means that, within the story, we have no means of knowing that any of it happened.

This is consonant with the idea of the Messianic Secret itself. For the Messianic Secret deals with the historical problem of the non-recognition of Jesus by demonstrating it to be essential to the nature of his message and work; and it anticipates the criticism that Mark's theology is innovative, by providing a historical account that shows it to have been known but concealed from the beginning. The ending at 16.8 contributes to both these ends. It is also a part of the wider mystery within the Gospel, and of 'a mysterious character' to which Wrede refers, and of which the Messianic Secret is itself a part.[20]

It would be easy to assume that the decision that the Short Ending is original leads to our reading Mark without reference to the others. But the truth is not so simple. Let us recall the various forms in which the text is presented:

1 The Short Ending
2 The Intermediate Ending
3 The Long Ending
4 The Long Ending with either a critical symbol or a note between verses 8 and 9
5 The Intermediate Ending plus the Long Ending (with or without notes)
6 The Long Ending containing the Freer Logion.

It will be observed that in both forms 4 and 5, the text had to be read in what might be called a compound way. In form 4, you had

---

[20] 'An older period of New Testament scholarship often spoke of the Gospel of Mark having a mysterious character. We find this already in Schleiermacher... This much seems certain to me: that if Mark's Gospel were to come to light for the first time today from some tomb ... many of the features belonging to it would be recognised without the slightest difficulty, whereas at present a certain critical habit of mind refuses to look at them at all' (W. Wrede, *The Messianic Secret*, tr. J. C. G. Grieg (Cambridge and London, 1971), pp. 146, 148).

the option of not reading verses 9–20, and the option of reading them. But whichever option you chose, you were aware of the other one. The same, with extra complications, applies to form 5. We are in no different a situation today. In what we have said about the Short Ending, we are sharply aware of its distinctive character in contrast to the other text forms. The fact that we have decided that the Intermediate and Long Endings are secondary does not mean that we have forgotten that they exist, or that we can now read Mark with its Short Ending as though we had never read it with its Long Ending. We are therefore not in a position to say that the Long Ending can be forgotten. The fact is that it stands as the ending which has been dominant for the reading of Mark for most of the text's history. Thus, even if one insists on a single original text of Mark, one cannot escape the need to be aware of the fact that all the text forms affect our interpretation of it. This fact is true whichever ending one believes to be original. So, while readers of the Bible are in disagreement with regard to the text of Mark which they read, they have this in common – the different forms in which the text exists.

Finally, textual criticism has, by patient and generally unspectacular work, managed in the course of the last 150 years to recover the Short and original Ending of Mark. To read the Gospel with this ending is to read a new book. This new book offers radical theological interpretations which had been wholly stifled by the ecclesiastical pieties of the Intermediate and Long Endings. Let it be said only by the unimaginative and those who know nothing of the past that textual criticism is insignificant or unnecessary.

CHAPTER 9

The last three chapters of Luke

> It is impossible to write except by making a palimpsest of a
> rediscovered manuscript
>
> Umberto Eco, *The Island of the Day Before*

Hitherto we have studied small blocks of material, a dozen verses
or so at most, which either show extensive variation or are
altogether secondary. In this chapter we study a different phenomenon, the effect on a longer passage of a number of variations
scattered through it. At the same time, we are able to observe the
way in which traditions, and with them texts, continued to grow
and to change in the earliest centuries and beyond.

The final chapters of Luke are the most suitable for this study.
The whole text of Luke has, as we have discovered on several
occasions already, been the subject of extensive revision. The most
notable of all such assaults was that of Marcion, and there can be
little doubt that his drastic revision had an unsettling influence on
the text, even if direct influence is found but rarely. It is in the final
chapters that uncertainty about Luke's text becomes most prominent, not only among the ancient witnesses to the text, but also
among modern scholars. Significantly different versions of the last
two and a half chapters of the Gospel have been accepted in the last
120 years.

We are fortunate in having to hand a recent and exhaustive
edition of the material, in the International Greek New Testament
Project's edition.[1] The information that it contains will form the

---

[1] *The New Testament in Greek. The Gospel According to St. Luke. Part Two, Chapters 13–24*, edited by
the American and British Committees of The International Greek New Testament
Project (Oxford, 1987).

foundation of what is provided below. I shall not always cite all the witnesses which it adduces.

The beginning of the problem of these chapters is the 'Western non-interpolations'. In fact, the very beginning is the name itself, which must be explained carefully. The phrase was coined by Hort in the introductory volume of *The New Testament in the Original Greek*. Many though his merits were, he was sometimes capable of writing remarkably turgid prose. The difficulty arises because he desires to be scrupulously accurate. In studying the evidence, Westcott and Hort were impressed by the fact that there are a number of verses in Luke 22–24 which are present in the Codices Sinaiticus and Vaticanus, but lacking in Codex Bezae. An examination of these passages led them to the conclusion (on the grounds of internal evidence) that Codex Bezae was correct in omitting them. But Sinaiticus and Vaticanus were their Neutral Text, that which they considered to be original, while Codex Bezae was a member of the Western Text, a generally corrupt and unreliable version. Hence the phrase 'Western non-interpolations'. A 'non-interpolation' is an omission, and 'Western' refers to the text supporting them. If we think of them as 'Western omissions', we shall not be far wrong. But of course it is not that the Western text has omitted something but that the Neutral Text has added something. It would have been simpler to describe the passages as 'Neutral interpolations'. This, out of trust in the Neutral tradition as a whole, Hort declined to do. Moreover, he and Westcott did not remove the doubtful verses from their text. All that they did was to print them within double square brackets.

The Western non-interpolations are not found only in Luke's Gospel. They include Matthew 27.49. This is the account, referred to already, of the piercing of Jesus' side.[2] In addition, they listed a dozen other passages which they thought might be of the same kind (that is, material wrongly added to the Neutral Text).[3] These passages are

Matthew 9.34; 21.44; Mark 2.22; 14.39; Luke 5.39; 10.41f.; 12.19, 21, 39; 22.62; John 3.32; 4.9.

---

[2] See p. 41 above.   [3] Westcott and Hort, Vol. II, p. 176.

But the main group of passages is

Luke 22.19–20; 24.3, 6, 12, 36, 40, 51, 52.

We shall deal with each in turn as we study the chapters.

THE LAST SUPPER

Luke 22.14

The first passage is a small detail with which copyists had difficulties: 'he sat at table, and the twelve apostles with him'. There has always been widespread reluctance to describe Judas Iscariot as an apostle. The problem is solved in different ways. The minuscule manuscript 348 (copied in 1022) replaces 'twelve' with 'eleven'. Some manuscripts, including the second hand of Codex Sinaiticus, omit 'apostles'. The Sinaitic Syriac and some forms of the Georgian version replace 'apostles' with 'disciples'. Others omit 'twelve'. These include P75 ℵ* B D 157 and a few other medieval manuscripts, and most of the Old Latin tradition. The support for this reading leads most modern editors to print it (as does the RSV). 157 was produced in about 1122. It may be recalled from Chapter 4 that it contains a striking number of agreements with Codex Bezae. It is a rare medieval witness to readings of that ancient text-type. The reading 'twelve apostles' is supported by ℵc A C W Θ f1 f13 and the Byzantine text, as well as Marcion. Its manuscript support, against that for the omission of 'twelve', might lead us to believe it to be secondary. But that it is the harder reading, and that the others avoid the implication that Judas Iscariot was an apostle seems incontestable.

22.16

It is stated that Marcion's text omitted this verse. For the reconstruction of Marcion's version of Luke, we are dependent almost wholly on the hostile evidence of two of his adversaries, Tertullian writing not long after Marcion's death and Epiphanius, the fourth-century Bishop of Salamis and writer against heretics. It is to the latter that we are indebted here. There are places in which we must suspect that Marcion's text contaminated the manuscript tradition. But that is not the case in this place, for there is no other evidence for its omission.

22.19–20

This is the best known and most discussed of the Western non-interpolations. Here, in parallel columns, are the text of D and of ℵ B in verses 17–20.

D	ℵ B
[17]And taking the cup	[17]And taking the cup
giving thanks he said	giving thanks he said
Take this	Take this and
divide it amongst yourselves	divide it amongst yourselves
[18]For I say to you	[18]For I say to you
henceforth I shall not drink of	I shall not henceforth drink of
the fruit of the vine,	the fruit of the vine,
until the kingdom of God comes.	until the kingdom of God comes.
[19]And taking bread, giving	[19]And taking bread, giving
thanks he broke it, and gave it	thanks he broke it, and gave it to
to them, saying	them, saying
This is my body.	This is my body, that is given for
	you. Do this in remembrance of
	me.
	[20]And the cup likewise after
	supper, saying
	This cup is the new covenant in
	my blood,
	that is shed for you.

The shorter text (in which the Greek and Latin columns of D concur) is shared by most of the oldest Old Latin manuscripts: e a b ff[2] i l. Several of these we describe for the first time. Codex Corbeiensis (ff[2]) is manuscript from the a fifth century – perhaps from the first half[4] – which was produced in Italy. Its editor has described it as a particularly carefully transcribed text, and one that

---

[4] He does not explicitly say that it is from the first half of the century, but this is my interpretation of the evidence presented by E. A. Lowe, *Codices Latini Antiquiores: A Palaeographical Guide to Latin Manuscripts Prior to the Ninth Century. Part V, France* (Paris and Oxford, 1950, repr. Osnabrück, 1982), No. 666.

is very free from harmonisation.[5] These factors add significantly to its importance as a witness of this shorter reading. Codex Vindobonensis (i) is of a late fifth-century date. It exists now only as fragments of Mark and Luke. It is a beautifully written purple manuscript, produced 'presumably in Italy, and probably in the North'.[6] The Curetonian Syriac omits verse 20 (the Sinaitic, the other Old Syriac manuscript, contains it). The situation is complicated by the fact that several of the witnesses have a different order. The African Old Latin Codex Palatinus (e) and Italian Codex Veronensis (b) and the Curetonian Syriac have the verses in the order 16–19a–17–18–21, thus imitating the better-known sequence of bread before cup. The Sinaitic Syriac has the order 16–19–20–17–18–21, achieving the same result. The Peshitta Syriac omits verses 17 and 18, and contains verses 19b and 20.

The ℵ B text is, with sundry variants, attested by all other witnesses.

In order to understand the nature of the problem, we need to look at the various eucharistic traditions in the New Testament. We can at once set aside the Fourth Gospel, which has no institution narrative. There remain 1 Corinthians 11.23–5; Mark 14.22–5; Matthew 26.26–9. There are, inevitably, variants in them all, but nothing with as significant an effect on the sense as that in Luke. Here are the three passages in parallel, from the Revised Standard Version's text.

1 Corinthians 11.23–5	Mark 14.22–5	Matt. 26.26–9
	[22]And as they were eating,	[26]Now as they were eating,
[23]For I received from the Lord what I also delivered to you, that the Lord Jesus on the night when he was betrayed	he	Jesus
took bread,	took bread,	took bread,

---

[5] E. S. Buchanan, *The Four Gospels from the Codex Corbeiensis*, Old Latin Biblical Texts 5 (Oxford, 1907). Buchanan is perhaps over-enthusiastic in claiming that with regard to harmonisation, it 'is more free from this influence than any extant Latin or Greek manuscript' (p. vii).

[6] Lowe, *Codices Latini Antiquiores: A Palaeographical Guide to Latin Manuscripts Prior to the Ninth Century. Part III, Italy: Ancona-Novara* (Oxford, 1938, repr. Osnabrück, 1982), No. 399.

(1 Corinthians 11.23–5)	(Mark 14.22–5)	(Matthew 26.26–9)
[24]and when he had given thanks, he broke it,	and blessed, and broke it, and gave it to them,	and blessed, and broke it, and gave it to the disciples
and said,	and said, 'Take;	and said, 'Take, eat;
This is my body which is for you. Do this in remembrance of me.	this is my body.'	this is my body.'
[25]In the same way also the cup after supper,	[23]And he took a cup, and when he had given thanks he gave it to them, and they all drank of it. [24]And he said to them,	[27]And he took a cup, and when he had given thanks he gave it to them,
saying		saying
		'Drink of it, all of you;
'This cup is the new covenant in my blood.	'This is my blood of the new covenant, which is poured out for many.	[28]for this is my blood of the covenant, which is poured out for many for the forgiveness of sins.
Do this, as often as you drink it, in remembrance of me.'		
	[25]Truly, I say to you, I shall not drink of the fruit of the vine until that day when I drink it new	[29]I tell you, I shall not drink again of this fruit of the vine until that day when I drink it new with you in my Father's kingdom.'
	in the kingdom of God.'	

We now have five texts – 1 Corinthians, Mark, Matthew, and Luke twice. They divide into three groups: Matthew goes with Mark and longer Luke with 1 Corinthians, while shorter Luke stays on its own. The very fact that longer Luke seems so like 1 Corinthians should make us question it. For here, it seems, a harder short text may have been harmonised to a parallel passage. That the parallel is in a letter of Paul and not another Gospel does not matter, given the way Paul speaks of the tradition, as received from the Lord.

It is very hard to proceed in this investigation without assuming so much from the Christian tradition of the eucharist that we deprive the individual narratives of their significance. It is also difficult to approach the problem without writing a separate treatise. In order to recover the distinctive Lukan tradition with reasonable brevity, we shall just have to propose some ideas with little or no detailed evidence.

Meals feature quite largely in Luke. Jesus eats with all sorts of people, and is sometimes criticised for his indiscriminate choice of table companions (5.30). This interest in table fellowship is extended to many parables, such as that of the two sons (Chapter 15) and of the rich man and Lazarus (Chapter 16). The same emphasis is found in the early chapters of Acts, where it is a prominent feature of Luke's account of the primitive Christian community. Like Mark and Matthew, Luke tells the story of the feeding of the five thousand (he omits that of the four thousand). But, unlike Mark and Matthew, he avoids using language that makes any link between the feeding of the five thousand and the last supper. Instead, he links the feeding with the meal at Emmaus, with the sequence of actions: taking – blessing – breaking – giving (Luke 9.16; 24.30). In the following resurrection story, Jesus asks for food and they share with him a piece of fish (24.42; compare 9.13 and see below). Thus the risen Jesus maintains his tradition of table fellowship. In the early chapters of Acts, the early church preserves it in 'the breaking of bread' (the phrase also used at Luke 24.35). This phrase drops out of Luke's narrative, to reappear in the final chapters (it is found in chapters 2, 20 and 27). The shorter narrative of the last supper does not belong within this sequence. It is a rite more or less just handed over – the cup is given with the brief instruction 'Divide it among ourselves.' They are to do this 'in memory of me'. Jesus has no part in this. He will eat and drink only in the kingdom of God. There is virtually no liturgical elaboration, and above all no reference to the death of Jesus. Only in 22.28–30 does Luke unite the table fellowship of Luke–Acts with the last supper:

You are those who have continued with me in my trials; and I assign to you, as my Father assigned to me, a kingdom, that you may eat and drink at my table in my kingdom, and sit on thrones judging the twelve tribes of Israel.

Only after the parousia will the table fellowship with Jesus be restored, and it is this which the act of fellowship at the last supper anticipates.

It is in the absence of any reference to the death of Jesus that shorter Luke stands out most markedly as an original contribution. Matthew follows Mark in interpreting the institution in the light of Jesus' atoning death; longer Luke follows 1 Corinthians along a similar path. But shorter Luke rejects the Markan interpretation altogether. As we have seen repeatedly, that reading is to be preferred which avoids harmonisation. Harmonisation is primarily a matter of sense and theology, and only secondarily of wording. This leads us to conclude that shorter Luke is to be preferred. For longer Luke harmonises on two counts: in wording with 1 Corinthians, and in sense with Mark (who is here Pauline in thought).

It might be concluded that shorter Luke is undisputed champion of the field. But not so. The tide of scholarly opinion has long flowed in favour of the longer text. Verses 19b–20 were included in Nestle–Aland[25] within double brackets. They appear in the twenty-sixth and twenty-seventh editions without reservation as an integral part of the text. In the words of the editors of that edition, 'Most (though not yet all) of the exegetes under the influence of nineteenth century theories have yielded to the overwhelming evidence attesting the originality of Luke 22:19b–20 in the Gospel text, recognizing that for the presentation and perspective of the gospel of Luke it is not the "shorter", but the "longer" account of the last supper that is authentic.'[7] Whether *all* exegetes will ever yield to this inevitable progress remains to be seen. I for one have always preferred the shorter text, but more by instinct than from a thoroughly worked out argument and (because of the majority opinion) slightly shamefacedly. I am delighted that a doughty champion has now sprung to the aid of the shorter text. Its defence by Ehrman in *The Orthodox Corruption of Scripture* is brilliant. Here is overwhelming evidence for the other side.

<hr/>

[7] Alands, *Text*, p. 311.

My argument as it is presented above is as far as I had got before
Ehrman's work appeared. It may be seen that there is a point which
links our views. He starts by noting that Luke did not understand
Jesus' death as atoning. But (he goes on) such a point of view was
inadequate in the eyes of early orthodox writers, who consequently
brought Luke into line with the other texts as part of their
campaign against heresy, especially docetism. He cites two writers
in support of his case: Irenaeus and Tertullian.

But vain in every respect are they who despise the entire dispensation of
God, and disallow the salvation of the flesh ... But if this indeed do not
attain salvation, then neither did the Lord redeem us with his blood, nor is
the cup of the Eucharist the communion of his blood, nor the bread which
we break the communion of his body.[8]

[Jesus] likewise, when mentioning the cup and making the new testament
to be sealed 'in his blood', affirms the reality of his body. For no blood can
belong to a body which is not a body of flesh.[9]

Ehrman brings together other kinds of evidence in defence of the
shorter text. But it is probably this exploration of theological
reasons for the creation of the longer text that is the most important
part of his argument.

   The debate on this passage has been important methodologi-
cally, because it is one of the small group of passages in which
Westcott and Hort preferred Codex Bezae and its allies to
Vaticanus. It is an acknowledgement that internal evidence must
come first, for it is only after its readings have been scrutinised and
the value of its readings acknowledged that a manuscript is
pronounced good. That confidence in its quality is then brought to
bear upon other less certain passages. It is such a process which has
led to the restoration of the longer text. But there are two other
matters not to be forgotten. It is important to consider carefully
those readings in a manuscript which go against the grain of its
habits. Thus shorter readings in the generally expansive Codex
Bezae demand particularly thoughtful scrutiny. This point struck
Hort most forcibly. And the possibility of a group of readings

---

[8] Irenaeus, *Against Heresies* 5.2.2, cited in B. D. Ehrman, *The Orthodox Corruption of Scripture*
   (New York and Oxford, 1993), p. 197.
[9] Tertullian, *Against Marcion* 4.40, cited in Ehrman, *The Orthodox Corruption of Scripture*, p. 209.

presenting a special case is a perfectly reasonable one. It is part of the purpose of this chapter to show that the final chapters of Luke contain just such a group. Above all, it is necessary to show how, why and when the text was changed and readings introduced. It is Ehrman's contribution to have shown all that in a *tour de force* of exposition.

22.35–7

According to Epiphanius, these three verses were omitted by Marcion.

22.43–44: THE AGONY IN THE GARDEN

[43]And there appeared to him an angel from heaven, strengthening him. [44]And being in agony he prayed more earnestly; and his sweat became like great drops of blood falling down upon the ground. (RSV)

There are five texts here.

1. The words are omitted by P[69] P[75] ℵ[c] A B N R T W 0211, some minuscule manuscripts (including four members of Family 13), and Lvt (f) Syr[s] sah boh[mss] Arm[mss] Gg (I.II). P[69] is a third-century manuscript. It is one of the few papyri to contain a text with marked similarities to that found in Codex Bezae.[10] 0211 is a seventh-century representative of the Byzantine text. The symbol Gg (I.II) denominates some of the oldest materials in Georgian. This version is derived from the Armenian, and perhaps Syriac stands between the Armenian[11] and the Greek. But the version should not be dismissed because of these derivations. It is a valuable witness to early types of text (as early as the fifth century) for which there is little other evidence.[12]

---

[10] The evidence needs careful handling. See J. K. Elliott, 'Codex Bezae and the Earliest Greek Papyri', in D. C. Parker and C.-B. Amphoux (eds.), *Codex Bezae: Studies from the Lunel Colloquium, June 1994*, NTTS 22 (Leiden, 1996), pp. 161–82, pp. 169–72.

[11] See p. 125 above.

[12] See most recently J. N. Birdsall, 'The Georgian Version of the New Testament', in B. D. Ehrman and M. W. Holmes, *The Text of the New Testament in Contemporary Research: Essays on the* Status Quaestionis. *A Volume in Honor of Bruce M. Metzger*, SD 46 (Grand Rapids, 1995), pp. 173–88.

2.   The words are copied but marked with a critical sign in Δ 230 1295 1424 syr^h boh^9 ^mss. Δ is an unusual ninth-century manuscript of the Gospels, with an interlinear Latin translation. It was evidently copied by someone trained in writing Latin and not Greek. Its text is said to be Alexandrian in Mark, and Byzantine elsewhere. 1424 is the oldest (late ninth- to early tenth-century) member of a very extensive family named after it. It was claimed by Streeter as remote evidence for the Caesarean text. The group has yet to be fully studied.

3.   Verse 44 is omitted by 13* 826 (both members of Family 13).

4.   Family 13 (except 174 230) includes the passage after Matthew 26.39. This is due to the use of the verses as a lection in the Byzantine Maundy Thursday cycle, between readings from Matthew. Thus 13^c 346 828 983 1689 have verses 43–4 twice, and 13* 826 have verse 43 twice.

5.   The remaining witnesses, including ℵ* D f^1 565, contain the verses. The earliest witnesses to the passage are Justin and Irenaeus.

The support for and against is similar to that in a number of other passages, including some which we have studied, such as Mark 16.9ff., Luke 11.2–4, John 7.53–8.11. P^75 B support the shorter text. The situation is quite different from the Western non-interpolations, except that here too there is very good cause for accepting the shorter text. Again, theological moulding has been at work.[13] Perhaps the most telling indication is that the two verses are at variance with Luke's view of the events in the garden (and elsewhere in the passion), which includes excising material in the tradition which show Jesus to be other than calm and confident; material such as Mark 14.33f., that 'he began to be greatly distressed and troubled' and said 'My soul is very sorrowful, even to death.' It would thus have been possible for Luke to have been interpreted docetically, presenting a Jesus who was not a real human being suffering in both mind and body. Their references to

---

[13] The case presented is that of Ehrman. As well as *The Orthodox Corruption of Scripture*, see Ehrman and M. A. Blunkett, 'The Angel and the Agony: The Textual Problem of Luke 22:43–44', *CBQ* 45 (1983), 401–16.

the agony in the garden are made, by both Justin and Irenaeus, in order to counter just such a view. That the verses were added to Luke in order to substantiate the Gospel's orthodoxy is the best interpretation of the evidence. Their appearance in Matthew in Family 13 may be due to the influence of the Byzantine lectionary system, which formed the Gospel for Thursday in Holy Week by linking Matthew, this passage and John.

22.47

Most witnesses record that Judas drew near to Jesus in order to kiss him. But D and a number of other witnesses, principally Greek and Latin, provide a version which includes the information given by Matthew (and Mark) that the kiss was a sign indicating the person who should be arrested. The harmonisation is interesting, in that it is not simply a *verbatim* transference of the material, but a slight revision, or rather a number of independent revisions, so that Matthew's words will fit the Lukan context better.

22.49–51: THE SERVANT'S EAR

These verses are, according to Epiphanius, omitted by Marcion. Here, his activity may have left a trace in the manuscript tradition, for verse 51 is omitted by 0171. This manuscript was produced in about 300, and is thus one of the earliest extant majuscules. It is extremely fragmentary, containing only about a dozen verses each of Matthew 10 and Luke 22. Its text has been thoroughly studied, and has proved to be of considerable interest. It is described succinctly by the Alands as 'paraphrastic'.[14] Its text here moves closer to Mark, for Mark records the mutilation but not the healing.

The healing of the servant is given in slightly longer ways in D, most Old Latin witnesses and one Armenian manuscript. D has 'Stretching out his hand he touched him and his ear was restored'; Lvt (l) is the longest, reading 'Stretching out his hand he touched his right ear which had been cut off and his ear was restored.' They seem to be attempts to resolve the question whether Jesus touched the severed ear or the man's head.

---

[14] Alands, *Text*, p. 123.

22.62: PETER'S REMORSE

The verse ('And going out he wept bitterly') is omitted by 0171[vid] and the Old Latin. The abbreviation 'vid' indicates that the manuscript is fragmentary, and that its missing text has been worked out by calculating the amount of space available. There is too little space for the words 'And going out he wept bitterly' to have been present in the manuscript. This verse, identical with Matthew 26.75, was discussed in Chapter 7.[15] Without it, Luke's story of Simon Peter's denial lacks the theme of remorse. There is no obvious reason why a scribe should deliberately omit the reference, and the likelihood is that the words are a later addition from Matthew.

23.1–5: JESUS BEFORE PILATE

According to Epiphanius, Marcion added to the accusation of perverting the nation (verse 2) that Jesus had been 'destroying the law and the prophets'. This, which perfectly fits Marcion's belief of what Jesus had done, was taken into the text of some Old Latin manuscripts – e b c ff² i l q – and subsequently even into a couple of Vulgate manuscripts. The words are from Matthew 5.17, with the trifling omission of 'not'.

In verse 5, two Old Latin manuscripts provided an added complaint against Jesus:

and he turns our sons and wives away from us, for they do not baptise as we do, nor do they purify themselves (Codex Palatinus (e))

and he turns our sons and wives away from us, for he does not baptise as we do. (Codex Colbertinus (c))

This is one of a number of places where c preserves an ancient African reading. Perhaps it is no coincidence that this manuscript, copied in the twelfth century in Languedoc, an area which long resisted the incursions of the Vulgate, among Albigensians, should reproduce this text, even without its final clause.

[15] See p. 117, n. 18 above.

23.17: BARABBAS

Now he was obliged to release one man to them at the festival.

This verse is omitted by P75 A B L Π and some other witnesses, including a small number of Latin and Bohairic manuscripts. Π is a ninth-century principal witness of a group named Family Π after it. Its text is related to that found in Codex Alexandrinus. The verse is placed after verse 19 in Codex Bezae and the Old Syriac and Ethiopic versions. It is included here, with variants, by all other witnesses. The fact stated in the verse is expressed in all the other Gospels (Matthew 27.15; Mark 15.6; John 18.39), but with wording that is quite different. This variation in wording might lead one to suppose that the verse is original to Luke. But that some of the principal manuscripts omit it, while others include it elsewhere, are two points that provide a strong case for its being an addition. The fact that the wording is not identical with the synoptic parallels does not matter, for we have already come across such harmonisation in which the interpolation is adapted.

It might on the face of it appear that the story is meaningless without this clause. But Luke's narrative is complete enough without it: Pilate offers to release Jesus, but the crowd decide that, if somebody is going to be released, they would rather have Barabbas, a man whose crimes Luke highlights. The evangelist is more interested in the crowd's irrational behaviour than in the motives for Pilate's actions. Again, the shorter text is to be preferred.

THE CRUCIFIXION

A small variant in verse 32 is due to embarrassment at an unintentional implication of Luke's text. The text of P75 ℵ B reads 'Two other criminals were also led out...' All other Greek witnesses read, through a reversal of the order of two words, 'Two others, criminals, were also led out...' Lvt (l) adds at the end of the verse that their names were 'Joathas and Maggatras'. A sixteenth-seventeenth-century note in Latin in a margin of Codex Bezae reads 'The thieves crucified with Christ: Gemas on the right, Demas on the left'.

As Jesus is crucified verse 34 reads 'And Jesus said, "Father, forgive them; for they know not what they do."' This verse is omitted by P⁷⁵ ℵᶜ B D* W Θ 0124 579 1241 Lvt (a bᶜ d) Syrˢ Copˢᵃʰ Copᵇᵒʰ ᵐˢˢ. 0124 is a part of a now widely scattered Graeco-Coptic manuscript of the sixth century. Its text does not clearly belong to any major group. A little of this support is that also accorded the Western non-interpolations. (The words were added to D in the second half of the sixth century.) But the presence of P⁷⁵ ℵᶜ (the words were written but then placed within brackets by the scribe, and then reinstated by an important fifth-century corrector) B casts a quite different complexion on the problem. What are we to make of it? Probably the most obvious explanation is that its omission is a consequence of Christian anti-semitism. This is much more likely than that the verse is a piece of floating tradition which came ashore in this appropriate spot.

It is interesting to note that the presence of P⁷⁵ and B amongst the witnesses against this reading led Nestle–Aland²⁶ to print it in double brackets, while in the Western non-interpolations the longer text is printed without brackets. There is no stronger proof of the extent of the edition's dependence on particular manuscripts. But in such a matter no manuscript is necessarily proof against prejudice.

At 23.35 the words in which the passers-by describe Jesus vary. 'His Chosen One' is omitted by 047 and the African Old Latin witness Codex Palatinus (e). Otherwise the variation is in the first phrase. B reads 'if he is the Son the Christ of God, the Chosen One', and P⁷⁵ f¹³ syʰ cop have 'if this man is the Christ the Son of God, the Chosen One'; D, which puts the address into the second person, has 'if you are the Son of God, if you are Christ the Chosen One'. There are a number of other variants, but the majority of remaining witnesses read 'if this man is the Christ, God's Chosen One'. It is understandable how such a formulation may have changed according to developments in the exegetical and theological issues at stake in exegesis.

At the end of verse 37, Codex Bezae, Codex Colbertinus and the Old Syriac versions add an episode:

D   Putting a crown of thorns on him
c   Then they put a crown of thorns on him
Sy^s   And they also put on his head a crown made from thorns
Sy^c   And they put on his head a crown made from thorns.

This episode is found in the other Gospels in an earlier mocking, that by the soldiers (Mark 15.16–20 and parallels), which Luke omits. The wording is not *verbatim*, and the sequence of events is not the same. Both these facts are worth noting. The first affords a parallel with several other passages which have already been discussed in this chapter. The second is similar to the way in which the piercing of Jesus' side is inserted by some manuscripts in Matthew *before* Jesus' death, while in John the incident happens *after* it.

Beyond these illustrative points, we note – yet again – the phenomenon of harmonisation.

The words of the unrepentant thief in verse 39 are omitted totally by Codex Bezae and Codex Palatinus (Old Latin e). They are replaced in l with the words of the passers-by in Mark 15.27 (and Matthew 27.40), 'You who would destroy the temple and in three days build it, save yourself now and come down from the cross.'

At 23.44–5 a number of marvellous events are described:

there was darkness over the whole land until the ninth hour, while the sun's light failed; and the curtain of the temple was torn in two.

The Christian Palestinian Aramaic version[16] has a spectacular addition:

and the moon hid its light and the stars fell and rocks split and graves were opened and the bodies of many saints arose and were seen by many.

Cyril of Jerusalem variously records that the sun was eclipsed and that the sun was eclipsed for one hour. Codex Vaticanus reads not 'the sun was darkened', but 'the sun was eclipsed'. Although references to an eclipse sounds more scientific, a solar eclipse could not occur at the time of the full moon. One could interpret the evidence in several ways. On the principle that the harder reading is more likely to be original, one would follow B. In addition, it is

---

[16] This version has also been known as the Palestinian Syriac or as the Jerusalem Syriac. But the title used here (abbreviated as CPA) is to be preferred.

consonant with Luke's style to adopt a more sophisticated language (Matthew and Mark only record that there was darkness). On the other hand, is the impossible event of an eclipse intended to emphasise the horror of all creation at this event?

The rending of the temple veil is removed in Codex Bezae to the end of verse 46, with the wording 'And the veil of the temple was rent.' This is the order found in Matthew (27.51) and Mark (15.38). Jerome records another version of the veil story:

In the Gospel which is written in Hebrew letters, we read not 'The veil of the temple was torn' but 'the lintel of the temple, of wonderful size, was broken'.[17]

Other traditions record that a voice or voices were heard. None of these has left its mark on manuscripts of Luke.

In verse 48 two lectionary manuscripts add 'the earthquake and' after 'seeing'. At the end of the verse, several sets of words are put into the mouths of the crowd. The Old Syriac manuscripts agree in

And saying 'Woe to us! What hath befallen us? Woe to us from our sins!'

An eighth- or ninth-century manuscript of the Vulgate that preserves some Old Latin readings, and so is cited for them (under the symbol g[1]), reads

saying 'Woe to you [*sic*] for the things that have befallen you today because of our sins; for the desolation of Jerusalem has drawn near.'

THE BURIAL OF JESUS

Verse 52 in Codex Colbertinus adds that 'When Pilate heard that he had died, he glorified God and gave the body to Joseph.'

We are told (23.53) that Jesus' body was placed in a tomb that had not yet been used. This is developed in Jerome's comments. He twice states that it was a tomb 'in which nobody was laid before him or after him'.[18] The same tradition is found in Augustine of Hippo, *On the Trinity*.[19]

---

[17] Jerome, Letter 120.8.2. He records similar information in his commentary on Matthew (27.51).
[18] Jerome, Letter 48.21; *Against Jovinianus* 1.31. In both passages he is collecting evidence for the virginity of Jesus and of Mary.   [19] 4.9.

Luke, unlike Matthew and Mark, does not mention the stone over the tomb until the next story (24.2). But a number of manuscripts supply the reference here – 265^c 700 1071 2757. Further embellishment surrounds the description of the stone. In many manuscripts it is a *large* stone – U 13 16 and others, with Bohairic and Ethiopic witnesses. U is a ninth-century Byzantine manuscript. Far more dramatically, Codex Bezae records that 'placing it [the body] in it, they set against the tomb a great stone which twenty men could hardly roll away'. This tradition is supported by 0124, many Sahidic manuscripts and the Old Latin Codex Colbertinus. Its presence was first noted in D, and Rendel Harris devoted some space to its study.[20] He concluded that its origin was a Homeric cento. This was a poetic form created by the drawing together of words and phrases and lines from Homer to make new poems recording events in the Gospels. A modern example of a cento may be found in the compilation *100 Hymns for Today*. Number 47, 'Jesus, Lord, we look to thee', is a cento compiled from verses by Charles Wesley. The text in the Greek of D is a somewhat halting hexameter, owing its origin to the description of the stone which Polyphemus drew across the mouth of his cave, too large to be moved even by twenty-two stout four-wheeled carts.[21]

As the women go to the tomb in 24.1, D 0124 and some Sahidic manuscripts add from Mark (though D puts it into indirect speech) that the women ask who will roll back the stone for them.

THE RESURRECTION

24.3

And entering they did not find the body of the Lord Jesus.

The last four words are omitted by D (Greek and Latin) and six Old Latin witnesses (e a b ff^2 l r^1). These constitute the second 'Western non-interpolation'. Their character as secondary is due to the fact that they explain the sense, and that the sense is orthodox, in that

[20] J. R. Harris, *Codex Bezae: A Study of the So-called Western Text of the New Testament*, Texts and Studies 2.1 (Cambridge, 1891), pp. 47–52.   [21] *Odyssey* 9.241–2.

they stress that it was indeed the body of the Lord Jesus which had lain in the tomb.

The meaning when the verse ends at 'body' could be interpreted favourably by those who believed that the heavenly Christ had left the physical body before Jesus died. To put it differently, the additional words make it clear that, in Ehrman's phrase, the body that was placed in the tomb was also the body that left it.[22] The case that the verse was expanded to preserve Luke's orthodoxy is strong. Of course, that the meaning without the addition could be claimed as support for heresy does not mean that Luke himself had that intention in writing. He could hardly be expected to anticipate and pre-empt future debates.

There is another variant, the omission of 'the Lord'. This is supported by a few medieval Greek manuscripts (representing several different types of text), the Old Syriac, the Arabic and Persian versions of Tatian's Diatessaron, one manuscript of the Bohairic version, and the text of the sermons of a fifth-century Bishop of Ravenna, Peter Chrysologus. The support is early, certainly in the Old Syriac and also perhaps as the reading of Tatian, if the reading of the two principal eastern witnesses is deemed sufficient evidence. But the support is also widespread, both geographically and chronologically. Is this another instance of a well-known reading which has only just survived? As Ehrman points out, the phrase 'the Lord Jesus' occurs nowhere in the Gospels (except Mark 16.19!). It is used in Acts. Like the short text of D, but to a lesser degree, this reading is open to the suspicion of heterodoxy. Can one posit a three-stage development of this text, from 'And entering they did not find the body' through 'And entering they did not find the body of Jesus' to 'And entering they did not find the body of the Lord Jesus'?

24.6

He is not here, but is risen.

The omission of these words is the third Western non-interpolation. The short text is read by Codex Bezae and the same Latin

---

[22] Ehrman, *The Orthodox Corruption of Scripture*, p. 219.

witnesses as the previous one, with the support this time of a Georgian version. The words are fairly similar to Mark 16.6 'He is risen, he is not here', and to Matthew 28.6 'He is not here, for he is risen as he said.' They are not identical to either. This to some has been evidence that Luke was adapting his source. But it is only another free harmonisation. We have again to enquire what the sense of the passage is like without them. In both Matthew and Mark the words to the women are 'You seek Jesus who was crucified,' In Luke this is changed into a question: 'Why do you seek the living with the dead?' The words 'He is not here, but is risen' are redundant after the proclamation contained in the question. But again, a later writer might choose to make Luke more explicit on this vital point, by adapting a well-known phrase from the other synoptists.

Codex Colbertinus (Old Latin c) adapts the end of verse 5 and has its own text here: '"Why do you seek Jesus of Nazareth? He is risen from the dead."'

24.12

But Peter rose and ran to the tomb; stooping and looking in, he saw the linen clothes by themselves; and he went home wondering at what had happened.

The entire verse is omitted by D Lvt (e a b l r¹), the fourth Western non-interpolation. Without them, the first part of Luke's resurrection account ends in a very down-beat way. the women tell 'the apostles; but the words seemed to them an idle tale, and they did not believe them'. After what we saw of the ways in which the ending of Mark was developed, the addition of verse 12 should come as no surprise to us, emphasising as it does the different response of Peter. The verse is a summary of John 20.3–8, in which both Peter and the other disciple go to the tomb, but omitting the other disciple and concluding with Peter going home (a comparable detail is found in the Gospel of Peter[23]). The fact that it is such a brief summary again reminds us of the Long Ending of Mark, in

---

[23] 'But I, Simon Peter, and Andrew my brother took our nets and went away to the sea.' The closeness of the analogy depends on where the interpolator of Luke thought that Simon Peter lived. Presumably, as in Mark 1, it is Capernaum, and so that he went fishing would be a natural inference (Gospel of Peter 12).

which several pericopae are thus abridged. In addition, the verse contains a couple of non-Lukan features.

ON THE ROAD TO EMMAUS

The distance from Jerusalem was somewhat uncertain in the tradition. The distance of seven stadia is recorded by Codex Palatinus. One Arabic manuscript has fifty. A better-attested variation is 160 stadia (about eighteen miles), supported by ℵ K* N Θ Π Lvt (g¹) Lvg (4 mss) syr (h) (2 mss), the rest of the Arabic and the oldest Georgian versions.

The tendency to provide names for unnamed biblical figures has proved irresistible for many (as for l in the crucifixion scene).[24] The two disciples on the road are often given names in the Latin tradition: e b ff² r¹ and the late fourth-century commentator known as Ambrosiaster give, with sundry variations between them,

a village sixty stadia from Jerusalem, by name Emmaus and Cleopas.

In verse 23, the Old Syriac reads '. . . had seen a vision of angels there and we were amazed'.

IN THE UPPER ROOM
24.36

As they were saying this, Jesus himself stood among them and said to them 'Peace to you!'

This is another Western non-interpolation: 'and said to them "Peace to you!"' is omitted by D Lvt (e a b ff² l r¹). The identical words are used in John 20.19, a similar story about a resurrection appearance within doors. It should at once be noted that the verb 'said' is in the Greek a historic present, an idiom found about 150

---

[24] See B. M. Metzger, 'Names for the Nameless in the New Testament: A Study in the Growth of Christian Tradition', in *Kuriakon: Festschrift Johannes Quasten*, ed. P. Granfield and J. A. Jungmann (Münster, 1970), pp. 79–99.

times each in both Mark and John, but rarely in Luke.[25] But the main question to be asked is whether, if it were original, there could have been any motive for omitting it. There is no theological reason, so one must conclude that it was omitted accidentally. But an obvious mechanical explanation for this is lacking, and the suggestion lacks substance. The conclusion must be reached that the words are a harmonising addition from John, supplementing Luke's account.

The words are further expanded by G (a ninth-century Byzantine manuscript), P, some minuscules, some Old Latin manuscripts including Colbertinus, the Vulgate, the Peshitta, Harklean and Christian Palestinian Aramaic version and other versional and patristic evidence. In them, Jesus says 'Peace to you! It is I, do not be afraid.' The last words are closest to John 6.20.

24.40

And when he had said this, he showed them his hands and his feet.

The witnesses for the omission of these words are the same as the previous Western non-interpolation, with the added weight of both the Old Syriac manuscripts. It is hard to escape the conclusion that the words are taken from John 20.20. There are variants in both verses which obscure the issue slightly. But they do not affect the main point. Here, as in verse 6, the words are not necessary. Their purpose is found in verse 39, and they are brought from John to supplement Luke.

24.43

And taking it before them he ate.

To this a number of witnesses add (with minor variation) 'And taking what was left he gave it to them'. They are K Π* 6 13 161* and a number of other minuscules, the oldest Georgian version, the

---

[25] Only at 8.49 does Luke preserve one of Mark's historic presents. Excepting the passages 24.12 and here, which are both additions, only at 7.40; 11.37; 11.45; 13.8; 14.7; 16.29; 19.22 do manuscripts attest Luke providing one of his own. See Sir John Hawkins, *Horae Synopticae: Contributions to the Study of the Synoptic Problem* (Oxford, 1899), pp. 113–19. Only in the third of these is there no serious manuscript variation.

Curetonian Syriac, the Harklean (which, however, puts an asterisk to indicate its doubts about the words' authenticity), the Ethiopic, some Bohairic manuscripts, the Arabic, the Old Slavonic, the Old Latin witnesses aur c r¹, Augustine in his commentary on the Psalms and in a sermon, and Pseudo-Vigilius of Thapsus. The last of these is a treatise *Against Varimadus the Arian* once ascribed to the African bishop Thapsus, but now believed only to be by an unknown contemporary, and thus from Africa in the period 445–80. The addition is thus extremely ancient, and widespread. It owes its origins perhaps partly to John 21.13. But it must also be likely to be due to the need (to which we have already seen that the longer text of the Last Supper, 22.19b–20, also bears witness) to introduce eucharistic theology into Luke.

24.51

While he blessed them, he parted from them, and was carried up into heaven.

The penultimate Western non-interpolation consists of the omission of 'and was carried up into heaven'. The support for it is slightly more extensive; ℵ* D Lvt (e a b ff² l) Syrˢ Gg (I) and Pseudo-Augustine, *Letter to the Catholics about the sect of the Donatists*. The first hand of Sinaiticus may or may not be a useful witness, for this is a copyist who is prone to omit phrases by mistake. We have therefore to view such evidence with scepticism, since it does not go against the characteristics of the scribe. The words were inserted in the fifth century. The Pseudo-Augustine tract is a document written in 405 in north Africa, no longer believed certainly to have been written by Augustine himself. Gg (I) is the oldest translation of the Gospels into Georgian, a copy known as the Adysh manuscript.

The consequence of the longer text is to harmonise the ending of Luke with the beginning of Acts. It makes quite plain that Luke is describing the ascension. Again, we should pay serious attention to the possibility that this text is tidying up loose ends and ensuring that Luke's orthodoxy is complete.²⁶ With the addition, there can be no doubt about the physical ascension of Jesus. Without it, we

---

²⁶ Again, see Ehrman, *The Orthodox Corruption of Scripture*, pp. 227–32 for both this variant and the next.

have simply 'While he blessed them, he parted from them.' Read with Acts 1, this makes perfect sense. But once Luke and Acts are separated by one or more Gospels, something clearer may have been required.[27]

A different explanation has been proposed by E. J. Epp.[28] Noting that Codex Bezae omits 'he was taken up' at Acts 1.2, 'he was lifted up' at verse 9, and 'into heaven' at verse 11, he concludes that its text represents an attempt to reduce the ascension as 'an observable transfer from earth to heaven'.[29] Most recently, A. W. Zwiep has challenged Ehrman's interpretation of the evidence in Luke.[30] He claims that it is not that the Alexandrian text is an orthodox corruption, but that the shorter text is a heretical corruption. Thus he sees the same tendency at work in the D text of Luke as Epp found in its text of Acts.

We do not have to assume that the ending of Luke and beginning of Acts have to be consistently treated by the manuscripts. It might be that the Alexandrian text is emphasising the bodily ascension in Luke, and the D text avoiding it in Acts. But the debate illustrates how seriously theological issues must be taken in studying the history of the text.

24.52

And they worshipping him returned to Jerusalem with great joy.

D Lvt (a b ff² l) (r¹ is damaged here) Syrˢ and the same Pseudo-Augustine treatise omit 'worshipping him'. It is the final

---

[27] In no manuscript does Acts come directly after Luke. In only the Curetonian Syriac, the Cheltenham Catalogue (a tenth-century copy of a list of New Testament books produced in about 360) and in the Latin commentary on the Gospels wrongly ascribed to the second-century writer Theophilus of Antioch (written in Gaul in about 500) is Luke either listed or copied as the Fourth Gospel. A Coptic vocabulary suggests that such an order was also known in Egypt. See B. M. Metzger, *The Canon of the New Testament: Its Origin, Development, and Significance* (Oxford, 1987), pp. 296f. Also, I have argued that Codex Bezae was copied from a manuscript with the order Matthew–Mark–John–Luke (and from a separate copy of Acts). D. C. Parker, *Codex Bezae: An Early Christian Manuscript and its Text* (Cambridge, 1992), p. 116.

[28] 'The Ascension in the Textual Tradition of Luke–Acts', in *New Testament Textual Criticism: Its Significance for Exegesis. Essays in Honour of Bruce M. Metzger*, ed. E. J. Epp and G. D. Fee (Oxford, 1981), pp. 131–45.   [29] *Ibid.*, p. 142.

[30] 'The Text of the Ascension Narratives (Luke 24:50–53; Acts 1:1–2, 9–11)', *NTS* 42 (1996), 219–44.

western non-interpolation. We must again ask whether these words, once included, would have been likely to have been omitted. Again the answer must be in the negative, and again mechanical error is not plausible. What the words do is to place the final verse in a somewhat different light. Without them, the Gospel ends 'And they returned to Jerusalem with great joy, and were continually in the temple blessing God.' This ending, which balances the opening in the temple as Zechariah burns incense, is in line with the continuity of observance which the apostles show in the early chapters of Acts. The simple addition of a reference to the apostles worshipping Jesus changes this quite markedly, for it makes their temple observance secondary to their worship of Jesus. Such an alteration may date from a period when the continuity of earliest Christianity with Judaism had been forgotten. It might even have the same motivation as the omission of 23.34. Once again, we must distrust such a reading. Here, yet again, the shorter text is to be preferred as representing Luke's intentions.

In our investigations we have uncovered evidence in rather more than 40 verses out of the last 167 of Luke's Gospel, about a quarter of them. Some of the readings might be best described as quaint (see especially 23.53 and 24.13). In several others we can see, as in so many other places, a difficulty or an unfortunate phrase being removed (such as 22.14 and 23.32). But the sum total provides incontrovertible evidence that the text of these chapters was not fixed, and indeed continued to grow for centuries after its composition. In Codex Colbertinus we have the striking example of a thirteenth-century manuscript with a particularly distinctive (and sometimes very ancient) form of text. The authenticity of a number of these passages (the western non-interpolations and 'Father, forgive them') have been fiercely disputed in modern times. But we should not isolate these well-known and much-discussed examples from the whole trend of the preservation of these final chapters. If we recognise these expansions as a part of the way in which early Christianity continued to use Luke 22–4, then two of the objections which modern scholars have made to Westcott and Hort's support for the shorter text will be overcome. The first of these is that the support for the shorter text is small and comes from a suspect group of witnesses. But overall, every type of text provides some expansion in these chapters, be it Western, Alexandrian or Byzantine. There was a tradition of expanding the text, and all witnesses succumbed to it in one way or another. With this recognition goes the removal of the second objection, that there could be a group of readings requiring special treatment. The real group is the entire text of Luke 22–4, which requires special treatment because of the extent to which it continued to grow.[31] Within this growing text, the Western non-interpolations are a distinctive sub-group marked out particularly by its anti-docetic emphasis.

We have in these pages discussed the comparative merits of different manuscripts, and we have discussed the comparative claims to originality of competing readings. Textual critics are often divided between those who consider the quality of the manuscripts supporting a reading to be the crucial factor in determining the original text and those who consider the readings on their own intrinsic merits with little or no reference to the witnesses supporting them. In the study of the last chapters of Luke, an approach is to be advocated which begins neither with the character of the witnesses nor with the reasonableness of the readings, but with the nature of the way in which the text was passed on down the generations.

It is towards the recognition of this that the present enquiry has been moving: that, behind the various texts and groups of witnesses there may be observed a tradition that permitted and encouraged the expansion of the Lukan passion narrative. A consequence of such expansion was an erosion of Luke's distinctive, non-Markan treatment of the death of Jesus. The main reason for it was precisely that his distinctive version provided heretics with biblical support for their views.

At the same time, the Marcionite tradition provided, from the second century, an alternative abbreviated and revised Luke,

---

[31] A note on my use of words such as 'expand', 'grow' and 'develop'. Revisers and readers expand or develop a text (in addition, the word 'develop' is either transitive or intransitive); such a text grows. I do not wish to differentiate too sharply between the meanings of the word. Of course, in the precise meaning of the word a text can grow only by being expanded. It can develop by being either expanded or cut or changed. But the word 'growth' expresses something of the continuing life of the copied text.

whose very existence certainly contributed to the lack of an authoritative text, and some of whose readings found their way into codices of the four Gospels.

We are accustomed to associate legendary accretions with apocryphal Gospels. Here, we find a number appearing in canonical Luke. The Gospel story continues to grow within as well as beyond the canonical pages. We might say that Luke is not, in these early centuries, a closed book. It is open, and successive generations write on its pages.

CHAPTER 10

The development and transmission of the
Fourth Gospel

Like – but oh, how different!
William Wordsworth, 'Yes, it was the mountain Echo'

Almost all the material examined so far has been found in the Synoptic Gospels. Only the spurious story of the woman taken in adultery, whose presence in the Fourth Gospel is almost accidental, has led us into its pages. This chapter will do little to redress the balance, for its purpose is not to introduce variants but to discuss a methodological question which demands our attention. Many of the most important variants in the Fourth Gospel are small changes of vital theological significance, such as the variant 'only God' or 'only Son' at 1.18. None of these will be discussed.[1] Instead, one longer passage of little theological significance will serve as a prologue to the main question.

The story of the angel at the pool is, after the story of the adulterous woman, the most significant legendary accretion on whose inclusion the manuscripts differ. The RSV at 5.3 reads

In these lay a multitude of invalids, blind, lame, paralyzed.

To this A^c C^3 D W^s Θ Ψ 063 078 fam^1 fam^{13} and most later manuscripts, with the Latin, Peshitta and Harklean Syriac versions and some Bohairic witnesses, add (the square brackets indicate words omitted in one or more of these witnesses)

---

[1] I refer the reader again to B. D. Ehrman, *The Orthodox Corruption of Scripture* (New York and Oxford), where some of them are discussed.

waiting for the moving of the water. 4For an angel [of the Lord] went down [at certain seasons] [into the pool], and troubled the water: whoever stepped in first [after the troubling of the water] was healed of whatever disease he had.

The first hand of A and L have only verse 4, without the addition to verse 3. As the shortest text (P66 P75 ℵ B C* 0125 syrᶜ cop) stands, the man's words in verse 7 'when the water is troubled' assume what is introduced here, and what he then says ('while I am going another steps down before me') is open to expansion. The shorter addition provides basic information. The story of the angel is a fuller explanation that found its way into the text.

Thus we have two stories, the woman and the angel, which were not originally parts of the Fourth Gospel.

Before we deal with the main questions of the chapter, another small detail requires our attention. It sheds further light on the process of conjectural emendation. At John 19.29, the Revised Standard Version records that 'they put a sponge full of the vinegar on hyssop and held it to his mouth'. Hyssop is a not particularly large, bushy herb, and seems peculiarly ill-suited to this purpose. The sixteenth-century commentator Camerarius proposed that for the Greek word *hyssōpō* (hyssop), *hyssō* (javelin) should be substituted. This reading has since been found in two medieval manuscripts, 476* and 1242. However, although this reading makes far better sense, it has rarely been accepted, for two reasons, one based on external and the other on internal criteria. The first is an argument as follows: 'It is unlikely that two late manuscripts preserve the original text. Moreover, one of them has been corrected to *hyssōpō*. It is therefore far more likely that *hyssō* is an error.' There is a flaw in this argument. The two medieval manuscripts may be in error for *hyssōpō*. But it does not follow that *hyssōpō* is not therefore itself corrupt. Rather, what has been established is the fact that such an error is possible. The second reason is that it is possible to find significance in an allusion to hyssop. In Exodus 12.22, Moses instructs the elders that, when they have killed the passover lamb, they are to 'Take a bunch of hyssop and dip it in the blood which is in the basin.' The reference might therefore be an allusion to Jesus as the passover lamb. The problem is that, where a text is accorded such reverence and studied so carefully, a mystic allusion might be found in almost any error. Against such over-elaboration, the words of Bultmann bring common sense: 'It is scarcely believable that Jesus should be designated as the Passover lamb through the statement that a sponge with vinegar was stuck on a hyssop stem.'[2] Here is a conjecture which would have been accepted in such a narrative in any other kind of text. It should be accepted here.

It is a cliché of Johannine studies that while in the Synoptic Gospels the sayings of Jesus are gnomic utterances, often strung together to make a larger block, and the episodes are briefly told, in the Fourth Gospel he speaks in developed and extensive discourses and the narratives are longer and more detailed. These marked differences have led to a study of the origins of the book which look for successive stages of composition and reordering. This has sometimes led to quite complicated schemes, in which the work of one or more redactor may be determined. The work of Rudolf Bultmann is the best-known example.[3] Whatever degree of development and redaction has been discerned, two matters recur. One is that the final chapter has every sign of being a later addition to the Gospel. That its twentieth chapter is enough on its own, and that 20.30–1 provide an excellent conclusion, has long been widely agreed. The other matter is one of order, in particular of chapters 5 and 6. The view that the sequence of events is more plausible were the order of these two chapters reversed is perhaps not generally held, but is still a matter demanding serious consideration.

There is no manuscript evidence whatsoever for either the omission of Chapter 21 or the reversal in order of Chapters 5 and 6. Because of this, it is usually said that the matter is one of literary criticism and of the 'prehistory' of the text, and has no connection with textual criticism. This statement is flawed.

In Chapter 7, the practice of conjectural emendation was discussed and approved. We saw that this practice was generally applied to brief words and phrases (such as the example we have just examined from John 19.29). But we also noted, in another connection, the conjecture of Fee (developing views previously

[2] R. Bultmann, *The Gospel of John: A Commentary* (Oxford, 1971), p. 674 n. 2.
[3] Bultmann, *The Gospel of John*.

advanced) that 1 Corinthians 14.34–5 is a later addition. We might also note that a scholar named Straatman conjectured that 1 Corinthians 15.56 was an interpolation. What is the difference between removing a word on grounds of style and sense and removing a passage? There is no difference. Whether one or twenty or two hundred words are removed, the character of the act as conjectural emendation does not change. We found good stylistic and literary evidence that the story of the woman in 7.53–8.11 was not Johannine, and it is on those grounds as much as those of the manuscript witness that they are removed from the text. The evidence with regard to Chapter 21 is also stylistic. To conclude that it is therefore secondary is a conjectural emendation.

For several reasons, however, the issue has been obscured. Those who have argued for the secondary character of John 21 have argued as exegetes in commentaries or monographs and papers devoted to the issue, while editors of the Greek New Testament have turned away from conjecture and seen their task as presenting the best text they can muster on the basis of the available witnesses. In addition, the act of removing a whole chapter must be considered brave, or even rash, and so caution has played a part.

But there is no difference between conjectural emendation and literary theories about the development of the Fourth Gospel. To emend conjecturally is to decide that all surviving manuscripts are in error, and thus that earlier copies (including the autograph) must have read something else. To argue that John 21 is secondary is to argue that there once existed one or more copies of John (including the autograph) without it.

Suppose that this earlier copy was like the text reconstructed by Bultmann. Would it still be a copy of John? If we accept that it was, then Bultmann's text is of John conjecturally emended. If we consider the difference to be so great that his reconstruction gives us not John but a source of John, is this reconstruction still achieved by conjectural emendation? The answer is yes, although we would be unlikely to give it that name. For what is offered is still a text that once existed in a manuscript or manuscripts now lost, which we have recovered by scrutinising the text common to all the surviving manuscripts. We have already met this question (in Chapter 3), in the form 'When does a copy of Luke become a copy of Mark?'

Of course, it might be argued that the difference between literary critical or source theories and conjecture is the difference between earlier and final forms of the text. Thus, the final form of John includes Chapter 21, and has Chapter 6 after Chapter 5. A conjecture would make an alteration within this shape. But this distinction is to beg the question. If we recall our study of several 'Minor Agreements' in Chapter 7, and of the endings of Mark in Chapter 8, we may see that it is precisely this distinction between literary developments towards a final form and textual criticism that our enquiries are showing to be false.

If the answer given in the last paragraph seems unsatisfactory, it is because the distinction between conjectural emendation and literary reconstruction is an artificial one. It is artificial because the distinction is based on the category of written texts. But this is not the fundamental category with which we are dealing, for the written texts are only a part of the process by which the traditions about Jesus were passed on. The traditions were told and retold, written and rewritten, in oral tradition and in successive versions of texts. The adulterous woman, the angel at the pool, the lakeside breakfast are all traditions about Jesus against whose place in John a case can be made. Whether the manuscripts are unanimous or not in their opinion cannot tell us more than whether or not any of them records a divergent text; that is, whether a divergent text has been preserved in those manuscripts which have survived.

Perhaps one could look at the matter quite differently. If John once existed without Chapter 21, and later came to include both Chapter 21 and the story of the woman in 7.53–8.11, an edition which prints the one but not the other might be said to present an intermediate form of the text, since both are accretions. Would it not be more justifiable to print it either with both or without both?

But there still remain two differences between source and literary criticism on the one hand and textual criticism on the other. The first difference is that textual criticism works for the most part with hard evidence, differences between the manuscripts which really and undoubtedly (if I may use such words) exist. The study of the formation of the Fourth Gospel, by distinction, has no such hard evidence. It proceeds from what is known to what may be deduced but is unknown. Its evidence is circumstantial, not direct. Even though all that has been said is true, this difference must be important in our perceptions of the two branches of study, and the weight which we accord to their findings.[4]

The second difference follows. Source and literary criticism as they have traditionally been understood depend upon textual criticism, upon the evidence and conclusions of its pursuit. Although textual criticism has often been considered simply as a necessary preliminary to the interesting part, the picture that has emerged is that it provides the firmest (indeed the only firm) evidence for the way in which the text of the Gospels was perceived and treated in the early centuries, and that any reconstruction of what happened before the formation of the Gospels must be compatible with what can be demonstrated from the manuscripts to have happened after it.

The tools of literary and of textual criticism cannot be uniformly applied to every text. They must begin with the special character of the material and the circumstances surrounding its preservation. It is evident that the Fourth Gospel presents the tradition in a unique way. The difference in the character of the variant readings demonstrates that it was transmitted differently from the other Gospels. The point may be demonstrated by the obvious fact that there is rarely the opportunity to harmonise, and thus harmonisations are rare.

One small detail which bears this out is the unexpectedly large number of papyrus witnesses to John's Gospel which contain *hermeneiai*, lots for fortune telling (see p. 27 above). That as many as six out of the twenty-three papyrus copies contain them is unlikely to be coincidence.[5]

Perhaps its presence in the same book as the other Gospels (since

---

[4] I had written this chapter before learning of M.-E. Boismard and A. Lamouille, *Un Evangile pré-johannique* (4 vols., Paris, 1993). The authors believe that the Homilies on John by the Greek writer John Chrysostom contain evidence of a Greek text older than that represented in the manuscripts of the Gospel. This shorter text had, they believe, been preserved in Antioch. This approach is unusual, in using textual evidence to recreate an earlier literary stage of the text. It advances much further in this direction even than Ehrman's article on the story of the adulterous woman (see Chapter 6 above). The claim should be treated with caution.

[5] B. M. Metzger, 'Greek Manuscripts of John's Gospel with "Hermeneiai"', in *Text and Testimony: Essays on New Testament and Apocryphal Literature in Honour of A. F. J. Klijn*, ed. T. Baarda et al. (Kampen, 1988), pp. 162–9; see further B. Outtier, 'Les *Prosermeneiai* du Codex de Bèze', in D. C. Parker and C.-B. Amphoux (eds.), *Codex Bezae: Studies from the Lunel Colloquium, June 1994*, NTTS 22 (Leiden, 1996), pp. 74–8.

at least the third century) has led us too easily to treat it as the Fourth Gospel. That is to say, its proximity to Matthew, Mark, and Luke has led us to pay more attention to the similarities than to the differences between it and them. Certainly, all that we have found in these pages leads us to recognise that the formation of the Gospels and the manuscript copies of them is a continuum: the traditions about and surrounding the acts and sayings of Jesus. But it does not follow that one should therefore attribute precisely the same characteristics to every Gospel and to the way in which it was copied. We must not overlook the variety of types of text and traditions of copying that may exist within the continuum.

CHAPTER 11

From codex to disk

I will not allow books to prove anything.

Jane Austen, *Persuasion*

Before attempting in these final chapters to explore the positions towards which our investigations have led us, it is necessary to summarise the conclusions which have so far been reached as a result of the examination of each problem or set of problems.

In Chapter 1, a basic question was asked, whether the task of textual criticism is to recover the original text. The answer was that it may be, but does not have to be. Examples were taken from Shakespeare and Mozart, to illustrate the way in which textual criticism has changed in recent years, from assuming its role to be the recovery of a single original and authoritative text to discovering an approach which takes as its starting point the recognition of the distinctive circumstances of particular documents and types of documents, and which pays more attention to the intrinsic value of successive versions. That such a change in perception has been one of the motivations for this book need hardly be stated.

The historical survey of the material in Chapter 2 led to the discovery of one set of circumstances surrounding the documents with which we are concerned. These circumstances are the physical characteristics of the copies containing them. Although this has hardly been touched on, it is an important point for consideration in these final chapters. The central chapters addressed a number of textual problems. It was possible to approach them in different ways, and different issues arose from each. The Lord's Prayer in Matthew and Luke was found to reveal two tendencies: in the one, Luke was harmonised to Matthew; in the other, both Matthew and Luke grew independently. We scrutinised the theory that there is a single original prayer behind the independent versions of Matthew and Luke.

The sayings of Jesus on marriage and divorce afforded the opportunity to examine the use of the traditions in modern debate. Given the number of forms in which these sayings exist, the question of their value in establishing authoritative moral teaching is very sharply posed. We concluded that the early church rewrote the sayings in their attempt to make sense of them, and that a single authoritative pronouncement is irrecoverable. It follows that there is no dominical prescript on which church discipline can call as its authority.

The story of the adulterous woman highlighted the way in which traditions have authority because they are used and not because they are part of an authoritative text.

A study of several of the Minor Agreements led to the conclusion that the development of the Gospel material in the period after the activity of the evangelists does not permit the kind of scrutiny required for documentary explanations of their relationships. The attempt was made to emphasise that developing traditions are not the same as documents.

The endings of Mark's Gospel brought us on to a number of literary questions, of the way in which to provide a new ending is to rewrite a story. With Eusebius' solution to the problem of double endings we met the interesting idea that *both* are to be received.

Turning to the final chapters of Luke, we examined a significant number of passages which were added to the Gospel in order to emphasise its orthodoxy. This revision was only one part of the way in which the text, or rather the traditions which it carries, continued to grow long after the evangelist had laid down his pen.

Finally, the shortest chapter discussed the Fourth Gospel. It became clear that the distinction between literary and textual reconstructions is artificial. The continuity in the development and history of the material is not broken but preserved by the written texts.

We shall return to these several matters at various points in the closing chapters. This brief summary has simply served to recall the main points.

The conclusions which we draw from these investigations consist of two principal points. Although there is no reason why all the evidence should support the same findings, these two points may be substantiated from every chapter of this book – and could be further established with far more evidence than there has been room to present. The first point concerns the physical characteristics of the tradition which we have examined; the second, the degree and nature of the textual variation.

THE PHYSICAL CHARACTERISTICS OF THE TRADITION

The summary at the beginning of this chapter touched on the importance of the physical characteristics of the copies of a text for the way in which it is understood. This may easily be illustrated from experience. The Latin Vulgate Bible had two columns from the very beginning, and this distinctive layout has been preserved virtually throughout the English Bible tradition. Only when a version has been perceived as a radically new departure by its producers has any other format been used. Thus, Tyndale's English Testament has a single column to the page. In this, it followed the precedent set by Luther's German version.[1] But its successor, Miles Coverdale's version (1535), reverts to the familiar format.[2] The Douai New Testament has a single column (because it is *not* the Vulgate?). The New English Bible abandoned the double column layout in favour of a single column with extremely long lines, but its successor the Revised English Bible has reverted to the traditional format. We know what a traditional Bible will look like in all particulars: black leather binding with gold lettering,

---

[1] The French version of Jacques Lefèvre (1523) also imitated Luther. The reforming versions were recognisable by their appearance. The significance of this was not lost on contemporaries: 'it was common in the sixteenth century for the opponents of dangerous innovators to counter their editions by producing others which imitated them closely in appearance and even used their text, castigated and with polemical editorial matter'. M. H. Black, 'The Printed Bible', in *The Cambridge History of the Bible: The West from the Reformation to the Present Day*, ed. S. L. Greenslade (Cambridge, 1963), pp. 408–75, p. 437.

[2] Such reversion in format is often paralleled by conservatism in text (to which we shall return below). For example, the Authorised Version (two columns) contains renderings which go behind Tyndale to the Wycliffe Bible. See Gerald Hammond, 'What was the Influence of the Medieval English Bible upon the Renaissance Bible?', *Bulletin of the John Rylands Library* 77 (1995), 87–95.

double columns, small print and thin paper. Not only does the English-speaking world know the Bible by its format, it also formulates its view of the contents according to it. This has led some to believe that something different, such as bright paper covers, will encourage new readers, by this process of reasoning: some people consider the contents of the Bible to be boring; this is because it has a boring format; give it a new and contemporary appearance and layout, and they will change their view of the contents.

But the importance of the form in which a writing is embodied goes deeper than this. It is of the essence of the writing. The present chapter will attempt to demonstrate this.

Greek manuscripts of antiquity were written without spaces between words, with little punctuation, and with no universally accepted practices of accentuation.[3] The important fact that all reading consisted of speaking the text out loud is to be attributed to this. Without many useful scribal conventions, the reader needed to rely more than we do on the guidance of the spoken sound to convey the sense. In addition, the choice of words to act as signposts (in particular conjunctions and particles of various kinds) and the choice of word order were essential tools for the prose writer to convey the shape and sense of the text to the reader. If there are no full stops and no capital letters for new sentences, then a conjunction will have to serve the purpose. Moreover, the structures and balanced periods acquired through a training in rhetoric enabled the writer to shape the prose so that the reader could follow it.[4] In none of these matters are the early Christian writings different from the rest of the literature of the Hellenistic world. But the basic differences can be and are so easily forgotten that these requirements in the construction of prose are here stressed. Today we have a sophisticated set of tools of punctuation, spacing and typefaces, and our prose reflects it. We can indicate a

---

[3] The same is true, *mutatis mutandis*, of Latin manuscripts. The question mark, for example, is of ninth-century origin.

[4] The recognition of the role of rhetoric in the New Testament writings is now well established. For its place in the sixteenth century, see the introduction to my translation of Philip Melanchthon's *Scholia on Colossians*, Historic Texts and Interpreters in Biblical Scholarship (Sheffield: The Almond Press, 1989). A recent approach called Discourse Analysis pays attention to the role of marking words and word order in the text.

question by an interrogation mark rather than by wording, and stress a word with italics instead of strengthening it by its place in the sentence. In antiquity, the clarity of the author's style had to convey such nuances, so that the reader's thoughts could piece them out in spite of the imperfections of scribal convention. The physical appearance of his text on the page was a prime consideration for the writer, even though it was all that he could conceive of and the consideration was thus partly unconscious.

It has been stressed that one of the most significant features of the early Christian Gospel book was that it was a papyrus codex. The Hebrew Scriptures were copied on parchment rolls, Greek literature on rolls of papyrus. The papyrus codex, whether invented by the Christians or not, was first used by them for a class of writings. It declared the Gospels to be neither sacred text nor high literature, but something both different and impermanent. The papyrus codex was at first no more than an enlarged notebook. We have seen that the first generations valued the oral tradition above written documents. The mean format of their Gospels makes them aids to those memories. It has also been suggested that they were in a more convenient shape for Christian missionaries to carry with them.

But it cannot have been long before this serviceable but undistinguished format proved to have unexpected virtues. Anyone who has measured wall-paper in decorating a room will know of one noteworthy feature of a roll, that it can be open only at one place at a time. To find a new place requires rolling up the first. In a codex, however, you can mark the original page with your finger or a slip, and then turn up as many more as you have fingers or slips to spare. The roll was and continues perfectly adequate for reading a text. But the codex provided new opportunities for comparing texts. You could keep your place in Mark, turn to Matthew, Luke and John, and compare them with each other. Thus, although the earliest codices probably did not contain all four Gospels (our evidence on the matter is insufficient to be categorical), the codex form encouraged the bringing of them together. It should be noted in passing that scholars and scribes of antiquity did not have desks on which to spread out their work, and that the difficulties of comparing more than two books are likely to have been considerable.

Thus, the reading of one Gospel in comparison with another was facilitated and therefore encouraged by the format which had been adopted, by the physical characteristics of the copies. This profoundly influenced the way in which early Christians read and interpreted them, and no less affected the development of the text (above all in harmonisation). This in turn led to greater sophistication in the tools for comparison, most significantly with Eusebius' creation of canon tables.[5]

The introduction of the lectionary again altered the character of the text, simply by making a selection, and then by providing the passage with a predetermined theme, and placing it in a particular liturgical and theological context.

The fourth century saw further innovations. The adoption of parchment instead of papyrus as the material from which the codices were made accorded the Gospel books a stature and a permanence which were new to them.[6] The introduction of biblical majuscule as the hand in which biblical manuscripts were generally copied increased their distinctive appearance and with it their separateness. Biblical majuscule was evolved out of a high-quality book hand known to us from some impressive rolls, amongst which copies of Homer stand out, of earlier times. It had begun to be used for biblical manuscripts in the third century. But it was in the fourth that it achieved a full flowering, in such magnificent manuscripts as the Codices Sinaiticus and Vaticanus. Apart from such outstanding monuments of Christian calligraphy, the parchment codex written in biblical majuscule became the normal way in which the Gospels (or any other part of Scripture) were produced. From the fourth century on, such a book is as instantly recognisable as a Victorian family Bible.

Thus was completed the codex's transition from its innovative character and lowly status in the emergent years of Christianity to the triumph of its technology as the bearer of the canonical texts in the late fourth century. That this development is a part of the formation of the New Testament canon is evident. Writers on the history of the canon should not neglect the evolution of the codex

---

[5] Similar issues are broached from a different perspective in Frank Kermode, *The Genesis of Secrecy* (Cambridge, Mass.), with which the present approach may be compared.

[6] There are parchment codices surviving from the third century, and papyri from as late as the seventh. But the preponderance shifted in the fourth.

from notebook to work of art. For without the physical copy there is no document.

The codex, then, is a fundamental contributor to the character of the Gospels. But there is something even more fundamental. Above all, the tradition is one of manuscripts copied from other manuscripts. For the first fifteen hundred years of their transmission, this is how they were passed down. That there was no other way of doing it is not the point. The fact is not one touching externals only: it is one that defines the nature of the Gospels. For it is of the essence of a manuscript tradition that every copy is different, both unique and imperfect. It follows that while early Christianity may have come to make lists of authoritative books, there were no authoritative copies of them. One has to make a few exceptions, such as Origen's Hexaplar, a copy of the Old Testament with six versions in parallel columns. There is no evidence that it was ever copied in its entirety; it was a reference tool, deposited in the library at Caesarea. We have seen how the emergence of standard texts, the Byzantine, the Syriac Peshitta or the Latin Vulgate, attempted to establish authoritative text-types, which must be the closest thing to authoritative copies which could be achieved. But our concern is with the earliest centuries, before such texts emerged. The most remarkable thing about that period is the great diversity between the witnesses. In the second century there was very great variety, and within it very great support for the kind of text to which from later centuries Codex Bezae and the Old Latin and Old Syriac versions alone bear witness. The further back we go, the greater seems to be the degree of variation so that our earliest substantial evidence, the citations of Justin Martyr, bears almost less resemblance to any later text than that of any other writer. This degree of variation was not an unfortunate aberration on the part of second century Christianity. It was part of the way in which they copied their codices. Thus, their character as a *manuscript* tradition is integral to the nature of the Gospels.[7]

---

[7] Again, some of these matters have been broached from other angles. M. W. Holmes ('Codex Bezae as a Recension of the Gospels', in *Codex Bezae: Studies from the Lunel Colloquium, June 1994*, NTTS 22, ed. D. C. Parker and C.-B. Amphoux (Leiden, 1996), pp. 123–60) cites W. J. Ong: 'manuscripts, with their glosses or marginal comments (which often got worked into the text in subsequent copies) were in dialogue with the world outside their own borders. They remained closer to the give and take of oral expression'

The contrast with the age of printing could not be greater. The discovery that it was possible to produce hundreds of identical copies led to a new confidence in the book's authority, and with it the assumption that the identical copies represent an authoritative edition. The uniformity that is the essence of the printed book masked the difference between authoritative books and authoritative copies, so that what could not be claimed on behalf of any individual manuscript could be claimed for an edition. The cheapness and availability of the printed Bible enhanced its attractions to those who followed Tyndale in wishing every ploughboy to recite it at his horse's tail. The future was with this vision, for the influence of the English Bible on the development of our culture has been profound.

Another part of the programme of humanists and reformers was the recovery of Greek culture and of patristic theology, and again the printing press proved an invaluable ally. For a scholar like Erasmus could edit a writing or the works of an ancient writer and, when it was done, go on to another secure in the knowledge that the material which he had gathered now existed in a hundred libraries, and no longer in a few manuscripts available haphazardly. They returned to the fountainhead of western thought, and the printing press was the conduit which brought the waters to all who thirsted. We have seen that it was this search for the original that led to the printing of the Greek Testament, and applaud the aim, even if the spring proved less pure than Erasmus had hoped. But of course, the achievement was to return to the Greek, and that his choice of manuscripts was unlucky must not blind us to the value of the achievement.

However, one consequence of the age of printing has been unfortunate. The ability to produce a huge number of identical copies of the Greek New Testament led to a new concept of the text as authoritative. The difference between the text itself and the printed copy became obliterated. Previously, all copies were manuscripts which differed between each other, and each copy was

(*Orality and Literacy: The Technologising of the Word* (London and New York, 1982), p. 132, quoted by Holmes, p. 151 n. 118). Holmes' reference is in the context of an enquiry into the nature of an 'edition' in antiquity. See also, in the same collection of papers on Codex Bezae, J.-M. Marconot, 'Les marques d'oralité dans Codex Bezae' (pp. 65–73).

both accurate and at fault. But now, each copy was a totally accurate copy of the printing, and could therefore be regarded as a representative of an authoritative text. Thus the written text of Scripture acquired, especially in Protestantism from the seventeenth century, a status that conferred a power which was really that of the press on the document produced. Nowhere can this be seen more clearly than in the stubborn and idolatrous defence of the Received Text which has continued ever since its imperfections were revealed.

There is also a respect in which the printed book is well suited to preserving the text of the Gospels. We have already noted that many readings came into existence early and continued to appear in manuscripts over a long period of time. They live to a great age. The stability of the printed edition matches that longevity, both by its ability to achieve a broad geographical spread and by the far greater likelihood of survival. Only one accident befalls a manuscript for it to be lost. Several hundred have to happen for an entire printing to be lost. For example, the story of the man working on the sabbath, found in a single manuscript of about 400 and nowhere else, turns up again over a thousand years later in a printed text edited in Geneva, Beza's first edition of 1563. He found it in the manuscript when it passed into his possession, and included it as part of the New Testament.[8] Even had Codex Bezae been subsequently destroyed, the text would still be available to us in many copies. It is this stability which, with several centuries of patient work, has placed modern scholarship in the remarkable position of being the first generations to have sufficient evidence to attempt an account of the development of the Gospel text in the early centuries.

It may be this matching of characteristics which is the reason for an aspect of textual criticism which marks it off from most other departments of biblical studies. While in many areas fashions change quickly, and books and theories go out of fashion very soon, the textual critic regularly uses older books. Tischendorf's great eighth edition of the 1860s is indispensable; his edition of the very difficult palimpsest Codex Ephraemi Rescriptus (1843) has yet to be

[8] E. Bammel, 'The Cambridge Pericope: The Addition to Luke 6.4 in Codex Bezae', *NTS* 32 (1986), 404–26.

superseded. Much may be learned from the eighteenth-century editions of Mill (1707) and Wettstein (1751–2). Walton's Polyglot (1654–7) has sometimes to be consulted. Sabatier's edition of the Old Latin materials (1743) is only now being replaced gradually by the new Beuron edition. This is the smallest selection. Nineteenth-century monographs, and transcriptions and collations of all periods, continue to be of value in the discipline. The fly leaves of some copies, bearing the names of successive scholars who have used them, bear witness to this.

The adoption of the codex and the invention of printing were the two most significant developments in the history of the Gospels. We stand at the end of the second age, that of printing, and on the threshold of a third, that of the electronic text. The most obvious application of the computer to textual criticism is in the storage and retrieval of the texts of witnesses. But the more far-reaching will prove to be in the perception of the text. To describe the significance of the new kind of text when we are in the midst of discovering it is probably impossible. All that we can do is to hazard a guess at what is to come. But one advantage of this brave new world is that we can look in a new way at both the previous epochs through which the transmission of the Gospels has passed, and see them from a fresh perspective.

It is easier now to see the effect of printing on the character of the text, and to see also how different it was from the manuscript tradition. In some ways the electronic text may be more similar to the manuscript than to the printed book. For the move is again towards individuality. The student buys an electronic text, installs it on the machine, and is then able to manipulate it by changing readings, reordering the text, deleting or adding material, and storing notes. The addition of notes might be analogous to the growth of the chain of excerpts of the commentary manuscript, to the Gloss of the medieval schools, or to the notes in the translations of Luther and Tyndale. That apart, the end result of the process will be as unique as a manuscript. It will be different in that very few manuscripts were privately owned, in any age; but the personalised electronic text is private. How this will affect the concept of official texts is a matter for speculation. How will the text read in worship be influenced by the electronic text? Will there be an increasing difference between lectionary texts and private texts? We know from Chapter 2 that a separate lectionary text would not be a new phenomenon.

But in another respect this private text may be far from private. By sending it on the Internet, I could put a girdle round about the earth in considerably less than forty minutes. My privately produced text, the product of my scholarship or preconceptions or ignorance, could obtain at once as wide a currency as a printed book, and a far greater one than any manuscript.

There is another respect in which the computer may provide new life for an old form. The great polyglots are some of the crowning achievements of the first two centuries of printing. They begin with the first *printed* Greek New Testament, the Complutensian Polyglot. Volume 5, printed first in 1514, gave the New Testament in Greek and Latin. Volumes 1–4, which contained the Old Testament, in Hebrew, Greek and Latin, were printed in 1517. There followed other polyglot Bibles, including that of Antwerp. The age of the polyglot was crowned by that of Brian Walton, published in London between 1654 and 1657. The New Testament volume contained the Gospels in Greek, Latin (Vulgate, reproducing two editions), Syriac (Peshitta), Ethiopic, Arabic and Persian. Such achievements of scholarship and typography have not been rivalled since. But the ease with which one can switch between languages on a computer suggests that scholars will soon be using modern polyglottal tools.

It will be recalled that Erasmus relied for his Greek New Testament largely on a single manuscript, which he prepared for the printer with marginal notes and corrections. Only when it was deficient or plainly erroneous did he desert it. That is, he did what he might have done had he been preparing it for a scribe to make a copy for him. With the passage of time, the comparison of manuscripts led to a more sophisticated process. Today, a printed critical edition is produced by comparing the witnesses, and deciding which to follow at each point of difference. Such a text is called eclectic. The Received Text is itself of this character, for by the time that it became fixed it had been revised a number of times against a number of authorities. An example of an eclectic reading was mentioned in Chapter 5. We saw that Greeven's text of Mark

10.11f. was a combination of the versions of ℵ B C and of A Byz. I can remember being puzzled by this phenomenon when I began to study textual criticism. When I turned from reading a verse to the apparatus at the bottom of the page, I could not find a manuscript which had the text I had read. I had to piece together the constituents which had made up this form of text. Thus, there are five manuscript forms of the text read by various groups of witnesses. But what was printed is a sixth, one for whose existence there is no attestation, and which is provided on the authority of the editor. While each *half* of the saying is attested in ancient witnesses, the *two halves together* are not. It is by this selection of readings that the editor creates a text.

If this practice were detected in a manuscript tradition, we would call it conflation, and we saw that all the texts of the Gospels are to a greater or lesser extent subject to it. Thus, for example, the Byzantine text of Luke 6 was a combination of elements from both the other two texts that we examined. Throughout its history, the Gospel transmission has thus been subject to a so far endless process of presenting the materials in ever new combinations of readings. The advent of the computer offers new opportunities in this regard. The scribe and the editor of the printed book have to be content with one form of text at a time. The electronic manipulation of data is making it possible to switch between many different forms of the text in the blink of an eye. One of the main consequences of this is that the *context* of a piece of text is changed. In a roll it is the column and perhaps its neighbours; in a codex it is the open page; on the screen with several windows or – even more potently – in a search programme, the context is greatly expanded.[9]

We come back to the question of the significance of its physical form for a text's nature. I find it hard to grasp the physical nature of an electronic text, even when I am told that it consists of minute patterns of magnetism on a disk. I know that what I see on the screen is a graphic representation of data which are stored within

---

[9] More could be said upon this matter. But one of my research students is at work on this area, and I wish to leave the field clear for him. On the subject, see further R. A. Kraft, 'The Use of Computers in New Testament Textual Criticism', in B. D. Ehrman and M. W. Holmes (eds.), *The Text of the New Testament in Contemporary Research: Essays on the Status Quaestionis. A Volume in Honor of Bruce M. Metzger* (Grand Rapids, 1995), pp. 268–82.

the machine in a format of which, being a textual critic and not a computer scientist, I cannot begin to conceive, although I know that the structures which make this possible are written in a specialist language. I know also that I can almost instantly turn this ghostly text into a printed page. It is perhaps part of the distinctiveness of the electronic text that it exists in several dimensions, on screen and on disk and as hard copy. It no longer has a single mode of existence. What the significance of this will be for the Gospels has not yet emerged. But one change is a change of context. In a roll, the context was the column that was open at the time. In a codex, it is as many pages as you can mark and turn back to. In an electronic text, the power of the word search means that the context is as wide as the data base. If the Gospels are stored with the entire corpus of Greek literature, then it is possible to find every occurrence of such and such a word or phrase in the Gospels and everywhere else. In another data base, containing only some types of literature, the context would be different. Even more significantly, the relationship between the Gospels themselves is different, for they can be manipulated and compared in new ways. We do not yet know to what developments this will give rise.

At present, there is one feature of the publishing of electronic texts that affords a very precise comparison with the early years of the printing press. Erasmus printed a Greek Testament, but his text was of poor quality. Many electronic texts are available which are taken from poor editions, very frequently with no indication of the edition presented. One sees advertisements for Latin Bibles and Greek Bibles with no indication *which* Bible is being offered. And, at present, one is more likely than not to get the text without the variant readings at the bottom of the page. The painful experiences of the early critical period will be repeated, unless some care is taken.

Regarding electronic texts, another matter should be remembered. Both manuscript and printed books are not only seen, but also handled. Fine parchment and high-quality paper, leather bindings and tooling are to be felt. The electronic text is present to the reader behind a barrier. While the writer is closer to the text because of the ease with which it can be manipulated, to the user it is remote, accessible only at a remove by the use of the keyboard. A book may be kissed as a relic or held aloft as the Gospel or sworn upon as something sacrosanct. It is hard to see such use ever being made of a diskette.

In one further respect the physical format of the copy has been of very great significance in the development of the role of the Gospels in the church. It is the matter of contents. A book in the older sense of the word is a division of a work. Thus, Homer's *Odyssey* is divided into twenty-four books,[10] Milton's *Paradise Lost* into twelve, and so on. The book was originally the convenient length of a roll (Latin *volumen*, hence our word 'volume'; the 'three-volume novel' was for long the convenient division into small volumes of books that today make, more often than not, unexceptionable paperbacks). The roll no more has a maximum length than a piece of string has, but it is more convenient in some lengths than others, and thirty-five feet is generally said to be the upper limit.[11] (Of course, the other variables of the height of the roll and the size of the writing are significant in determining the amount of text one could get into a roll.) It is also generally said (I have not checked it) that the Gospel of Luke, the longest of the four (and the longest book in the New Testament) would fill a roll. A codex, however, could contain more. In fact, from the third century onwards it was possible to read all four Gospels in a single codex. One might assume that the next stage would have been the extension of this to the entire New Testament or even the entire Bible. But – and this is the important point – complete Greek Bibles, even complete New Testaments, were very rare. We saw that Constantine commissioned a set of fifty Bibles. Only four such copies exist from antiquity: Sinaiticus, Alexandrinus, Vaticanus and Ephraemi Rescriptus. Of course, they were not produced as one *volume* in our sense of the word, but several matching volumes.[12] Copies of the complete New Testament are also surprisingly rare. There are fifty-seven catalogued, all of them minuscules; and a further one majuscule (Ψ 044) and

[10] The precise antiquity of this division is disputed.

[11] F. G. Kenyon, 'Book Division in Greek and Latin Literature', in *William Warner Bishop, A Tribute*, ed. H. M. Lydenberg and A. Keogh (New Haven, 1941), pp. 63–75.

[12] These manuscripts are in fact inconsistent in the books which they contain: Sinaiticus includes the Shepherd of Hermas and the Epistle of Barnabas in its New Testament; Vaticanus (presumably in error) omits the books of Maccabees (also, its final leaves are missing, so we cannot be certain of what it contained at the end).

147 minuscules have everything but Revelation.[13] This is a small proportion of the total. It has to be concluded that a complete New Testament was a rarity in every age of the manuscript period of textual transmission. Yet from the beginning the printed Greek New Testament contained all the books recognised as canonical in Greek and Latin Christendom. The main influence here is the medieval Latin Bible, where the whole was included in a small volume. That a Greek New Testament contains what it does is so natural to us that we need to be particularly careful to remember how much more a theoretical than a real entity the Greek New Testament was, until the invention of printing. It was far more a creation of northern European medieval and Renaissance technology than it was of early Christian thought. The overwhelming popularity of the complete vernacular Bible is even more evidently a modern phenomenon. The main point to which I wish to draw attention is that the canon in the form that we know it is the product of technological development. The manuscript tradition of the Gospels, when once it had become the custom to copy them together, generally copied them as a separate codex from other canonical texts.

It remains to be seen how the electronic text will affect our concept of the canon. All that is certain is that it will demonstrate how little canonicity is a 'given'.

The Gospel texts can be properly understood only by recognising the significance of the medium in which they are transmitted. We thus conclude this section with the beginning. Their origins and early transmission were as manuscript copies. It is with the physical reality of their existence that our interpretation of them must reckon. A part of this reality consists of the slow developments and endless variety of the successive copyings of manuscripts. It is to this that we now turn.

THE TEXTUAL VARIATION

The most obvious fact to be gathered from the preceding chapters is of the greatest importance: that there is extensive variation

---

[13] These and further statistics are in Alands, *Text*, pp. 78f. Some of the manuscripts containing all the New Testament are copied by more than one scribe. It may be that they are separate manuscripts that were bound together at a later date.

between the manuscripts. We have seen repeatedly that, while readers of the Gospels have got used to the idea that there are differences between them, they have largely overlooked the fact that there are often as great, if not greater, variations between the manuscript copies of each Gospel. The text of the Gospels is not rigidly fixed. It would be better to say that the tradition of the deeds and sayings of Jesus is not rigidly fixed. This may be demonstrated in two ways: the general degree of variation, and the existence of free texts. The general degree of variation consists not in a statistical proportion, but in the number of *significant* places where the wording of an account or a saying varies. Of course, the argument from statistics is double-edged. If one is arguing to discount the significance of the number of variant readings in a text, then that there are any at all will remain embarrassing.[14] The security of the dominical material has often been defended by the evidence that the seven major editions from Tischendorf's last (1872) to the twenty-fifth of Nestle–Aland (1963)[15] agree in the wording of 62.9 per cent of the verses of the New Testament. Note that this is *not* the same as saying that they agree in 62.9 per cent of the wording of the New Testament. The proportion ranges from 45.1 per cent in Mark to 81.4 per cent in 2 Timothy. The figures for the Gospels are shown in the first of the two tables.

	Total number of verses	Variant-free verses	Percentage
Matthew	1071	642	59.9
Mark	678	306	45.1
Luke	1151	658	57.2
John	869	450	51.8

This is also expressed in the second table by the number of variants in these seven major editions on each page of the twenty-fifth edition of the Nestle text:

[14] Fredson Bowers, *Textual and Literary Criticism* (Cambridge, 1966), p. 2.
[15] The others are Westcott and Hort, von Soden, Vogels, Merk, and Bover. For bibliographical references, see Alands, *Text*, Chapter 1. The statistical information is derived from Tables 1 and 2 (pp. 29f.).

	Total variants	Variants per page
Matthew	567	6.8
Mark	556	10.3
Luke	637	6.9
John	567	8.5

This represents *something* of a consensus, but it should be realised that, especially in the last half-century, there has been a steady change in thinking which means that the twenty-sixth edition of Nestle–Aland is different from its predecessor in over five hundred places. We are still catching up with the task of collecting, never mind evaluating, the evidence that has been gathered in this century. But it is not the amount of variation that is most significant, although even that is greater than has sometimes been allowed. It is the significance of the difference in the passages where the witnesses differ. We have seen that the addition of a dozen verses at the end of Mark is to rewrite the previous sixteen chapters, that the words of Jesus on divorce are written down in many different forms, and so on. If the degree of variation which we have found were to exist even in only one of the passages we have studied, the matter would require a serious evaluation of the nature of the tradition. Moreover, we have seen that it is often in important and difficult sayings and ideas that the differences occur, rather than in less significant narrative sections.

Comparison with other traditions makes the point even clearer. The Masoretic Text of the Hebrew Scriptures preserves the sacred writings with extraordinary accuracy. Such variation as there is within it is confined to small, generally orthographic details. The tradition is accompanied with much information about the numbers of words, mid-points of books, and other precise details which insist upon total accuracy. And the very activity of the scribe is also set by rules. Most strikingly, the permissible number of mistakes is clearly set out. If the scribe should write a higher number of errors, then the page must be scrapped and a new start must be made. This point must stand, even though the study of the Samaritan Pentateuch, and the recovery of much older materials from Qumran, which not infrequently agree with the Septuagint against the Masoretic Text, have shown that there was more than one type of text in earlier times. The significant fact is that the Masoretic Text, once it emerged, did not change.

The text of the Koran, while it contained variation in its earliest stages, was quickly regularised, and any copy divergent from the norm was destroyed.

The example of the Masoretic Text shows that, where a totally reliable manuscript tradition is required, human beings have the capacity to achieve it. The fact that the New Testament text has so much variation cannot therefore be due to incapacity.

The comparison with the Koran is also instructive. Because of Christianity's quite different relationship to the state in the first centuries, there was nobody in the earliest centuries who was in a position to impose uniformity on the text. From the fourth century on, we see the emergence of controlled texts in different regions – for example, the Greek Byzantine text, the Syriac Peshitta, the Coptic Bohairic and the Latin Vulgate. But there was never an ecumenical norm. And, even before many Greek manuscripts had been discovered, the comparison of the versions led scholars to recognise the diversity of texts in use in Christendom. The great polyglots of the sixteenth and seventeenth centuries provided the material for this discovery. As has been said, Walton printed the Gospels in Syriac, Ethiopic, Arabic and Persian. The Gothic and Bohairic versions first became known through the Greek Testament of Fell (Oxford, 1675).

We learn from the analogy of the Masoretic Text that it is not impossible for a manuscript tradition to be fixed, preserving itself with almost perfect accuracy. But the early transmission of the Gospels shows not only no such accuracy, but no attempt to achieve it. Fidelity in copying does not depend upon whether copyists are able to attain high levels of accuracy, but whether they attempt it. This comparison brings to mind the debate about the reliability of the earliest traditions, which were oral. It is often argued that, in a culture in which oral tradition was more significant, the memories of Jesus' hearers will have been better prepared to retain his words with perfect accuracy. This may or may not be the case. But the more important question than whether they could is whether they *tried* to remember them with perfect accuracy. The variation between the Gospels answers the question with regard to the earliest oral tradition, and the variation between the manuscripts with regard to the written tradition. If we accept that it was possible in that culture to remember more accurately, and that it was possible to transcribe with a very high degree of accuracy, the evidence that early Christians at least sometimes did neither gains in significance.

It is thus possible to show, by comparison with other traditions, what kind of text that of the Gospels is not. It is harder to find a suitable language to describe what it is. The terminology which I adopt here is to characterise the text of the Gospels as a free, or perhaps as a living, text.

I have regularly referred to the difficulties and intriguing problems of the second-century text. This period has long been known to have been one of great significance. It has even been argued that almost all important deliberate variations in copying were first made before the year 200.[16] Even though this is an overstatement, there is no doubt that just as the traditions reached a high degree of variation in the first generation, so the written tradition was at its most fluid in the first century of its existence. There are analogies for this in other textual traditions. We have seen that the variation in the ending of Mark, in the story of the adulterous woman and in other passages came into existence at a very early period.

The first attempt to establish a controlled text of which we know is the early Alexandrian text of P75, from about the last decade of the second century. Everything which we know about the earlier period suggests that, whatever desire to control the text there might have been, there was little opportunity for individuals or groups to enforce it. It was only with the emergence of powerful church leaders from the fourth century that standard texts began to emerge. And, as we have seen, the success of all of these was local. Thus, it was long before the text of the Gospels lost its initial freedom. This book has illustrated that freedom with regard to a number of passages. No manuscript of significance is untouched by it. Attention to individual units of variation can mask that fact. The words in the Revised Standard Version 'Some ancient witnesses...' conceal from the reader the vital information whether

---

[16] This was the view of G. D. Kilpatrick.

these are the same or different each time. There is a contemporary move in textual criticism to put the variants back together again in order to discover the shape of the story within each witness. Again, it is not the amount of variation which matters, for a number of small changes may shape an entire passage or even book.[17] But we are not speaking only of small changes. That there was a free text is best illustrated by Codex Bezae. This manuscript contains unique readings on every page. Significant features of its text of the Gospels, many of which we have already noted, include extensive harmonisation (in all there are over 1,200 examples), the introduction of material about Jesus from elsewhere, and a tendency to rewrite or to alter the text, frequently in a more colloquial style. The evidence is presented in Chapter 3 and elsewhere, and need not be repeated. The same characteristics may be found in its text of Acts, which is considerably longer than that generally known, and contains extensive rewritings of passages, to the extent that we have what could be described as a separate version of Acts.[18] This text is even willing to change the content of the apostolic decree of Acts 15: it omits the reference to what is strangled, adding 'and that whatsoever they would not should be done to them ye do not to others' (Acts 15.20). This free version developed by stages, which can be at least partially reconstructed.[19] In recent years, it has been demonstrated that Codex Bezae everywhere presents a separate version. Its text of Matthew is the most secure, but even it has been shown to be a careful revision.[20]

A minority of scholars have maintained that Codex Bezae is not a free text, but the oldest and most authentic form. Others have argued that it *sometimes* presents the best text. Whichever of these

---

[17] We may recall the example of *King Lear* from Chapter 1. I cite again the words written by the editors in explaining their decision: 'It is not simply that the 1608 quarto lacks over 100 lines that are in the Folio, or that the Folio lacks close on 100 lines that are in the Quarto, or... It is rather that the sum total of these differences amounts, in this play, to a substantial shift in the presentation and interpretation of the underlying action... We believe, in short, that there are two distinct plays of *King Lear*, not merely two different texts of the same play' (William Shakespeare, *The Complete Works*, general editors Stanley Wells and Gary Taylor (Oxford, 1986), p. xxxv). That copies of the First Folio differ from one another is a further problem. I refer to it here, because it illustrates a problematical aspect of the transition from manuscript to printed copy.

[18] It has been translated by J. M. Wilson, *The Acts of the Apostles Translated from the Codex Bezae* (London, 1924 (1923)).   [19] See D. C. Parker in *Codex Bezae*.

[20] Holmes, 'Codex Bezae as a Recension of the Gospels'.

positions is correct, the present argument is unaffected. For the fact stands that sharply divergent texts survive.

Although it has sometimes been claimed that the free-text form of Codex Bezae is of a late date – the work of the manuscript's scribe, or of 'an outstanding early theologian of the third/fourth century'[21] – there is substantial evidence that it is as old as the second century. The evidence most perplexing to those who believe that the Alexandrian text is the best, and to those who continue to favour the Byzantine form, is that the second-century materials available to us show no knowledge of either. It is with such texts as Codex Bezae, the Old Syriac and some Old Latin witnesses – all those considered most aberrant by later standards – that second-century witnesses concur most regularly. The reconstruction which emerges from current study is that the text represented by Codex Bezae was formed in Rome in about the middle of the second century. Few would have confidence in tracing it further back, although C.-B. Amphoux has argued that this text came into being in Smyrna in approximately 120.[22] Be that as it may, the age of the text of which Codex Bezae is a later representative is important, for the following reason: the study of this ancient text has generally focussed on a single question, what is its claim to be original? There is, however, another question which must be asked: does this remarkably free text preserve the earliest Christian attitude to the tradition? That is, does its freedom reveal that it preserves the spirit of the primitive use of Jesus' words, precisely because the letter has been altered? If that is the case, then the quest for a single authoritative text is in itself a distortion of the tradition. But this is to anticipate the final chapter.

[21] Alands, *Text*, p. 69.
[22] See pp. 205–6 below. Although there is no evidence to contradict it, I have also yet to see any evidence to support this thesis.

CHAPTER 12

The living text

To me the charters are Jesus Christ, the inviolable charter is
his cross, and death, and resurrection, and the faith which is
through him;– in these I desire to be justified by your prayers.
                              Ignatius, *To the Philadelphians* 8.3

Man's need to write books is a great injury; it is a violation of
the Spirit compelled by necessity, and is not the way of the
New Testament.
      Martin Luther, *Sermon on the Gospel for the Feast of the Epiphany*

In the previous chapter, two facts were stressed: that the Gospel
texts exist only as a manuscript tradition, and that from the
beginning the text grew freely. It is from these facts that all
questions of interpretation and all theological formulations must
start. Concepts of biblical inspiration, or any other doctrinal
formulations, which fail to take account of these two key facts are
based on *a priori* theorising or prejudice, and not on the actual
character of the writings. An attempt will be made in this final
chapter to explore some of these matters. We begin where the
previous chapter ended.

SCRIPTURE AND TRADITION

The interest and significance of the second century cannot be too
highly stressed. One development within it attracts our attention
here. Papias, early in the century, is actually cited by Eusebius as
preferring oral to written traditions about Jesus: 'I supposed that
things out of books did not profit me so much as the utterances of a
voice *which liveth and abideth.*'[1] In such a context, it is unlikely that

---

[1] Eusebius, *History of the Church* 3.39. See J. Stevenson, *A New Eusebius*, revised edition
(London, 1987), p. 47.

written texts can have been free from alterations or additions from trusted oral sources. For example, may not a saying received at one remove from an eye-witness have been more highly estimated than the version of Luke, whose authorities were, as he himself confesses, other written accounts? But we must recognise that, regardless of whether Papias preferred oral or written tradition, what he wanted was *tradition*. This tradition was handed down in several ways, and in the handing down was retold and rewritten. The texts did not have an existence independent of scribal activity, and their use in the churches. In the beginning there were traditions about Jesus. Then there were Gospels, a part of these streams of tradition. Later still, four Gospels were placed together, and the question of the accuracy of the traditions became subordinate to the claim for the authority of the writings. Yet, even then, the character of all manuscript copying meant that there was a continuing interplay between the Scripture – the text copied – and the tradition – the person engaged in the process of copying in and for the church. That is, we have a double interaction of Scripture and tradition in the copying: the one arising out of the fluidity of the early period, the other out of the inevitably provisional character of all manuscript copies.

Then there came printed texts. Here we have a claim for authority made on behalf of texts that, instead of being provisional (unique attempts to copy a text in the knowledge that the result will be imperfect), can be reproduced exactly thousands or millions of times.

A point follows from this, one which is necessary if we are to understand the character of a manuscript as opposed to a printed tradition. There is a sense in which there is no such thing as either the New Testament or the Gospels. What is available to us is a number of reconstructions of some or all of the documents classified as belonging to the New Testament – some of these reconstructions are manuscripts, say P[75] or Codex Vaticanus; others are printed texts like Nestle–Aland. Textual criticism makes it clear that the text is in a sense inaccessible to us. The fact that the recovery of the original text is a task that remains beyond all of us sets a question mark against any claim that we can in any sense 'possess' the text – literally or metaphorically.

We have several times in the preceding pages discussed the difference between the study of the variation between the manuscripts (textual criticism) and the study of the earliest written stages of the Gospel traditions (source criticism). The conclusion towards which we are drawing is that modern scholarship has placed too much significance on the compilation of the four Gospels as a final stage in the growth of the traditions. According to the predominant view, the literary activity of the evangelists marked an end to the fluidity which had hitherto characterised the traditions about Jesus. The reconstruction which has emerged from the present study is that the text and with it the traditions remained fluid for centuries, and that the work of the evangelists did not end when they laid down their pens. This may be demonstrated most clearly from the phenomenon of harmonisation.

Harmonisation has often been regarded as a levelling process by which the differences between the separate Gospels are removed, a process in which much of the evangelists' individuality and colour is lost. It has become increasingly clear to me that this is only a part of the process. In examining the last chapters of Luke, I am struck by the creativity of many harmonisations: either the wording is altered (as in the use of 1 Corinthians in 22.19b–20) or the added material is put into a different place (as in the crowning with thorns). That is to say, harmonisers used the evangelists with the same degree of freedom as Matthew and Luke had used Mark. They reword and reorder the material. That such harmonisations are found centuries after the compilation of the Gospels is incontrovertible evidence that the traditions continued to live, that is, to grow.

The same process can even be seen at work in later processes of copying. It is quite rare to be able to demonstrate that two manuscripts are related as exemplar and copy. In the two instances which I have examined and tried to prove, the text copied has not been precisely preserved, and I could not find any rationale for the changes that were made by the copyist.[2]

The most radical contemporary approach to the formation of

[2] D. C. Parker, 'A Copy of the Codex Mediolanensis', *JTS* N.S. 41 (1990), 537–41; pp. 172f. of *Codex Bezae: Studies from the Lunel Colloquium, June 1994*, NTTS 22, ed. D. C. Parker and C.-B. Amphoux (Leiden, 1996).

the Gospels is that of C.-B. Amphoux. He has argued that only in about 120, in Smyrna, were the mass of traditions that originated with and about Jesus first set out in the form in which we know them, as the four Gospels Matthew, Mark, Luke and John. Only then did the Gospels come into existence. This is the oldest text form of which we know. Its chief surviving representative is Codex Bezae. This text went through various developments at Rome in the course of the second century, including the activities of Marcion. The Alexandrian text of P75 was formed out of those Roman materials. Let us ignore for a moment the historical questions which might be asked of this reconstruction, and concentrate on the theory which it represents. At a stroke, all the various edifices of source criticism have been swept away, and the distinction between it and textual criticism redefined. The principal creative literary stage has been moved later in time by fifty or more years. And *all* the surviving texts have been shown to be artificial creations. There is less point in looking for an original text, for even the oldest is quite a late formation. Moreover, the different text-types were formed to serve quite different purposes. It is the logical outcome of this that Amphoux's project of editing the text of Mark's Gospel provides not a single text with other witnesses given as variants, but a number of major witnesses in full, each on its own line.[3]

To draw all these points together: the traditions about Jesus flow through the early church. The writing of Gospels by their evangelists represents certain confluences in the stream, ones which are not directly available to us. We might better think of them as stars in the expanding universe of early Christianity. The copyings of these texts represent further confluences (or stars), of which a few have survived. To a greater or lesser extent, they make the Gospels available to us. Then there are printed texts, more

---

[3] For further views regarding changing perceptions of the goal of the discipline, see B. Aland and J. Delobel (eds.), *New Testament Textual Criticism, Exegesis and Early Church History: A Discussion of Methods*, Contributions to Biblical Exegesis and Theology 7 (Kampen, 1994). For an account of the past century of textual criticism, which illustrates how the discipline has developed, see J. N. Birdsall, 'The Recent History of New Testament Textual Criticism (from WESTCOTT and HORT, 1881, to the present)', in *Aufstieg und Niedergang der römischen Welt*, Part II: *Principat*, Vol. XXVI, Section 1, *Religion (Vorkonstantinisches Christentum: Neues Testament (Sachthemen))* (Berlin and New York, 1992), pp. 99–197. See also my 'The Development of Textual Criticism since B. H. Streeter', *NTS* 24 (1977), 149–62.

authoritative and persuasively authentic forms of the tradition. All are the traditions about Jesus. In no sense may the Gospels be regarded as independent of the traditions. They convey part of the early tradition, and are transmitted to us only by and as tradition. In fact, Scripture is tradition.

J. Neville Birdsall has suggested an approach without the distinction:

> if we must cope, pending more satisfactory resolution, with a text containing many variations, some unresolved, in what position are we in our use of scripture in theology, and in the life of the church? I suggest that a way forward is to treat our knowledge of scripture as knowledge of scripture within the church, and not only as a foundation document separate from the church. The variations will then be treated as themselves part of the scripture, showing us not only the original, but the church's understanding of it.[4]

This position is not incompatible with the one proposed in this chapter. There are two differences. One is that, if we speak of manuscripts rather than of variant readings, we find that the variations consist not of discrete items, but of unique copies. The other is that I suggest that, metaphorically as well as literally, we find the original text in the variations.

THE MANUSCRIPT GOSPELS

That the Gospels in their earliest form exist only as manuscripts, as individual representations of ink on papyrus or parchment, was described as their embodiment. The word 'embodiment' could be misleading. It is not used so as to refer to some kind of prior, higher or ideal existence of the text apart from its physical existence as manuscript. If this sense of the word has any use here, it is certainly not the text which has an independent existence. For the very idea of book has no meaning without the physical reality. To determine to write a book is to begin to make marks on sheets of material, the end being a pile of such sheets fixed together. The word 'embodiment' is used, because it expresses the writer's intention in taking ideas and oral traditions and preaching and turning it all into a solid, physical body.

[4] J. N. Birdsall, *Textual Criticism and New Testament Studies: An Inaugural Lecture delivered in the University of Birmingham on 10 May 1984* (Birmingham, 1984).

The early Christian Gospels exist for us only as a pile of manuscripts (in which we include the manuscripts used by fathers in their citations). The ultimate (and sometimes the only) purpose of textual criticism has been perceived to be the use of this ever-growing pile to recover the original texts of the four evangelists. In one respect this is evidently justifiable. The surviving manuscripts constitute the minutest fraction of those that ever existed, and we have no extensive remains older than the end of the second century. The attempt to discern earlier forms of text, from which those known to us are descended, is an essential task in the critical study of Christian origins.

It does not follow that it is also necessary to recover a single original text. We have seen that the process of choosing readings in the attempt to recover an original text leads to the creation of new text forms. The problem with this approach was formulated by the example of Mark 10.11f. We studied five forms of these verses, which were all created out of particular settings in the early church. The sixth, formed by the fusion of two halves into a new whole, has to be justified by proposing a credible context for it in early Christianity.[5] The difference is that we *know* that the other sayings existed, and that their differences are a testimony to the ways in which the church interpreted the tradition.

The quest for a single original text of the Gospels is driven by the same forces that have sought a single original saying of Jesus behind the different texts of different Gospels. Both quests are dubious. We found several ways in which the concerns and formulations of the sayings on divorce differed. In particular, the purpose and context of Matthew 5.32 was very different from those of Mark 10.11f. It is common to solve such problems by ascribing such differences to redaction. But there are other solutions. Why should not Jesus have addressed both of these related issues in different and perhaps contradictory ways? Why should he not have expressed different ideas at different times? On what grounds could one deny the possibility of this? Would it not be doctrinaire to do so? To suggest that differences between sayings as they are recorded in different Gospels may have arisen out of his speaking

[5] I leave aside the question whether such a fusion should be regarded as conjectural emendation.

on the subject more than once has often been a piece of apologetic, designed to show that the divinely inspired Gospels are not inconsistent. But this is certainly not our purpose here. For, whether Jesus spoke on divorce once or twice, or four times (once for each episode in the Gospels), whether he delivered one way of praying to the disciples or two, the problem is not resolved. For we have more than two versions of the Lord's Prayer, and not four but twenty different sayings on divorce. It must be stressed that the problem is not a new one. We have seen both Origen (in Chapter 4) and Eusebius (in Chapter 8) struggling with it. It is a problem that is integral to the tradition, and one (again witness Mark 16) of which the copyists were aware.

Is the tradition of Jesus' sayings on divorce best understood by attempting to recover a single original text of each of the four passages, and then from those four a single original saying of Jesus? Or is it best understood by recognising the role of all the text forms as interpretations of the tradition? With the distinction between Scripture and tradition removed, the way is open to advocate the latter. We saw that at Matthew 19 Duplacy considered the original text to be irretrievable. That is a telling point. But the question is not whether we *can* recover it, but why we want to. There is an analogy with the debate whether the earliest Christians were *able* to pass on accurately the traditions (specifically, the teaching of Jesus). The existence of the free-text form shows that the real question is why they chose *not* to.

Expressed most starkly, the issue is whether the attempt to recover a single original text is consonant with the character of the free-manuscript tradition, or whether it is driven by external demands: in particular, those of the churches for authoritative texts (see Chapters 5 and 6) and of scholars for a sure foundation on which to build their theories (see Chapter 7). Our analysis of the material can leave no doubt in the matter.

It is important at this point to emphasise that the manuscripts are not only transmitters of the tradition. They *are* the tradition. Or rather, they are a part of the tradition. There are two things to be said here.

First, we are rejecting the idea that there is a greater reality *behind* what we have. Manuscripts do not carry a tradition. They *are* that tradition, for the text has no existence apart from those copies in which it exists. The only distinction necessary to be recognised is that there is a difference between the copies in which it now exists and those in which it has existed at various times in the past. It might be objected against my argument that there is a greater reality, and that it consists in those copies in which the tradition once existed in its earliest form. There are good reasons why those earliest copies are of particular interest to us. But the situation is complicated by the fact that attitudes have changed so frequently since Mark put pen to paper, and that these attitudes have – of course! – affected the tradition itself. We live at our place in the development of the tradition, and are dependent on those who threw away or copied and then threw away the materials that had come to them. We have done our best to free ourselves from this dependence, by diligently seeking out the copies they had thrown away. But we cannot escape some measure of it. But even more significant than this historical position is the fact that as written documents, the Gospels now exist only in those forms in which they are known to us. Our business is with making sense of these materials which we have received, documents produced and preserved within the church. Part of that task is to produce hypotheses about lost copies. But the written tradition survives only in the written copies that still exist. That is all the written tradition available to us.

Second, written tradition is only a part of the tradition. The oral tradition is often seen as ending at some point in the early church, so that we today are wholly dependent on the written text. But it is not so. One should think instead of an oral tradition extending unbroken from the lips and actions of Jesus, since people have never stopped talking about the things he said and did. Sometimes the oral tradition has been influenced by the written tradition, and sometimes the influence has been in the opposite direction. The written and oral tradition have accompanied, affected and followed one another.

It is as the written tradition which has survived and as the oral tradition which we have received that the tradition lives. The surviving manuscripts and the spoken word are not simply bearers of some prior living tradition. They are the living tradition. The studies of this book have made clear to me that we think, write and talk as inheritors of this tangled written and oral tradition. We cannot empty our minds at will, and form an image of Jesus only out of the materials which we select. Even if only one or none of the forms of the Lord's Prayer is original, we cannot rid ourselves of knowing all of them. Be the story of the adulterous woman never so late, it has had its influence upon our image of Jesus. We may reject material, but we cannot rid ourselves of the knowledge of it. This applies not only to textual criticism, but to all studies of the historical Jesus. However many sayings we may reject, we cannot undo the influence they have had in our minds on the sayings which we preserve as authentic.

It may seem that the argument is moving towards the conclusion that the quest for the earliest forms of the text is worthless. But it is not, because the attempt to recover early text forms is a necessary part of that reconstruction of the history of the text without which, as this book has been at some pains to demonstrate, nothing can be understood. But, even if very ancient, even the original texts, could be recovered or reconstructed, the ambiguity of the definitive text would not be at an end. Even though many historical questions would be answered, our interest in the history of the text would not cease. Theologically, there would be no resolution of the central problem. For the heart of the matter is that the definitive text is not essential to Christianity, because the presence of the Spirit is not limited to the inspiration of the written word. We have already approached this from the point of view of a false distinction between Scripture and tradition. Examining it in the present context, one is struck by the fact that a belief in single authoritative texts accords to the Spirit a large role in the formation of Scripture, and almost none at all in the growth of the tradition. Once the distinction has been abolished in the way that we have attempted above, it is possible fully to acknowledge that the very life and whole life of the church is in the Spirit.

When we accord significance to *all* the text forms as a part of the tradition, are we thereby affirming a pluralism in which contradictory forms of sayings of Jesus, for example, on divorce, have equal weight? No, because we are not attempting to ascribe to all forms of the tradition the authority which traditionally has been accorded to only one. Instead, we argue this: the church came into being through the Spirit, as the community of the Spirit. The oral and written tradition together were and remain a principal element in the church's finding its calling. But the tradition is manifold. There are four quite different Gospels, none with a claim to authority over the other three; there is no authoritative text beyond the manuscripts which we may follow without further thought. There is a manifold tradition to be studied and from which we may learn. But once that is done, the people of God have to make up their own minds. There is no authoritative text to provide a short-cut. Difficult though it often is in practice to accept such a situation, it at least allows us to find an alternative approach to the multiplicity of variant readings which represent the divergent interpretations of early Christianity. Rather than looking for right and wrong readings, and with them for right or wrong beliefs and practices, the way is open for the possibility that the church is the community of the Spirit even in its multiplicities of texts, one might say in its corruptions and in its restorations. Indeed, we may suggest that it is not in spite of the variety but because of them that the church is that community.

It would be bravado to finish this book with a rhetorical flourish, as though this were the kind of matter that might be concluded. I shall therefore simply underline three points. First, the manuscript tradition lasted for fifteen hundred years. It would be quite misleading to treat it as a unity over against the age of printing. On the contrary, it went through many different phases. There was the emergence of the codex. There was a period of free development. There was also a move towards standard texts. There were translations into new languages and new cultures. There was continued interest in ancient copies, so that early text forms reappear centuries later. There is more than one way of working with a manuscript tradition. What is above all to be emphasised is that any study must start with the fact that it is a manuscript tradition.

Second, it is the tradition in some churches that, when the Gospel has been read at the eucharist, the book is lifted up with the words 'This is the Gospel of Christ.' Whether the book is manuscript or printed, the act is a declaration that it is this particular volume which is the Gospel. For the early Christian communities, the written Gospel existed as *their* Gospel book.

Third, this book has not been concerned with a process that is now ended. Scholars continue to discover fresh materials and to revise the text of the Gospels; translators provide fresh renderings, commentators new interpretations, and theologians new ideas. We have seen how much the printed text has changed since 1516, and have wondered what changes will be brought by the electronic text. Today's influences on the text of the Gospels are not those of the early centuries, but they may prove equally powerful. The text of the Gospels remains a living text.

Index of citations

214

Index of Greek New Testament manuscripts

Index of names and subjects

Acts, text of, 115, 201
Aids to readers, 19, 25, 27–8, 29, 185
Aland, B., 3 n. 1, 8 n. 1, 11 n. 7, 62 n. 13,
    127 n. 1, 155 n. 7, 159, 196 n. 13, 197
    n. 15, 202 n. 21, 206 n. 3; *see also*
    Nestle–Aland
Aland, K., 3 n. 1, 8 n. 1, n. 2, 11 n. 7,
    62n. 12, n. 13, 127 n. 1, 155 n. 7, 159,
    196 n. 13, 197 n. 15, 202 n. 21; *see
    also* Nestle–Aland
Alexandria, 26
Alexandrian text, 32, 39, 61, 74, 78, 83,
    112, 119, 127, 135, 137, 158, 171, 173,
    200, 206
Allison, D. C., 90 n. 8
Ambrosiaster, 168
Ammonian sections, 25, 125; *see also*
    Eusebian canons
Amphoux, C.-B., 119 n. 22, 157 n. 10, 180
    n. 5, 188 n. 7, 202, 205 n. 2, 205–6
Anderson, S. D., 67 n. 25
Antioch, 26, 180 n. 4
Antwerp Polyglot, 192
Apostolic Constitutions, 57, 58, 69
Arabic harmony, 20, 166
Arabic version, 168, 192, 199
Armenian version, 14, 99f., 125, 157, 159
Atticism, 43
Augustine of Hippo, 15, 164, 170
Authorised Version, 29, 33 n. 1, 50–1,
    77ff., 95, 126, 130, 184 n. 2

Baarda, T., 180 n. 5
Bammel, E., 44 n. 5, 45, 190 n. 8
Bauer, W., 22 n. 14
Bentley, R., 94
Berytus, 32
Beuron, 191

Beza, Theodore, 44, 190
Biblical majuscule, 24, 26, 187
Birdsall, J. N., 157 n. 12, 206 n. 3, 207
Black, M., 72 n. 31
Black, M. H., 184 n. 1
Blake, R. P., 135 n. 12
Blanchard, A., 18 n. 10
Blunkett, M. A., 158n. 13
Boismard, M.-E., 122, 180 n. 4
Book of Common Prayer, 29 n. 21, 59
Books in antiquity, 17–27, 119–20, 184–8
Bover, J. M., 197 n. 15
Bowers, F., 197 n. 14
Buchanan, E. S., 152 n. 5
Bultmann, R., 177, 178
Burgon, J. W., 127 n. 1, 130, 132, 135, 139
Burkitt, F. C., 33 n. 1, 99 n. 1, 143
Byzantine text, 32–3, 52–3, 59, 65, 70,
    78f., 82f., 85, 86, 90, 96, 97–9, 112,
    129, 131, 134, 150, 158, 165, 173, 188,
    193, 199, 202; *see also* Received Text

Caesarea, 188
Caesarean text, 55, 56, 61, 62, 78, 86, 112,
    125, 135, 158
Camerarius, 176
Carruth, S., 67 n. 25
Catullus, 113
Chase, F. H., 67, 68 n. 27
Cheltenham Catalogue, 171 n. 27
Clement of Alexandria, 16, 22, 107, 111,
    125, 136
Coates, M., 28 n. 29
Codex, origin of, 18–19, 186–8
Commentary manuscripts, 27, 191
Common Bible, 51
Complutensian Polyglot, 51, 192
Conjectural emendation, 113–16, 117,

New International Version, 77ff.
New Jerusalem Bible, 77ff.
New Revised Standard Version, 77ff.
Nîmes, Chapter Library of, 99 n. 2

Old Latin versions, 13–14, 15, 25, 32, 42,
  54, 56, 57, 79, 89, 96, 107, 111, 117 n.
  18, 126, 133–4, 150, 160, 169, 175–6,
  188, 191, 202
  a (Codex Vercellensis), 68, 81f., 96, 151,
    162, 165, 166–7, 168, 170, 171
  aur (Codex Aureus Holmiensis), 170
  b (Codex Veronensis), 81f., 151–2, 160,
    162, 165, 166–7, 168, 170, 171
  c (Codex Colbertinus), 68, 160, 162–3,
    164, 165, 167, 169, 170, 172
  d (Codex Bezae), 81f., 134, 162–3, 165,
    166–7; *see also* Codex Bezae (in Index
    of Greek New Testament
    Manuscripts)
  e (Codex Palatinus), 96, 151–2, 160,
    162, 163, 165, 166–7, 168, 170
  f (Codex Brixianus), 78, 157
  ff¹ (Codex Corbeiensis), 85
  ff² (Codex Corbeiensis), 68, 151–2, 160,
    165, 166–7, 168, 170, 171
  g¹ (Codex Sangermanensis), 63 n. 16,
    164, 168
  i (Codex Vindobonensis), 68, 151–2,
    160
  k (Codex Bobbiensis), 57, 70, 81–2,
    125–6, 133, 134
  l (Codex Rehdigeranus), 151, 159, 160,
    161, 163, 165, 166–7, 168, 170, 171
  q (Codex Monacensis), 160
  r¹ (Codex Usserianus), 165, 166–7, 168,
    170, 171
  (Codex Sangallensis), 158; *see also* Δ 037
    (in Index of Greek New Testament
    Manuscripts)
  African text, 14
Old Slavonic version, 14, 170
Ong, W. J., 188 n. 7
Oral tradition, 100, 102, 121, 203–207, 210
Origen, 16, 54, 56, 60, 62–3, 64, 68, 70,
  72–4, 84, 88f., 93, 108, 119–20, 125,
  136, 188, 209
Original text, recovery of, 3–7, 45–6, 91,
  207–13
Oulton, J. E. L., 99 n. 3
Outtier, B., 180 n. 5

Palaeography, 52–3
Pamphilus of Caesarea, 55, 62
Papias of Hierapolis, 16, 99f., 139,
  203–204
Papyri, 9, 24, 25, 186–7
Parchment manuscripts, 9–12, 24, 25, 187
Paris Bible, 28
Parker, D. C., 11 n. 6, 53 n. 3, 119 n. 22,
  157 n. 10, 171 n. 27, 180 n. 5, 185 n.
  4, 188 n. 7, 201 n. 19, 205 n. 2, 206
  n. 3
Patristic citations, 15–17, 132, 136
Pepysian harmony, 20, 28
Persian harmony, 20, 133, 166
Persian version, 192, 199
Peter Chrysologus, 166
Petersen, W. L., 20 n. 12
Pierpont, W. G., 130 n. 3
Porter, S. E., 72 n. 31
Printed Greek New Testament, 3, 29, 44,
  51–2, 189–90, 196, 204
Pseudo-Augustine, 170, 171
Pseudo-Theophilus of Antioch, 171 n. 27
Pseudo-Vigilius of Thapsus, 170

Q, 104f., 106
Quasten, J., 134 n. 10

Rauer, M., 68 n. 28
Received Text, 97–9, 126, 129–30, 190,
  192; *see also* Byzantine Text, Majority
  Text
Revised English Bible, 77ff., 184
Revised Standard Version, 38, 49–51,
  77ff., 105, 108–9, 124–5, 128, 150,
  152–3, 157, 175, 176, 200
Revised Version, 51, 52–3, 130
Roberts, C. H., 18 n. 10
Robinson, M. A., 130 n. 3
Rome, 202

Sabatier, P., 191
Samaritan Pentateuch, 198
Schleiermacher, F., 146 n. 20
Semitism in manuscripts, 43
Shakespeare, text of, 4–6, 182, 201 n. 17
Shepherd of Hermas, 195 n. 12
Skeat, T. C., 18 n. 10, 19 n. 11
Smith, M., 141
Soden, H. von, 97, 197 n. 15
Stephanus, Robert, 44, 97
Stevenson, J., 203 n. 1

Q - 45- 6